2005

China's New Nationalism

A

B O O K

The Philip E. Lilienthal imprint
honors special books
in commemoration of a man whose work
at the University of California Press from 1954 to 1979
was marked by dedication to young authors
and to high standards in the field of Asian Studies.
Friends, family, authors, and foundations have together
endowed the Lilienthal Fund, which enables the Press
to publish under this imprint selected books
in a way that reflects the taste and judgment
of a great and beloved editor.

China's New Nationalism

Pride, Politics, and Diplomacy

Peter Hays Gries

UNIVERSITY OF CALIFORNIA PRESS

Berkeley / Los Angeles / London

The publisher gratefully acknowledges the generous contribution to this book provided by the Philip E. Lilienthal Asian Studies Endowment Fund of the University of California Press Associates, which is supported by a major gift from Sally Lilienthal.

Portions of chapters 6 and 8 are based on work that has been previously published in *The China Journal*, *The Journal of Contemporary China*, and *International Security*. The nationalist slogans reproduced at the beginning of chapters 1–8 are from the Belgrade bombing protests of May 1999.

University of California Press
Berkeley and Los Angeles, California

University of California Press, Ltd.
London, England

Library of Congress Cataloging-in-Publication Data

Gries, Peter Hays, 1967–
    China's new nationalism : pride, politics, and diplomacy /
Peter Hays Gries.
      p. cm.
    "A Philip E. Lilienthal book."
    Includes bibliographical references and index.
    ISBN 0-520-23297-6 (alk. paper).
    1. Nationalism—China.   2. Anti-Americanism—China.
3. Japan—Foreign public opinion, Chinese.   4. Public opinion—
China.   I. Title: Pride, politics, and diplomacy.   II. Title.

DS779.215.G75   2004
320.54'0951—dc21   2003008451

Manufactured in the United States of America
13 12 11 10 09 08 07 06 05 04
11 10 9 8 7 6 5 4 3 2 1

The paper used in this publication meets the minimum requirements of ANSI/NISO Z39.48–1992 (R 1997) (*Permanence of Paper*).♾

For Mônica

Contents

Illustrations

Introduction

Dragon Slayers and Panda Huggers

On 1 April 2001, an American EP-3 surveillance plane and a Chinese F-8 jet fighter collided over the South China Sea. The EP-3 made it safely to China's Hainan Island; the F-8 tore apart and crashed. Chinese pilot Wang Wei was killed. A few days later, China's Ministry of Foreign Affairs called an unusual late-night news conference. Spokesman Zhu Bangzao, his rage clearly visible, declared: "The United States should take full responsibility, make an apology to the Chinese government and people, and give us an explanation of its actions."[1] Foreign Minister Tang Jiaxuan and President Jiang Zemin soon reiterated this demand. Secretary of State Colin Powell initially responded with equal bluntness: "We have nothing to apologize for." Viewing the aggressiveness of the Chinese jet as the cause of the collision, many Americans did not feel responsible. As Senator Joseph Lieberman said on CNN's "Larry King Live," "When you play chicken, sometimes you get hurt."[2]

The impasse was broken after eleven days of intensive negotiations. American Ambassador Joseph Prueher gave a letter to Foreign Minister

Tang: "Please convey to the Chinese people and to the family of pilot Wang Wei that we are very sorry for their loss. . . . We are very sorry the entering of China's airspace and the landing did not have verbal clearance." Having extracted an "apology" from Washington, Beijing released the twenty-four American servicemen being held on Hainan Island. In the Chinese view, Jiang, "diplomatic strategist extraordinaire," had won a major victory.[3] The American spin was quite different. Powell denied that America had apologized, again asserting, "There is nothing to apologize for. To apologize would have suggested that we have done something wrong or accepted responsibility for having done something wrong. And we did not do anything wrong." The conservative media was not so restrained. The *Weekly Standard* declared the People's Republic to be "violent and primitive . . . a regime of hair-curling, systematic barbarity."[4] A *New Republic* editorial asserted that "a non-Maoist tyranny in China is still a tyranny. . . . They are, in short, in transition from communism to fascism."[5] Chinese nationalism, the *National Review* maintained, is "psychopathological."[6]

Is China out to settle old scores with the West, or is China seeking to incorporate itself peacefully into the world system? Is China, in other words, an evil dragon or a cute panda? Westerners hold both views. Foreign-policy makers, businesspeople, and academics frequently sing China's praises. Former U.S. Secretary of State Henry Kissinger paints a rosy picture of Chinese intentions. "China is no military colossus," Kissinger argues in the *Los Angeles Times,* and has "the best of intentions." China, Kissinger insists, can be counted on to pursue its "self-interest" in cooperation—high praise indeed from a proud practitioner of realpolitik.[7] As China's economic reforms embraced the market, many in the West came to romanticize a business China that was thought to be capitalist, "just like us." In 1985, after six years of successful economic reforms in China, *Time* magazine even declared Deng Xiaoping "Man of the Year."[8] Western businesspeople have frequently served Beijing in exchange for access to China's consumers. Academic China watchers also tend to present a rosy picture of China, rarely speaking out on controversial issues such as human rights. Scholars like Andrew Nathan and Perry Link are the exceptions that prove the rule. Because they have spoken out against Chinese human rights violations, Chinese nationalists and government officials have subjected them to vicious personal attacks, and they have been denied visas to China. For example, Penn State's Liu Kang, one of the most virulent of China's anti-American nationalists, viciously attacks Link in his "A 'China Hand' Not Welcome in Beijing" section of the best-selling 1996 diatribe *The Plot to Demonize China.*[9]

Meanwhile, an odd alliance of politicians, celebrities, and journalists on the left and right join together in China bashing. On the left, a variety of politicians and actors have avowed a profound concern for Chinese human rights abuses and the fate of Tibet. Nancy Pelosi, congressional representative from northern California, feels so strongly about standing up for democratic values that she frequently joins conservatives in Congress to criticize China. Pelosi even has a special China human rights page on her Web site.[10] Actors have joined the politicians. Living in affluent southern California, but enraptured by Tibetan spirituality, Hollywood celebrities like Richard Gere and Steven Seagal have turned to the Dalai Lama for spiritual guidance and depicted Beijing as a ruthless dictatorship.[11] On the right, a "Blue Team" of conservative hawks has emerged on Capitol Hill to attack "panda huggers" and "Sinapologists." For example, William Triplett, coauthor of *Year of the Rat* and *Red Dragon Rising,* and a former staff member of the Senate Foreign Relations Committee, argues that China is a rising power determined to challenge the United States. He maintains that China's "dictatorial regime" is suppressing "the Chinese people's yearning for freedom and democracy."[12] To such dragon slayers, America must stand up for democracy, disciplining an evil and despotic China. The Western media often reinforces this message: journalists stationed in China, harassed by the Beijing authorities, frequently focus on the dark side of life in what they characterize as a land of tyranny.

Some Westerners have even argued both sides. After acquiring Hong Kong's Star TV in 1993, media mogul Rupert Murdoch declared satellite television an "unambiguous threat to totalitarian regimes everywhere." Beijing soon declared war on Murdoch's News Corporation, pronouncing satellite dishes illegal. Murdoch quickly surrendered, and has been kowtowing to Beijing ever since, first pulling BBC off of Star TV, and then canceling publication of the memoirs of the former British governor of Hong Kong, Chris Patten.[13] More recently, Murdoch's son James has parroted Beijing's shrill critique of the Falun Gong spiritual movement as a "dangerous . . . cult."[14]

China, it seems, means very different things to different people. American fears and fantasies about China reveal a great deal about the interests and ideals that shape the American political landscape. They do not, however, teach us much about the real China. Romanticizing and demonizing China, furthermore, dangerously distorts our understanding of Chinese foreign policies. The way that we talk about China influences the ways we interpret and respond to Chinese actions. And the way that we talk about China also influences the way that the Chinese (mis)understand us. Such trans-Pacific muddles help explain how the United States and China came to blows in Korea (1950–1953) and Vietnam (1965–1973). And a conflict over Taiwan remains a real possibility at the dawn of the twenty-first century. Our China policy debate must, therefore, see beyond such distortions to focus on the real China.

To understand Chinese nationalism, we must listen to the Chinese. This study, therefore, seeks to introduce Western readers to the views of China's new nationalists. Specifically, I focus on Chinese perceptions of China's two most important rivals: America and Japan.[15] There is real need for such a study. Recent academic and journalistic accounts have done an admirable job of recounting the American perspective on the United States' relationship with China.[16] But Chinese perceptions of this relationship are woefully neglected. This book, therefore, will introduce the rarely told Chinese side of the story. The neglected Chinese perspective on Japan and America is found in a wide assortment of Chinese materials expressing nationalist sentiments: movies, television shows, posters, cartoons, but particularly popular books and magazines published in mainland China since the early 1990s. Most of these materials were produced by a "fourth generation" of Chinese nationalists in their thirties. These young Chinese seek to distinguish themselves from their elders, and to make sense of their experiences in the "Liberal '80s."

Ironically, the "fourth generation" appears to find the new victimization narrative of Chinese suffering at the hands of Western imperialists appealing precisely because they, unlike older Chinese, have never been directly victimized. The first generation of revolutionaries endured the hardships of the anti-fascist and civil wars of the 1930s and 1940s. The second generation suffered during the Anti-Rightist Campaign and the Great Leap Forward of the late 1950s. And the third generation of Red Guards was sent down to the countryside during the Cultural Revolution of the late 1960s and 1970s. The fourth generation of PRC youth, by contrast, grew up with relative material prosperity under Deng Xiaoping and Reform in the 1980s and 1990s.[17] In their 1997 psycho-autobiography *The Spirit of the Fourth Generation,* Song Qiang and several of his coauthors of the 1996 nationalist diatribes *China Can Say No* and *China Can Still Say No* fret over their generation's materialism: "cultural and spiritual fast food has taken over." They are envious of the third generation who, "proud of their hardships," can celebrate them at Cultural Revolution restaurants like Heitudi ("The Black Earth") in Beijing, nostalgically eating fried corn bread, recalling the good old, bad old days. They then ask, "Are we an

FIGURE 1. "China will not be insulted!" Following the Belgrade bombing of May 1999, numerous popular books and magazines expressed outrage. Three of the books in this Beijing bookstall have titles declaring, "China cannot be bullied!" Photo courtesy of Richard Smith.

unimportant generation?" In a section entitled "How Much Longer Must We be Silent?", they lament that "we in our thirties are without a shadow or a sound. . . . It seems that we will perish in silence."[18] Many of this generation, it seems, have a strong desire to make their mark. And they seek to do so through nationalism.

Many "fourth-generation" nationalists today have self-consciously defined themselves against the "Liberal '80s." Sociologist Karl Mannheim long ago argued that the formative events of youth mark each generation.[19] Late-1980s experiences like the pro-Western "River Elegy" television sensation and Beijing Spring 1989 came at a pivotal time in the lives of Chinese nationalists now in their thirties. Today's nationalists frequently dismiss the 1980s as a period of dangerous "romanticism" and "radicalism"; they then depict themselves as "realistic" and "pragmatic" defenders of stability and order.[20] During the "May 8th" nationalist protests of 1999, for instance, one group of students demonstrated with a painting of what might best be described as the "Demon of Liberty." During Beijing Spring a decade earlier, Chinese students became famous for their statue the "Goddess of Democracy." This self-conscious superimposition of America as demon over America as goddess tells us far more about

FIGURE 2. Good America: The "Goddess of Democracy," 1989. Mao looks on as students protest in Tiananmen Square during Beijing Spring. Photo courtesy of AP/Wide World Photos.

FIGURE 3. Bad America: The "Demon of Liberty," 1999.
Students in Canton protest the Belgrade embassy
bombing. Source unknown.

changes in the worldview of Chinese youth since 1989 than it does about
the United States.

These and other Chinese voices can help us with the thorny problem
of just what exactly "Chinese nationalism" is. Because it is based upon
analysis of European history, the definition that nationalism arises when
nations seek to become states does not apply very well to China.[21] The
Western view of the nation as a uniquely *modern* institution is also problematic in the Chinese context. "China" has four millennia of documented
history, and two millennia of centralized rule. Did it only become a "nation" in the twentieth century? Historian Prasenjit Duara has gone to great

lengths to argue that premodern China's regions were linked to Beijing in a variety of ways, creating a widely shared notion of "China." Because premodern Chinese shared a common culture, he argues, they were the "first nation."[22] Other historians disagree, arguing, for example, that local religious practices accentuated regional differences, undermining consciousness of a common "Chinese" identity.[23]

Confucianism presents a further problem to those who want to define Chinese nationalism. One group of scholars holds that Confucianism and nationalism are incompatible: Confucian universalism, which holds that all peoples can become Chinese if they adapt to a Sinocentric civilization, mitigates against the idea of a Chinese nationalism that defines itself in contradistinction to other nations.[24] Other scholars, however, argue that "Confucian nationalism" is not an oxymoron: Confucianism allows for the reinforcement of cultural boundaries when barbarians do not accept Chinese values. The "universal" "all under heaven" *(tianxia)* can and often has become a closed political community.[25] Historian Lei Yi of the Chinese Academy of Social Sciences in Beijing has used the phrase "'Sinocentric' cultural nationalism *['Huaxia zhongxin' wenhua minzu zhuyi]*" to describe such views. The Confucian world was not "one big happy family" *(tianxia yi jia),* but extremely Sinocentric, involving a "fierce racism, rejection of other cultures, . . . and cultural superiority."[26]

Indeed, pride in the superiority of Confucian civilization is central to nationalism in China today. In 1994, Xiao Gongqing, an outspoken neoconservative intellectual, advocated the use of a nationalism derived from Confucianism to fill the ideological void opened by the collapse of communism.[27] Popular nationalists frequently evince pride in China's Confucian civilization. The cover of a 1997 *Beijing Youth Weekly,* for instance, has "Chinese Defeat Kasparov!" splashed across a picture of the downcast grand master. Two of the six members of the IBM research group that programmed "Deep Blue," it turns out, were Chinese-Americans. "It was the genius of these two Chinese," one article asserts, "that allowed 'Deep Blue' to defeat Mr. Kasparov." Entitled "We Have the Best Brains," the article concludes that "we should be proud of the legacy of '5,000 years of civilization' that our ancestors have left for us."[28] The Communist Party elite seems to concur. In 1995, for example, Vice Chair of the National People's Congress Tian Jiyun declared that "The IQs of the Chinese ethnicity, the descendants of the Yellow Emperor, are very high."[29] Confucianism, it seems, does not "thin out" nationalism, but is instead the very basis of China's new nationalism.

This book avoids such controversies in taking a social psychological approach to nationalism. As Elie Kedourie noted long ago, nationalism "is very much a matter of one's self-view, of one's estimation of oneself and one's place in the world."[30] Following social identity theorists, I loosely define national identity as that aspect of individuals' self-image that is tied to their nation, together with the value and emotional significance they attach to membership in the national community.[31] "Nationalism" will refer to any behavior designed to restore, maintain, or advance public images of that national community.[32]

Because Chinese politics often dictates that "surface and reality differ" *(biao li bu yi)*, the successful interpretation of Chinese materials is no easy task. China's emperors saw language as a tool of rule. Diction mattered. Two millennia ago, the *Art of Writing* demonstrated how language could be used to mold popular opinion. For instance, China's emperors commissioned literati to (re)write official dynastic histories to legitimate their rule. China's rulers could also be quite ruthless. Emperors from Qin Shihuang (ruled circa 1 B.C.E.) to Qianlong of the Qing Dynasty (ruled 1736–1796 C.E.) are famous for burning books and suppressing free expression.[33] Such actions forced China's literati to develop the art of "*indirection.*" Historical allegory—especially critiques of the corrupt practices of past emperors—was and is one form of "indirection" used to chastise present-day politics.[34] Western-style direct criticism, indeed, came to be seen as vulgar.

The reader of Chinese political materials is therefore challenged to listen to "the sound outside the strings" *(xianwai zhi yin)*, relying on a deep immersion in the historical and cultural context of Chinese politics today. Identical events or words can have different meanings in different contexts. The reader must "listen to the sound of the gong" *(luo gu ting yin)*. Is it rejoicing (a marriage), or mourning (a death)?[35] It is striking how often the actual meaning of a diplomatic statement is the precise opposite of what is literally said. Descriptions of China as "inferior" and "great," for example, cannot be read literally, but must be understood in their historical and political contexts. When tributary missions came to pay obeisance, imperial officials referred to China as "our inferior nation" *(biguo)* and the tributaries as "your superior nation" *(guiguo)*. They were so confident that China was the undisputed center of civilization *(wenming)* that they could afford the self-deprecation. By contrast, Chinese diplomats under the People's Republic have routinely referred to China as "great" *(weida)*. These diametrically opposite choices of diction point to an insecurity—central to today's nationalism—about China's international status.

Understanding the diplomatic tendency to say the opposite of what is meant helps one interpret China's relationships with other nations. It was only after reading the phrase "Sino-Japanese friendship" literally hundreds of times in a Beijing library, for instance, that I came to realize that the phrase frequently conceals animosity. Authors irate about Japanese atrocities in China, Japanese "historical revisionism," or the "revival of Japanese militarism" nonetheless use the phrase in the conclusions of their articles and books. While it is possible to speak of the feelings of both love and hate that many Chinese have for America, it is decidedly *not* possible to speak about a genuine Chinese "friendship" for Japan.[36] The Chinese viewed the Japanese as the paradigmatic "devils" *(guizi)* during World War II, and they continue to view them that way today.[37]

This kind of political interpretation requires more than just reading many Chinese books and magazines. A person who wants to do it well must also be sensitive to his or her own cultural standpoint: who you are shapes both what you choose to look at, and how you interpret it. Being a white American male undoubtedly had a major influence on my research experience. As a Caucasian in China, I am seen as a *"laowai,"* which means "foreigner" or even "Whitey."[38] Skin color immediately creates a distance between Chinese and Caucasians. The presence of an American presented an opportunity for many Chinese to vent their feelings—positive or negative—about the United States; Sino-American relations is not a subject an American in Beijing can easily avoid. And foreign men are the object of many Chinese nationalists' anxiety: the recurring figure of China as a raped woman has recently reemerged in nationalist discourse, and many of its young male exponents are enraged by the very idea of white men intimately involved with Chinese women.[39]

As a white American male writing about Chinese nationalism, therefore, I am likely to be the object of a good deal of suspicion.[40] The fate of Geremie Barmé, a white male and one of the West's most incisive observers of the Chinese cultural scene, is instructive. In 1995 Barmé violated a taboo by publishing an article, "To Screw Foreigners Is Patriotic," that exposed the racist dimension of Chinese nationalism. Popular nationalist Wang Xiaodong, writing under the pseudonym Shi Zhong, quickly penned a highly critical riposte in which he labeled Barmé an "extremist"—and asserted that Western academics are incapable of "understanding China."[41] I reject Wang's claim, as well as the position, advanced by other Chinese cultural nationalists and postcolonial theorists, that white males cannot understand China. Instead, I take comfort in the fact that Alexis de Tocqueville, a Frenchman with an outsider's perspective, produced one of the most astute analyses of American politics ever written, *Democracy in America*.[42] Westerners can understand China, and should seek this understanding.[43]

They cannot, however, do so in isolation. Where possible, I supplement my own readings of Chinese texts with Chinese analyses of the same texts.[44] Fortunately, the recent rise of popular nationalism has engendered extensive Chinese commentary. Numerous psychobiographies of the "fourth generation" of Chinese nationalists have been published.[45] As noted above, the authors of *China Can Say No* and *China Can Still Say No*, which marked the emergence of popular nationalism in 1996, later published a very revealing psycho-*auto*biography, *The Spirit of the Fourth Generation*. This secondary Chinese literature on Chinese nationalism provides an invaluable source of primary material, against which I have verified and developed my own views.

Perhaps my greatest challenge, however, has been assessing how my Chinese sources relate to each other. Chinese, like Americans, project their fears and fantasies onto our bilateral relations. China has its own fair share of Kissingers and Tripletts — America lovers and America haters. The challenge, therefore, is to figure out how the views of extreme nationalists are accepted by mainstream Chinese.[46] While nationalist views won headlines in 1996–97, they were likely accepted only by a small group of disaffected intellectuals. Following the 1999 American bombing of the Chinese embassy in Belgrade and the 2001 spy plane collision over the South China Sea, however, the propagators of anti-American views are now speaking to a much broader Chinese audience. Meanwhile, in America, two summer 2002 reports painted a dark picture of China's international activities. The Department of Defense's (DoD) *Annual Report on the Military Power of the People's Republic of China* focused on recent Chinese arms acquisitions and the threat they pose to Taiwan.[47] The United States–China Security Review Commission (USCC) then submitted its first annual report to the U.S. Congress, expressing concern that China's America policy is driven by a coherent set of expansionist goals. The report asserts, for instance, that "China is not a status quo country." Commissioner Arthur Waldron goes even further, asserting that China's "wide-ranging purpose" is to "exclude the U.S. from Asia" and "to threaten and coerce neighboring states."[48]

These developments do not bode well for twenty-first-century Sino-American relations. Words have consequences. Anti-American and anti-Chinese polemics are pernicious: they can easily spiral into mutual dehumanization and demonization, laying the foundation for violent conflict.

Chinese and Americans who paint rosy pictures of the bilateral relationship are irresponsible; we should squarely confront the dangers inherent in a relationship devoid of mutual trust. But it is Chinese America bashers and American China bashers who are the most dangerous. This book, therefore, seeks to present a balanced view of China's new nationalism— one that both acknowledges its legitimate grievances and recognizes its potential dangers.

維
護
民
族
尊
嚴

!!

*"Protect our national
self-respect!"*

CHAPTER I

Saving Face

8 May 1999. Midnight. In the skies over Belgrade, an American B-2 bomber dropped five two-thousand-pound guided missiles. All five hit their intended target. But it was not a Serbian arms depot, as their maps indicated, but the Chinese embassy. Three missiles exploded near the embassy's intelligence operations center. And three Chinese—Xu Xinghu and Zhu Ying of the *Guangming Daily*, one of China's premier national newspapers, and Shao Yunhuan of the New China News Agency—were killed in the blast. Twenty-three others were injured.

That night in Urumuchi, in China's far northwest Xinjiang Province, Yue Hongjian was eating dinner when he saw the news of the bombing on Central Chinese Television (CCTV). "I finished dinner with tears in my eyes," he later wrote, "and then wrote this poem":

You have gone.
We will think of you
always.

13

Your work and hopes
will be continued.
Please be at ease,
my compatriots.

You have gone.
But we will forever,
always,
think of you.[1]

Yue's poem is no masterpiece, but it is a powerful and pure expression of sorrow over the deaths of three total strangers. Meanwhile, two thousand miles east in Beijing, Su Zhengfan wrote in his diary, trying to express his feelings about the bombing, but found that there was "no way to calm my feelings of grief and indignation." That same night, on the other side of the Pacific, Zhao Guojun, a researcher at the University of British Columbia, hearing the news, had a lengthy discussion with several of his Chinese compatriots in Vancouver. They agreed that the bombing was of "hostile intent."[2] Chinese across the globe spontaneously poured into the streets to protest. Students in America and Europe demonstrated on university campuses and outside city halls and embassies. In Chicago, Chinese nationalists utilized e-mail networks to organize demonstrations on campuses and a joint protest march downtown. Chinese students carried pictures of the "three martyrs" and placards declaring, "Punish the war criminals!" and "Justice must be done!"[3] Meanwhile, in Rome, two thousand demonstrating Chinese shouted, "The Chinese people cannot be defeated!"

Back in China, nationalists were busy as well. Protests erupted in over two dozen major cities. The American consul's residence in Chengdu was firebombed. In Canton, a group of three hundred protestors broke off from the main demonstration to yell slogans in front of a local McDonald's, such as "Kick American hamburgers out of China!" and "Oppose invasion!"[4] In Beijing, students from prominent universities took buses to the embassy district on the other side of town to protest outside the U.S. embassy, shouting "Down with hegemonic politics!" Student leaders publicly presented protest letters to American diplomats. Many demanded revenge, chanting "Blood for Blood!" Protestors smashed embassy cars, removed and burned American flags, and threw gas bombs, rocks, and bricks at embassy buildings as soldiers looked on. The U.S. Ambassador to China, James Sasser, along with other American diplomats, was imprisoned inside the American embassy com-

FIGURE 4. The Belgrade bombing protests, 1999. Tens of thousands of students demonstrated in Canton on 9 May. Photo courtesy of AP/Worldwide Photos.

FIGURE 5. America imprisoned. Ambassador James Sasser looks out through broken glass the day after the U.S. embassy in Beijing was attacked by Chinese protestors. Photo courtesy of Harry Hays and the USIA.

pound for days. Protests were not confined to the streets: Chinese nationalists were also active on the Internet. Deluged by e-mail from China, the White House Web site in Washington, D. C., was temporarily shut down. Cyber-nationalists also hacked into the U.S. embassy's Web site in Beijing, inserting "Down with the Barbarians!" on the homepage.[5] Dozens of protest sites appeared on personal Web pages, and Chinese-language chatrooms were swamped.

The Communist Party also joined the fray. The China Internet Information Center, an official Chinese government Web site in English, constructed a Web page devoted solely to protesting the Belgrade bombing. The page contained links to translations of Chinese leaders' speeches, letters from common Chinese, opinion pieces, and a page entitled "International Community Responses." The latter consisted of links to 159 separate New China News Agency English-language reports—from Bangladesh to Mozambique—of various foreign leaders condemning the NATO bombing.[6] It clearly sought to demonstrate that "world opinion" and "justice" were on China's side.

In Washington, President Bill Clinton proclaimed the bombing a "tragic mistake" made because of outdated maps, and extended his "regrets and profound condolences" to the Chinese people. President Clinton's attempts to telephone President Jiang Zemin in Beijing were repeatedly rebuffed. Secretary of State Madeline Albright visited the Chinese embassy in Washington at midnight to express her condolences—and to discuss the safety of American diplomats in China. In Beijing, Chinese officials rejected the American faulty map scenario as "sophistry," and declared NATO apologies to be "insufficient" and "insincere." The Chinese media did not publicize Clinton's, Sasser's, or NATO Secretary General Javier Solana's public apologies until 11 May. Instead, they proclaimed the bombing a "barbaric" and intentional "criminal act."[7] A *People's Daily* op-ed entitled "This is not 1899 China" declared:

This is 1999, not 1899. This is not . . . the age when people can barge about in the world just by sending a few gunboats. . . . It is not the age when the Western powers plundered the Imperial Palace at will, destroyed the Old Summer Palace, and seized Hong Kong and Macao. . . . China is a China that has stood up; it is a China that defeated the Japanese fascists; it is a China that had a trial of strength and won victory over the United States on the Korean battleground. The Chinese people are not to be bullied, and China's sovereignty and dignity are not to be violated. The hot blood of people of ideas and integrity who opposed imperialism for over 150 years flows in the veins of the Chinese people. U.S.-led NATO had better remember this.[8]

The Belgrade bombing, in this Chinese view, was not an isolated event; rather, it was the latest in a long series of Western aggressions against China.

The "May 8th" protests marked a high point in a rising tide of popular nationalism in China. The protests may even mark a turning point in Chinese attitudes towards the United States and the current world system. China in the mid- to late 1980s had been notable for a decidedly positive vision of America.[9] By the late 1990s, that view had changed dramatically. Perceived American abandonment of Mikhail Gorbachev and Russia after the fall of the Soviet bloc, combined with Beijing's lost 1993 bid to host the 2000 Olympics (attributed to a devious U.S. Congress), precipitated an early 1990s shift in Chinese attitudes towards the United States. The fiftieth anniversary commemorations of World War II in 1995, the Taiwan Strait Crisis of 1995–1996, and the 1996–1997 fervor over the inflammatory *China Can Say No* and similar anti-American and anti-Japanese publications solidified the emergence of popular nationalism.[10] Following the Belgrade bombing in 1999 and the 1 April 2001 spy plane collision over the South China Sea, the views of parochial "say no!" nationalists, once thought extreme, gained wider currency among ordinary Chinese.[11] At the dawn of the twenty-first century, a new nationalism had emerged in mainland China.

The Enigma of Chinese Nationalism

How should the Belgrade bombing protests be understood? More broadly, what should be made of China's new nationalism? The "May 8th" protests shocked the U.S. media, which quickly blamed the Chinese government. A brief review of American newspaper editorials on 11 May 1999 reveals that most media outlets thought the Chinese people were not genuinely angry with America; rather, they were manipulated by Communist Party propaganda that called the bombing intentional. The *San Francisco Chronicle* protested that Beijing has "failed to tell its citizens that the U.S. attack was an accident and that President Clinton has apologized to Beijing." As *USA Today* stated, "China's state-controlled media aren't reporting to their public the U.S. apology officials say they want. It's no surprise that the usually pro-American Chinese are angry." Such "state-supervised anger," the *Boston Globe* wrote, was neither genuine nor popular. The "brutes of Beijing," it seems, were responsible for the Chinese people's anger and mistaken belief that the bombing was intentional, and the protests were yet another example of the "Communist menace."

The mainstream American media's portrayal of the Belgrade bombing protests fits in well with the dominant Western interpretation of Chinese nationalism in general: the Communist Party has constructed Chinese nationalism as a tool to legitimize its rule. With communism in crisis, proponents of this view argue, Party elite foment nationalism to maintain power. Thomas Christensen expressed this dominant argument succinctly in an influential *Foreign Affairs* article: "Since the Chinese Communist Party is no longer communist, it must be even more Chinese."[12] There is broad consensus in the West on the fundamental nature of Chinese nationalism today: it is "party propaganda," generated by the Communist elite for its own purposes.[13]

This mainstream view of Chinese nationalism is not wrong, but it is incomplete. Even the brief summary of the Belgrade bombing protests outlined above suggests that Western dismissals of Chinese nationalism as a tool of communist rule greatly oversimplify reality. Chinese nationalism cannot be interpreted in isolation, but must be understood in its international and historical contexts. Moreover, Chinese nationalism is not simply "party propaganda," since ordinary Chinese now play a central role in nationalist politics. And Chinese nationalism is not simply an "instrument" or "tool." Chinese, like all peoples, have deep-seated emotional attachments to their national identity. Hence, this book advances four interrelated arguments. First and second, Chinese national identity evolves in dynamic relationship with other nations and the past. Third and fourth, Chinese nationalism involves both the Chinese people and their passions.

Arguments in the West over the existence of a "China threat" frequently atomize and even demonize China. Is Chinese nationalism benign or malign? Is China a panda or a dragon? Such debates are dangerous because they treat Chinese national identity as autonomous and unchanging, ignoring the international context within which it evolves. Nationalism concerns the identity of nations, and identity does not develop in isolation. The China Internet Information Center's Belgrade bombing Web site, for instance, played up evidence of various foreigners' support of China's position. Similarly, in their account of the Rome protests discussed above, New China News Agency correspondents Yan Tao and Liu Ruting "quote" an Italian named Mario: "Like the Chinese people, the Italian people love peace and oppose war . . . If NATO persists in bombing the Yugoslav Federation, Italy should withdraw from this aggressor organization."[14] The centrality of foreigners' views of China to Chinese nationalism points to the dynamic, intersubjective nature of Chinese national identity. Just as personal identity emerges through our interpersonal relations, national identities evolve through international relations. Chinese identity is not static, but evolves as Chinese interact with the world. Chinese nationalists are thus extremely sensitive to the things that Westerners say about China. We would be wise, therefore, not to indulge ourselves in fits of China bashing.

Identities, personal and national, are also constituted in large part by stories about the past. Therefore, the ways Chinese imagine their "Century of Humiliation" at the hands of Western imperialists in the past have a powerful influence on the nature and direction of Chinese nationalism today. As the *People's Daily* noted in "This is not 1899 China," Chinese reactions to the 1999 Belgrade bombing were shaped in part by memories of China's semicolonial past. In summer 2000, the *Beijing Youth Daily's* Zhang Tianwei made the connection between past "humiliation" and current nationalism: "Until they achieve a rebirth, and their emotional scars have thoroughly healed, the Chinese people will carry their memories with them as they confront themselves, others, the present, and the future."[15] If Western China policies do not consider how Chinese nationalism is shaped by interactions with the West and evolving narratives of the national past, they may well push Chinese nationalism in a malevolent direction.

Moreover, the "party propaganda" view of Chinese nationalism dominant in the West too narrowly focuses on the Communist Party, dangerously overlooking the role of the Chinese people. The global and spontaneous nature of the "May 8th" protests should cast serious doubts on this top-down view. The Western media's argument that the Communist Party used "misinformation" about the bombing to manipulate the Chinese people like puppets cannot explain why the bombing also outraged Chinese outside China who had full access to the Western media, like Zhao Guojun and his colleagues in Vancouver. The 1990s witnessed the emergence of a genuinely popular nationalism in China that should not be conflated with state or official nationalism. Although the antiforeign impulses of popular nationalism in China often mirror party-line nationalism, popular nationalism's independent existence undermines the Communist Party's hegemony. The Chinese people are demanding a say in nationalist politics: the fate of the nation is no longer the Party's exclusive dominion. Western policymakers should also recognize that because the Party's legitimacy now depends upon accommodating popular nationalist demands, the Foreign Ministry must take popular opinion into account as it negotiates foreign policy.

The West's "party propaganda" view also focuses on the instrumental motivations of Chinese nationalists, dangerously dismissing their emotions as irrelevant. Many Chinese construed the Belgrade bombing as an intentional assault on Chinese sovereignty, another in a long line of Western insults. Seen as such, the bombing aroused a genuine anger that sought to right a wrong.[16] These passions are evident in Yue Hongjian's moving poem, Su Zhengfan's diary, and the drama of the worldwide "May 8th" protests. While some will always seek to "use" nationalism, it also has a vital affective component: we all have emotional commitments to our national identities. Chinese nationalists are no different—they are moved by considerations of both sense and sensibility.

In sum, Western academics and journalists tend to treat Chinese nationalism ahistorically and in isolation from other nations. And by highlighting "party propaganda," they dangerously trivialize the roles that the Chinese people and their emotions play in Chinese nationalism. I maintain that national identity, the past, the people, and the passions all play vital roles in nationalist politics everywhere. Chinese nationalism today is no exception. To make these arguments, I rely heavily on social psychology. The concept of *face*—the self displayed before others—will be central to my analysis.

The Many Faces of "Face"

Following the Belgrade bombing, "Ouyang from Wuhan" wrote a lengthy essay that he sent to the *Guangming Daily*. According to Ouyang, the American motive behind the attack was to humiliate China. To underscore his point, Ouyang uses the word *xiuru* (to humiliate) thirteen times, at one point deploying it in six consecutive sentences: "Chinese, this is actually Americans *humiliating* us! The American desire to *humiliate* us is no mere recent event. Blocking our hosting of the Olympics was a *humiliation*. Boarding the *Milky Way*[17] by force to search its cargo was a *humiliation*. Recent allegations that we stole their [nuclear] secrets are a *humiliation*. Similarly, the motive for the bombing of our embassy was to *humiliate* China." Once this goal is understood, Ouyang argues, American behavior starts to make sense. America's "compulsive lying" about the bombing, for example, is part of a larger plan: "Their goal is to humiliate Chinese, and the more absurd [their explanations], the more they can humiliate us."[18]

Chinese like Ouyang were not the only ones outraged and insulted by the unfolding events of May 1999. House Majority Whip Tom DeLay, for example, was infuriated by the Chinese reaction to the bombing. He later told a group of *Washington Post* reporters:

> I was on "Meet the Press" . . . right after the bombing of the Chinese Embassy in Kosovo [he meant Belgrade], and the [Chinese] ambassador [Li Zhaoxing] was on before me. And if you remember, he's kind of an obnoxious fellow and he's screaming and yelling about how bad the Americans were, and I had had it up to about here.
>
> So he's coming off the stage and I'm going onto the stage and I intentionally walked up to him and blocked his way. . . . I grabbed [his] hand and squeezed it as hard as I could and pulled him a kind of little jerk like this and I said: "Don't take the weakness of this president as the weakness of the American people." And he looked at me kind of funny, so I pulled him real close, nose to nose, and I repeated it very slowly, and said, "Do–not–take–the–weakness–of this president as the weakness of the American people."[19]

It is hard to say which is more shocking: DeLay's bullying, or his gloating about it later. However, most Americans, myself included, believed that the bombing was not deliberate and thus shared his dismay at the Chinese challenge to American integrity. Indeed, Ambassador Li had a very long week in Washington. In an interview on PBS's *NewsHour,* the mild-mannered Jim Lehrer pestered Li about Chinese skepticism that the bombing was an accident: "Yes, sir. But my question is: why would you think that it would not be an accident or a mistake? In other words, why would you think—to repeat my question, why would you think that the United States would *intentionally* kill Chinese citizens in downtown Belgrade?"[20] Lehrer, stunned by Li's skepticism, returned to the issue seven times in the course of his brief interview. DeLay and Lehrer, like most Americans, simply could not accept the Chinese challenge to their positive self-image. "How can they think that we Americans could do such a thing intentionally? We are not that kind of people!" was a widespread sentiment. It is notable that the bombing was rarely mentioned in the U.S. media without the qualifying adjective "accidental." An "accidental bombing" was very different from an "intentional bombing." It had very different implications for American self-esteem.

Ouyang, DeLay, and Lehrer were all motivated by a concern for *face*, the self revealed to others. "Saving" or "maintaining" face involves efforts to preserve what social psychologists call "ingroup positivity" or "collective self-esteem." To the extent that we identify ourselves as "Chinese" or "Americans," we seek to maintain the *face* or honor of our nations. Viewing the Belgrade bombing as the latest incident in a long history of Western aggression against China, Ouyang construed the blast to be a threat to his self-esteem as a Chinese. Similarly, DeLay and Lehrer viewed Ambassador Li's intransigence on the bombing as a direct challenge to their view of themselves as decent and respectable Americans, although their reactions to that challenge were dramatically different.

Some readers may object to the contention that Americans like DeLay and Lehrer care about saving face. Viewing ourselves as "rugged individualists," we Americans have a long tradition of passionately denying that we care "what society thinks."[21] We are, it seems, a nation of John Waynes and Lone Rangers—individuals who bravely chart their own courses. As sociologist David Ho notes, "The Western mentality, deeply ingrained with the values of individualism, is not one which is favorably disposed to the idea of face. For face is never a purely individual thing. It does not make sense to speak of the face of an individual as something lodged within his person; it is meaningful only when his face is considered in relation to that of others in the social network."[22] Indeed, the valorization of the rational individual central to Western civilization helps explain how the figurative *face* came to be a pejorative in the English language, meaning mere "pretense" or "façade." The word has developed a strong negative connotation as a false social appearance covering an unseemly inner reality. *Face* serves as a negative foil for a rational and genuine self.[23]

That foil has long been found in the Orient. To demonstrate the defects of the "Chinese racial character" and justify his Christian civilizing mission, British missionary Arthur Smith first associated the term *face* with the Orient in the late nineteenth century. *Face,* it seems, represented duplicitous Oriental "disguise."[24] Fearful of society—"the mob" and its unruly passions—classical Liberals began to use words like *face* to project their fears about society and the emotions onto the Orient, the realm of the mindless Yellow Horde. Paradoxically, the East came to represent both a passive "herd mentality" and a cunning duplicitousness to Western minds. This helped preserve the good qualities of individualism and rationality for Liberalism and the West.

The continuing association of *face* with the Orient can be seen in the titles of a pair of recent books about China: James Mann's *About Face: A History of America's Curious Relationship with China,* and John Garver's *Face Off: China, the United States, and Taiwan's Democratization.* Mann's engaging narrative dwells on the themes of secrecy and paradox: "It was a relationship beset with contradictions, a strategic marriage of convenience. . . . In private, some American leaders, particularly Nixon, could be candid about the regime they were dealing with. . . . Yet in public, American leaders presented their new relationship with China as something different."[25] Oriental duplicitousness can rub off. There is something "two-faced" about Nixon and others associated with this "curious relationship." It is a tale of intrigue, in which public appearances mask private realities.

In this book I seek to redefine the word *face* as a cultural universal. It is not uniquely "Oriental," but applies to all humanity—including Westerners. Against Americans' rugged individualist lore, I contend that the "self" does not exist in isolation. No man is an island. But neither is man a mere pawn of society: all humans have free will. As social beings, our identities emerge through social intercourse. *Face* captures the interplay of self and society in the process of constructing personhood.

Face also helps capture an interplay of reason and passion central to nationalism that can be seen in the intense emotion Ouyang and DeLay displayed following the Belgrade bombing. In *Face Off,* a fine analysis of the Taiwan Strait Crisis of 1996, Garver recognizes that "strong 'national feeling' may take on a life of its own." He insists, however, that "Great powers go to war over interests."[26] With "feeling" and "interests" presented as binary opposites, human behavior becomes impenetrable. The complexity of human motivation is an urgent problem in all of the social sciences. Garver's title *Face Off* evokes an image of America and China staring each other down. Because he reduced motivation to a choice between sense and sensibility, however, Garver was limited in his ability to explore *why* the Taiwan Strait Crisis occurred. Both power and pride motivated politicians in Washington and Beijing to play such a high-stakes game.

Face as a universal human concern can help us overcome the opposition of reason and passion common in social science, providing a more nuanced account of human motivation. There are both emotional and instrumental motivations for defending the "self shown to others." As sociologist Erving Goffman, pioneer in the Western study of *face*, observes, "a person . . . cathects his face; his feelings become attached to it."[27] People become emotionally attached to the image they present to the world. If *face* is assaulted, feelings are often hurt. But maintaining *face* also means maintaining authority. He who "loses face" loses status and the ability to pursue instrumental goals. An example of how emotions and authority both motivate public efforts to save face is the 1997 suspension of former Golden State Warriors basketball star Latrell Sprewell for physically assaulting his coach, P. J. Carlesimo, during a team practice. The athlete millionaire, it turns out, did not like his coach's "in your face" style. The incident quickly became national news. Dennis Wolff, Boston University's basketball coach, explained the dynamic: "If you tell a guy that you want him to improve his free-throw shooting, he takes it that you don't like him. You know, 'You're dissing me'.[28] . . . You can't embarrass players in front of the group. . . . But if you allow guys to dictate to you it's over."[29] In social settings—"in front of the group"—(dis)respect or saving face is no mere emotional matter: it is a way of maintaining authority. As Goffman has also noted: "Every day in many ways we can try to score points, and every day in many ways we can be shot down."[30] Both power and passion are implicated in such face-to-face combat.

Face can help us to understand how national identities are reshaped through international encounters and what the complex motivations are that drive nationalists. *Face* is not pretense; Chinese culture is not, as writer Ian Buruma asserts, a "culture of duplicity."[31] *Face* is present in *all* societies—even if many in the West are loath to admit as much—but it manifests differently in different contexts. "If a black coach kept coming after Sprewell after he said to stop, he would have been hit, too," argues African-American studies scholar William Banks, "But a black coach probably would have known better, [s/he] would have understood that . . . some current players are operating on street rules."[32] "Street rules" likely refers to the social norms governing life in inner-city America—norms that are very different from those governing upper-middle-class suburbia. The former, for instance, demand a public response to being "dissed." The latter assume precisely the opposite: that one disregard such "slights" as "beneath" one's response. This culture clash may in part explain how the Golden State Warriors incident occurred: coming from very different sub-cultures, Sprewell and Carlesimo likely had very different understandings of the rules that should govern their interaction at team practices.

As "dissing" suggests, the language of *face* varies across both time and place. In the West, we are most familiar with the language of "honor." In an elegant essay written almost seventy years ago, Hans Speier argued that, "A man's honor neither springs from his personality nor clings to his deeds"; it has a "double aspect," both dependent upon others' valuations yet also independent and absolute. Speier maintains that our current preference for the latter over the former is the product of a specific historical circumstance: the bourgeoisie's revolt against the nobility. "The modern individualistic notion of 'personal honor,' as independent from any others' opinion, is a polemic conception which served the middle classes in their struggle to overthrow the feudal conception of honor. The conspicuously honorable behavior of the nobility was devaluated to mere gestures, irrelevant politeness . . . against which was set up a realm of 'natural' inner quality accessible to everyone alike."[33] This conflict is ably captured in the 1995 movie *Rob Roy* about an eighteenth-century Scotsman's revolt against the local nobility. Liam Neeson, playing Rob Roy, explains to his son, "Honour is what no man can give you and none can take away. . . . Honour is a man's gift to himself." I disagree. Although we in the West may dislike it, honor, like face, depends in part on the opinions of others. In the movie, Rob Roy may reject the judgments of the nobility, but his honor depends in part on the respect his fellow Scotsmen confer upon him.

The language of honor is not just the stuff of Scottish legends; it continues to inform life in the West today, although it does so differently in different places. In their fascinating *Culture of Honor: The Psychology of Violence in the South,* social psychologists Richard Nisbett and Dov Cohen found that insults are a much more serious matter for Southerners than they are for Northerners. In a series of experiments conducted at the University of Michigan in 1995, students walking down a hallway were bumped into and called an "asshole!" Southern students were much more likely than northern students to respond aggressively to any subsequent affronts. For instance, Nisbett and Cohen sent their students down a hallway one at a time and had a burly football player walk down the center of the hall on a collision course towards them. Northerners were more likely to get out of the way quickly; Southerners were more willing to play "chicken" against the oncoming Wolverine. The differences were so

striking that Nisbett and Cohen suggest that the students may have interpreted the "asshole!" comment in qualitatively different ways. Northerners were likely to see the comment as reflecting upon the other person, not themselves, while Southerners were much more likely to take it
personally as a question of masculine honor.[34]

If the norms regulating *face* can differ *within* one nation, they can certainly diverge *between* nations. The Chinese and American cultures of *face*
are governed by very different sets of rules. Since foreign policy invariably involves the projection of domestic social norms onto the international arena, Americans and Chinese often expect international society to
operate by the same rules that govern their own domestic societies. And
because these rules often differ, the efforts of Americans and Chinese to
maintain *face* on the international stage can easily become conflicts. Like
Sprewell and Carlesimo, Americans and Chinese may take different expectations about appropriate conduct into their interpersonal and international encounters.

To better understand Chinese nationalism, Americans must understand
the "rules of the game" that Chinese take into interpersonal and intergroup encounters. An interrogation of China's *face* culture reveals the social norms that regulate the negotiation of identity and authority in China.
Chinese views of *face* can be understood at two levels: *lian* and *mianzi*.[35]
Sociologist Hu Hsien-chin defines the former as "decency" or "good
moral reputation" and the latter as an "extra reputation" achieved through
social accomplishments.[36] I focus on the social *mianzi;* my references to
face in the Chinese context are thus to *mianzi,* not *lian*. Chinese discussions of *face* use theatrical allusions, suggesting performances before audiences of popular opinion, whether these are individuals or groups.[37] A
person or group may "give" *face* to another through public praise or deference, or it may "leave" another *face* by not publicly exposing a *faux pas*.
Conversely, public criticism prevents one from "getting off the stage" —
stuck in the spotlight of public scrutiny.

In Chinese, therefore, *face* is not always a bad thing. In English, however, *face* is invariably used as a pejorative, as in "two-faced." It may be
helpful for the Western reader to think of *face* as denoting the more neutral term "honor." The "*face* game" is a battle over the zero-sum resource
of social status.[38] *Face* is thus fundamentally political, involving a contest
over power. Parties vie for *face*. Indeed, the metaphor of exchange is implicit throughout *face* discourse, but even explicit at times: one can try to
"buy" and "sell" *face,* for example, in exchange for goods and services.[39]
Transparent attempts to buy face are not always successful, as the nou-

veaux riches will readily attest. *Face* does not, therefore, imply that Asian political cultures are always "harmonious." The idea that Japanese have a "*wa* culture" of harmony is as absurd as arguments that Japanese are born into a "samurai" or "kamikaze" culture of violence. All societies experience cooperation and conflict. China is no exception.[40] Chinese will sacrifice relationships to protect *face*. It is not uncommon, for instance, to discover brothers who have lived in the same small village for years without talking. But *face* can also facilitate social intercourse. The fear of losing face can constrain behavior, promoting sincerity in social relations. The desire to maintain *face* can thus act as both a barrier to and a facilitator of social interaction.[41]

The same is true of intergroup relations in general and international relations in particular. Experimental work in social psychology has convincingly demonstrated that as social beings we identify ourselves with groups, imbue these groups with positive value, and go to great lengths to maintain "ingroup positivity" or group *face*.[42] Indeed, we can be very creative in our efforts to maintain *face* for our groups, altering comparisons that are threatening ("They may be good at X, but we are good at Y—and Y is more important"), shifting the values of group attributes (arguing that white society viewed "black" as ugly, the American "Black is beautiful" movement successfully challenged that view), changing the quality upon which two groups are compared ("They may have a strong economy, but we know how to party!"), and self-deception ("I think we're stronger, so we are stronger").[43]

In China, such psychological acrobatics are widely associated with Ah Q, the famous protagonist of Lu Xun's brilliant 1922 satire "The True Story of Ah Q." China's most famous twentieth-century writer, Lu Xun was highly critical of the negative influence a vain desire for *face* can have on Chinese behavior.[44] Ah Q, his extreme caricature of this failing, is well known for his "psychological victory technique" by which he maintains an inflated sense of himself.[45] For instance, after suffering humiliating public beatings, Ah Q frequently hits himself. Why? Ah Q sought to fool himself into thinking that he was actually giving—not receiving—a licking: "Presently [Ah Q] changed defeat into victory. Raising his right hand he slapped his own face hard, twice, so that it tingled with pain. After this slapping his heart felt lighter, for it seemed as if the one who had given the slap was himself, the slapped one some other self, and soon it was just as if he had beaten someone else—in spite of the fact that his face was still tingling. He lay down satisfied that he had gained the victory."[46] Turning defeats into victories, Lu Xun suggests, allows Ah Q to save face. Nationalists everywhere frequently engage in such face-saving self-deception. Many Chinese narratives of Sino-American and Sino-Japanese military encounters, we shall see, transform defeats into heroic victories with an Ah Q–like magic.[47] Such subtleties allow the authors of these accounts to maintain *face*.

To repeat, the universal desire to save face is not necessarily a source of conflict. Desires to maintain national *face* can even promote peaceful diplomacy. Contrary to the views of many liberals and realists in international relations, Chinese, Japanese, and Americans are neither innately pacifist nor hardwired for conflict. Instead, history and culture shape how we will construe and react to the events of world politics. It is the actions of individuals that will determine whether our need to view our nations positively—our need to save face—will lead to cooperation or conflict in twenty-first century East Asia.

American Arrogance and Chinese Vanity

Chinese contains a rich popular vocabulary for criticizing those who are too "thick-skinned" or "thin-skinned." Individuals with "thick skin" *(lianpi hou)* are resistant to popular censure. The more serious accusation that an individual "doesn't want *face*"*(buyaolian)* condemns individual profit-seeking as a selfish lack of concern for society. The charge that an individual "has no face" *(meiyoulian)* is even more severe: without a conscience, the individual has lost his or her humanity.[48] The "thin-skinned," by contrast, have an excessive concern for social approbation. *"Si yao mianzi huo shouzui"* refers contemptuously to an irrational willingness to suffer to maintain or gain *face*. Efforts to "put on airs" *(yao mianzi* or *zhuang menmianr)* are ridiculed as "hitting your cheeks to appear healthy/fat" *(da zhonglian yun pangzi),* and as "ringing hollow" *(diqi buzu).*

China's leaders are often too thin-skinned before domestic audiences and too thick-skinned before foreigners. They have been intolerant of domestic criticism, suppressing it brutally. The Tiananmen massacre is but one example of such thin-skinned behavior. However, Beijing's elite often appear to disdain international opinion by lying to foreigners. PLA chief Chi Haotian's 1996 claim that "I can tell you in a responsible and serious manner that not a single person lost his life in Tiananmen Square," for instance, is an example of thick-skinned behavior before international audiences, who, Chi surely realizes, witnessed the massacre on their own television sets.[49]

The more common dynamic in Sino-American relations, however, is a thick-skinned Washington and a thin-skinned Beijing. Unilateral American policies are often insufficiently attentive to Chinese opinion. Chinese elites, for their part, often appear overly sensitive about Chinese *face,* seemingly demanding that America petition China for approval before setting its Asia policies. American arrogance and Chinese vanity can even upset bilateral relations when American and Chinese interests and goals are congruent. Former Assistant Secretary of State John Holdridge has recently related, for example, how he received a tongue-lashing from the Chinese Ministry of Foreign Affairs during an official trip to Beijing in 1982. Although he had come to personally announce a unilateral U.S. concession—giving in on F-5 jet sales to Taiwan—China's diplomats were angry: "They were upset because China had not been a major player in the sequence of events leading up to my visit."[50] Process matters. Until Chinese and Americans learn to interact more harmoniously on the world stage, their common interest in a stable Asia-Pacific will not ensure peace in the twenty-first century.

A Confucian saying holds that "Petty people are irascible. If you draw close to them they are contemptuous of you. But if you are distant from them, they bitterly complain *[xiaoren wei nan yang ye, jinzhi ze buxun, yuanzhi ze nu].*" This book will reveal that China's parochial nationalists often act like such "petty people." When Westerners are accommodating, they are contemptuous. Nationalist Li Fang, for instance, wrote vainly in 1996 that "every American president now comes running obsequiously to China to make his report."[51] When Westerners are firm with China, however, many parochial nationalists angrily denounce the West as a big bully. In another article in the same magazine Li Fang vehemently denounces Americans as "arrogant, boastful, and showoffs."[52]

Fortunately, most Chinese would likely agree with the *Analects'* dictum that "a superior man is broad-minded, whereas a petty person is always resentful." They recognize, as the *Analects* also cautions, that "Intolerance of minor insults will ruin great projects."[53] If they are secure in the belief that China's national *face* is respected in the international community, the Chinese people will marginalize parochial nationalists like Li Fang and demand that their leaders behave like superior men.

CHAPTER 2

Chinese Identity and the "West"

讨
回
公
道
！！

"Restore justice!"

Washington Times national security correspondent Bill Gertz has dark suspicions about Chinese intentions: his writings are distinguished by the fears and fantasies that he projects onto China. In his 2000 book *The China Threat: How the People's Republic Targets America,* Gertz argues that "the China threat is real and growing." "The true nature of Chinese communism," he asserts, is the same as that of all dictatorships: "military aggression." Gertz goes on to equate engagement policies with appeasement: "the Clinton-Gore administration treated China the way Chamberlain treated Hitler."[1] Fears about a declining West become manifest when Gertz asserts that Clinton's engagement policy was "ridiculed by China's communist leaders as the abject weakness of a decaying Western society." Gertz, it appears, has direct access to a sinister "Chinese mind," about which he must warn the West. Gertz clearly identifies with Notra Trulock, a former Energy Department official that Gertz claims was harassed for exposing the alleged Chinese theft of American nuclear secrets, and other such Cassandras, whom he calls his "heroes": "Notra Trulock had dared to challenge the pro-China policies of Bill Clinton. . . . No good deed goes unpunished, as they say."[2] Substitute "Gertz" for "Trulock" and one can see how Gertz might conceive himself to be a valiant defender of American security, struggling fearlessly against China and those who would "appease" it.

Suspect as they may be, the writings of Gertz and other American China bashers should not be dismissed lightly. Like all identities, Chinese and American identities are dynamic, evolving in part through their mutual interactions. Because Chinese nationalists care intensely about China's "international image" (*guoji xingxiang*) and do not want any dirty laundry exposed in public, they pay close attention to the Western press. It is no coincidence that one of the very ugliest of China's anti-American diatribes, 1997's *The Plot to Demonize China,* focuses on real and imagined anti-China schemers in the Western press. Coauthor Li Xiguang, a New China News Agency reporter, even harbors a strong grudge against the rather pro-China *Washington Post,* where he spent several months as a visiting fellow.[3] Chinese nationalists pay close attention to Gertz and other American China bashers.[4] Accordingly, Gertz and others like him have a disproportionate impact on the shape and evolution of Chinese nationalism.

Disciplining America

The back cover of a special 1996 issue of the provincial Chinese magazine *Love Our China* displays smiling pictures of former Foreign Minister Qian Qichen, PLA chief Chi Haotian, and Trade Minister Wu Yi juxtaposed with unflattering pictures of their American counterparts: Warren Christopher, William Perry, and Charlene Barshefsky. A header in bold type declares, "A Colossus and a Bandit Test Their Strengths." The subhead explains, "The grand rules of Sino-American relations are that the kind discipline [*chengjie*] the barbaric." China's role as disciplinarian is highlighted by a large picture of a People's Liberation Army infantryman on the Chinese side of the page thrusting his bayonet towards the American "barbarians."

Such imagery inverts the "King Kong syndrome" satirized by Rey Chow, in which the U.S. media, Washington politicians, and Hollywood frequently construct China as a "primitive monster" that the West must punish.[5] The Bill Gertzes, Tom DeLays and Richard Geres of the West repeatedly depict China as the last bastion of despotism, thus positioning

FIGURE 6. Disciplining America. The back cover of a 1996 *Love Our China* declares that "a Colossus and a Bandit Test Their Strengths." A PLA infantryman reinforces the point. Source: *Love Our China.*

themselves as freedom fighters. American ideologues have long deployed the foil of Chinese tyranny to argue the virtues of American liberty.[6]

As the example from *Love Our China* reveals, however, the roles can be reversed: China can discipline too.[7] Just as many in the West use the "Orient" to define themselves, many in the East use the "Occident" to the same ends. The text on the back cover of *Love Our China*, for instance, begins with some contrasts: "China has 5,000 years of civilized history . . . while America has only 200 years of history." It then turns to insults: "Facing an ancient Eastern colossus, America is at most a child." "Emotion-cues," sociologist Candace Clark reminds us, "can be used to manipulate, reminding and counter-reminding each other of judgments of the proper place."[8] By "altercasting" America as a child, China can play the superior elder. "Altercasting," a basic technique of interpersonal control, involves the projection and manipulation of identities onto others to serve one's own goals.[9]

Following Edward Said's discussion of "Orientalism," Chen Xiaomei has labeled such Chinese uses of the West "Occidentalism," a "deeply rooted practice [in China] of alluding to the Occident as a contrasting Other in order to define whatever one believes to be distinctively 'Chinese.'"[10] Reversals of the relative status of China and the United States appear in descriptions of Sino-American relations that invoke relational metaphors. The teacher-student relationship, for instance, is a prominent metaphor in Chinese writings about America. Chinese as diverse as Sun Yat-sen, Chen Duxiu, and Mao Zedong all at one point looked to America as a "teacher" to be emulated. In 1904 future president Sun Yat-sen wrote, "We . . . must appeal to the people of the civilized world in general and the people of the United States in particular, for your sympathy and support . . . because we intend to model our new government after yours." May Fourth intellectuals also looked to America as a teacher. In 1918 Chen Duxiu, soon to be founder of the Chinese Communist Party, wrote glowingly of Woodrow Wilson: "All the speeches made by President Woodrow Wilson of the United States are open and above board. He can be regarded as the best man in the world." Prior to the outbreak of the Korean War, Mao Zedong also viewed America as a teacher. In 1946 Zhou Enlai told American General George Marshall that "It has been rumored that Chairman Mao is going to pay a visit to Moscow. On learning this, Chairman Mao laughed and remarked . . . that he would rather go to the United States, because he thinks that he can learn lots of things useful to China."[11] However, Mao soon became disillusioned and revolted against mentor America, whom he claimed had bullied, rather than instructed, student China.

Like Mao, today's young Chinese nationalists also claim to have rebelled against an America they figure as teacher. At the beginning of the 1996 anti-American sensation *China Can Say No,* Song Qiang confesses that in the 1980s he "worshipped" Ronald Reagan. By the 1990s, however, Song had come to view pro-American sentiment as an "infectious disease" to be purged.[12] In "Our Generation's America Complex," Li Fang similarly depicts America as a "teacher to rebel against."[13] Wen Ming is indignant in the *Beijing Review,* writing that Americans "think they are the chosen people and have the right to teach others."[14] Young Chinese are increasingly rebelling against their chosen teacher.

Many Chinese nationalists today clearly want to exchange roles within their teacher-student relationship with America. In 1996, Guan Shijie wrote in the English language *China Daily* that "the time has come for the West to learn from the East. The West should switch positions, and the teacher should become a student." This statement is both ironic and disappointing, because Guan is the director of "International and Intercultural Communications" at Beijing University, the birthplace of political liberalism in China.[15] His longing seems widespread, however, and is often revealed indirectly in seemingly apolitical discussions of the Chinese and English languages. For example, 1997's *Dragon History,* a psycho-autobiography written by members of the "fourth generation" of Chinese in their thirties, contains a section entitled "Whitey, Please Study Chinese." The author recounts an experience that he had reading a Chinese language textbook written for foreigners. One sentence read, "I'm determined to study the English language well. If I don't learn it well, I won't be able to find a spouse." Reading this line made the Chinese author feel "suffocated and resentful." He then shares a fantasy with his readers: "The sentence would clearly be much more enchanting if you just replaced the word 'English' with the word 'Chinese.'"[16] He thus expresses his desire for an inversion within the hierarchy, with China taking the superior position.[17]

Another way China's young nationalists revolt against the United States is by reversing the roles in another relationship metaphor: that of father and son. By depicting America as a child, China can be the father. After a lengthy tirade against American arrogance, for example, nationalist Li Fang sets things right by declaring that "America is still a child." He then relishes a discussion of his Singaporean brothers "whipping American ass."[18] (In 1994, American teenager Michael Fay was lashed four times as punishment for the crime of vandalism.) In his section of *China Can Say No,* Qiao Bian similarly declares the United States a "spoiled child" who changes the rules in order to win.[19] Again, altercasting America in the role of child, Li and Qiang depict China as a parent—and clearly believe that parents have both the right and responsibility to discipline their children.

Chinese national identity, in sum, is constructed in part through the ways that Chinese think and write about America. Ambivalence about their status vis-à-vis the United States is reflected in the use popular nationalists make of teacher-student and father-son metaphors to describe Sino-American relations. What Jin Niu has labeled a "teacher-student complex" *(shi-sheng qingjie)* is still pervasive in Chinese attitudes towards America, revealing Chinese anxieties about their own identity and position in international society.[20] Indeed, the West is central to the construction of Chinese identity today: it has become China's alter ego. As the sole superpower of the post–Cold War world, America symbolizes the West for China and for much of the rest of the non-Western world. For many, the global reach of American culture, industry, and military might make America *the* Occident.

However, although the United States provides China with an important foil, Americans are *not* ideal objects for Chinese identity dialectics, because they are so racially and culturally different from Chinese. It is simply too difficult for many Chinese to identify with "Western devils" *(yang guizi)*. The father-son relationship used to reinforce Chinese superiority over America is less prominent in describing relations with Japan, where an older brother–younger brother metaphor is more typical. Perhaps the greater distance between fathers and sons feels more appropriate for the Sino-American relationship, whereas greater similarity allows the Sino-Japanese relationship to be captured by the older brother–younger brother metaphor. Thus, although an assumption of fundamental difference underlies many Chinese writings about the West in general and about the United States in particular, an assumption of similarity underlies many Chinese writings about Japan.

Japan, China's Occident

Japan is not geographically west of China, but Chinese often include Japan in both the noun and adjective *"Xifang"*—"the West" and "Western." It is through Japan that Chinese have sought both to learn from the West and to understand themselves. That the idea and even the title for the popular 1996 anti-American book *China Can Say No* was inspired by Ishihara Shintaro and Morita Akio's 1989 anti-American *The Japan that Says No* is emblematic of Japan's continuing centrality to Chinese identity. Indeed, Japan has served as the primary reference point from which modern Chinese have defined themselves. Although America has come to represent the West *par excellence* for post–Cold War Chinese (and most non-Western peoples), Japan's proximity to China, the racial and cultural similarities Japanese share with the Chinese, and Japan's extensive interactions with China in the modern period justify its designation as "China's Occident." The vital analogue and inspiration for such a designation is historian Stefan Tanaka's 1993 argument that China has served as "Japan's Orient."[21] Tanaka argues that prewar Japanese used "the West and Asia as other(s) to construct their own sense of a Japanese nation as modern and oriental."[22] Chinese nationalists similarly use Japan and "the Occident" to build their own visions of China and its proper place in the world.

Because of the centrality of Japan to Chinese national identity, histories of Sino-Japanese relations raise extremely sensitive issues. Many Chinese assume a moral right to control discussions of the subject. The Shanghai Academy of Social Science's Wang Hailiang, for instance, reacted strongly to Yamada Tatsuo's 1994 history of Japan-China relations. Writing in a 1996 *Asia-Pacific Forum*, Wang declares that Yamada's views are "incorrect" and "cannot be accepted." Wang is angered that Yamada characterizes the second half of the nineteenth century as a period of "mutual reliance," and the twenty years centering around 1900 as an era of Japanese assistance to Chinese revolutionaries. Like numerous Chinese, Wang maintains that Japan, a "hungry wolf on the prowl" *(elang bushi),* had expansionist aims directed at China ever since the Meiji Restoration of 1868. To say that Japan assisted Chinese revolutionaries is "like saying that the Japanese made modern Chinese history." Wang's rage, however, is reserved for what he calls Yamada's search for an "objective explanation" for World War II: "Research all you want and you won't be able to change World War II's evil nature. . . . Invasion is invasion!"[23]

Many Chinese seem happier with Chinese histories of Sino-Japanese relations, or, better yet, with cooperative histories dominated by Chinese. The 1982 movie *The Go Masters,* about Chinese and Japanese *"weiqi"* or *"go"* players, is a fascinating example of such a joint project. A match set in 1924 is interrupted by World War II and not completed until thirty years later, on the Great Wall, symbolizing the triumph of Chinese civilization. Chinese moral superiority is also the subject of the film's many interpersonal relationships. A Chinese magnanimously forgives a repentant Japanese classmate after a fight. And masculine and feminine roles are also used to indicate Chinese dominance, as the son of the Chinese protagonist and the daughter of the Japanese protagonist fall in love. She is assimilated to Chinese culture, reaffirming Chinese superiority. Although Chinese clearly controlled *The Go Masters* project, Japanese participation confirmed Chinese *face* claims.

The closely intertwined nature of modern Chinese and Japanese history accounts for the unique way Chinese talk about their country's "friendship" with Japan. Although such phrases as "Sino-Japanese friendship" are frequently used by Chinese writers to remind Japanese of their indebtedness to China, they also confirm positive Chinese views of themselves.[24] Therefore, such phrases also contribute to Chinese productions of *face*. An example of how this works may be seen in the reaction of a group from the Institute for Japanese Studies at China's Liaoning University to a two-week tour of Japan in 1990. Writing in *Japanese Studies,* they claimed to have been overcome by the "friendliness" of their Japanese hosts. One incident, they write, particularly "warmed our hearts." Visiting a Japanese elementary school, they were greeted by "childish hellos" in Chinese.[25] This greeting was probably moving to the Chinese visitors because it reinforced a positive self-image of themselves as parents to Japanese culture at a time when the shock of witnessing firsthand the high Japanese standard of living was likely challenging their national self-esteem.

In contrast, when Chinese project negative self-images onto Japanese observers, it is with the anger of those who expect friendship but receive rejection. A Chinese survey provides a telling example of such projection. Administered to over 1,000 Chinese in Shanghai in 1996, the survey included the question, "How do Japanese view Chinese?" Reporting on their results in Fudan University's *Japan Research Quarterly,* researchers Chen Jian'an, Xu Jingbo, and Hu Lingyun note that 54 percent responded "with disdain," while only 27 percent responded "respectfully." The result surprised the authors, who open their article by indignantly asserting that "Westerners see both Chinese and Japanese as 'Orientals.' . . . This is a mistake."[26] The idea that Westerners might group Chinese together with Japanese infuriates them, but it originates not with Westerners, but with Chinese. The authors of the survey, by asking Chinese to imagine how others view them (clearly a recipe for projection) have set themselves up to be outraged.[27] It is noteworthy that the authors' response to the questionnaire results was to reject a distressing similarity to the Japanese that they had projected onto Westerners.

Indeed, Chinese can declare both similarity and difference with Japanese either to resist the West or to win praise from it. Similarity with Japan is often emphasized to create a "yellow Asia" in opposition to the "white West." Japan is especially useful as an example of non-Western modernization, satisfying the nationalist imperative to distinguish between modernization and Westernization.[28] For instance, Gao Zengjie writes in *Japanese Studies* that discussions of Chinese and Japanese differences are based upon the premise of commonalities, which he then enumerates. "Chinese and Japanese scholars," Gao concludes, "agree that modernization is not the same as 'Westernization.'"[29] Feng Zhaokui, Gao's colleague at the Institute for Japanese Studies of the Chinese Academy of Social Sciences (CASS) and China's foremost expert on Japanese economics and technology, also utilizes Japan in this manner in his section of the 1993 *Japan's Experience and China's Reforms*. Feng argues strongly against the idea, which he ascribes to "the West," that China's transition towards a market economy means that China is becoming like the West. Such a view, he declares, is a Western "disorder" *(maobing)*. Feng then lists similarities between China and Japan to demonstrate that the Chinese, like the Japanese, do not need to Westernize to modernize. He cites Japan's use of economic planning during its postwar takeoff to claim that, "just as the 'market' is not monopolized by capitalism (socialism also has markets); the 'plan' is not monopolized by socialism (capitalism also has 'plans')." His nationalist reaction to *his impression of the West's impression of China* even leads him to assert by the end of the chapter that "socialism is *better than* capitalism at integrating the plan and the market."[30] Similarity between China and Japan is thus used to create an Asia better than the West. Chinese superiority can also be established by depicting Japanese culture as similar to but derivative of Chinese civilization. As democracy activist Wei Jingsheng told writer Ian Buruma, "The Orient is China. Japan is just an appendage."[31]

However, to make the same argument that China is superior to the West, Chinese can also emphasize Japan's differences with China, and sometimes cast these differences as culturally Western. For example, in the 1996 *China Can Still Say No* Song Qiang, Zhang Zangzang and their coauthors insist on Chinese differences from the Japanese to assert Chinese superiority: "There is a saying that Japanese and Chinese are 'of the same culture and same race.' But I don't believe that Japanese are the descendants of Chinese. Although they also use Chinese characters and preserve some things from Chinese culture, Japanese lack Chinese generosity, kindheartedness, and modesty. Theirs is a different kind of blood."[32] In their 1997 psycho-autobiography *The Spirit of the Fourth Generation*, Song and his coauthors identify Japan with the West, asserting that the

Japanese "economic animals" are the "eastern heroes" of "Western materialism," inferior to "Eastern harmony."[33]

Many Chinese seem to move easily between depicting the Japanese as same and viewing them as different. In his *Brief History of Sino-Japanese Friendship,* for example, Ge Xin first writes that "looking over the history of friendship between the Chinese and Japanese peoples, Chinese have given more to Japanese than Japanese have given to Chinese." He thus establishes the *difference* between generous Chinese and the stingy, ungrateful Japanese. In the same paragraph, however, Ge continues, "Japanese enterprise management thought, greatly *esteemed by all the nations of the world,* mostly comes from Confucius, Mencius, and Sun Zi's *Art of War.*"[34] Ge, easily moving between depictions of Japan's difference from and similarity to China, shows how both may be used to *identify* China with Japan in ways that gain *face* for China before world opinion. China both becomes superior to Japan and basks in its reflected glory.[35]

Like Chinese writings about America, Chinese discussions of Sino-Japanese relations often invoke the Confucian "five relationships." The teacher-student and older brother–younger brother metaphors are particularly prominent. Altercasting Japan in the inferior role makes China its superior. For example, in his 1997 diatribe *Why Japan Won't Settle Accounts,* Li Zhengtang argues that for hundreds of years China was Japan's "benevolent teacher." In the Sino-Japanese War of 1895, however, "China lost to her 'student.'" He then asks, "How can we sons and grandsons of the Yellow Emperors forget for a moment this great racial insult?"[36] Li himself has not forgotten. The righteous Japan bashing expressed throughout *Why Japan Won't Settle Accounts* suggests that Li believes the "student" should be put back in his proper place. Li's anger seeks to reconstruct the *correct* teacher-student hierarchy with China in the superior position.[37]

In a more dispassionate academic account of the issue by Jiang Lifeng and a few of his colleagues at the Institute for Japanese Studies of the Chinese Academy of Social Sciences, the older brother–younger brother metaphor is used to the same ends. This relationship metaphor seems particularly suited to the Sino-Japanese relationship.[38] According to Jiang, China and Japan may fight, but they are still "brothers" sharing the "same culture and blood" *(tong wen tong zhong).* At issue is their "relative position." During the ancient period, China was superior and relations were "harmonious." In the early modern period, however, Japan became superior and a "competitive" politics damaged Sino-Japanese relations. Although Jiang and his coauthors do not explicitly state what the brothers' current relative positions are or should be, their view is revealed indirectly. Writing about the nations' respective attitudes toward their common history, for instance, they argue that the Japanese "seek psychological equality" by evading responsibility for World War II. This position implies China's current moral superiority. Jiang and his colleagues are also angered by the "high posture" they believe Japan has taken towards China since the mid-1990s, contending that the Japanese want to establish a "superior position."[39]

Chinese nationalists are very sensitive about issues of hierarchy and power in Sino-Japanese relations. Historian Arif Dirlik argues that when Chinese speak of "two thousand years of Sino-Japanese friendship" they seek to remind the Japanese of Japan's cultural indebtedness to China.[40] The same logic applies when Chinese claim that China and Japan are neighbors separated by "a mere belt of water" (*yi yi dai shui*). The phrase uses proximity to claim Chinese hegemony.[41] Dirlik's statement that "For the Chinese . . . history (as culture) represents a means of bringing symmetry to . . . an 'asymmetric' relationship," is questionable, however.[42] "Symmetry" suggests equality. The prevalence of teacher-student and older brother–younger brother metaphors in Chinese discussions of Sino-Japanese relations suggests that many Chinese see Japanese as morally inferior to them—not as equals.

A Clash of Civilizations?

Chinese identity does not exist in isolation. It evolves through the ways Chinese perceive their interactions with other nations, and especially through the ways they perceive their relations with the United States and Japan. Samuel Huntington's clash-of-civilizations argument provoked heated debate in mid-1990s China. Many Chinese pundits were upset by Huntington's idea of an Islamic-Confucian alliance against the West. Huntington, they argued, was paranoid: fearful about America's decline, he resorted to China bashing. But anger alone did not sustain the Huntington sensation in China. The idea of a clash between East and West pleased many Chinese nationalists, who embraced the image of China Huntington provided: "They see us as a threat! We've finally regained our great power status!"

Huntington's focus on race and culture also struck a chord with Chinese intellectuals, who have long defined "modern" Chinese history as beginning with the mid-nineteenth-century arrival of Western imperialism in China. Wang Jisi, Director of the Institute of American Studies at the Chinese Academy of Social Sciences, explained the appeal of Huntington to Chinese intellectuals: "An important reason Huntington's theory has provoked so much discussion in China is that his prediction of a clash of civilizations echoes a debate that has been going on within China for over a hundred years which revolves around a most sensitive issue for the Chinese: Are Chinese and Western cultures headed for convergence or collision? . . . As he sees it, the clash of civilizations is like the clash of national interests: Either the west wind prevails over the east wind, or vice versa. There can be no room for accommodation or convergence."[43] Many Chinese nationalists fear that modernization will lead to "peaceful evolution": cultural convergence or Westernization. By reifying cultural differences, Huntington creates space for a non-Western but modern China.

More importantly, however, Huntington confirmed Chinese nationalists' assertions that the West is in decline and that the twenty-first century will be China's era. In a 1995 issue of *World Affairs* (Beijing), Jin Junhui quotes Huntington on the rise of the non-West (in Jin's eyes, China)—"the peoples and governments of non-Western civilizations no longer remain the objects of history, as targets of Western colonialism, but join the West as movers and shapers of history." He continues that "Even as one criticizes the 'Clash of Civilizations,' . . . we should not be blind to some of Huntington's more incisive points."[44] Indeed, many Chinese read Huntington as arguing that China—not Islam—is the greatest threat to America. Writing in the influential *Reading* (Beijing) magazine in 1997, for example, Li Shenzhi asserts that Huntington states that "Chinese civilization is Western civilization's number one enemy." This view allowed readers like Li to view China as the number two power of the post–Cold War era. The reason for the demonization of China, Li further maintains, lies in Huntington's fears about the decline of the West: "This is unmistakably the tone of someone with no other choice, someone defending himself in retreat." He then revels in a description of the decline of the West: "Even though this U.S. melting pot has melted down all kinds of ethnic groups from Europe during the past 200 years . . . it is now clear that there are too many ingredients, too little old sauce, and not enough heat. The pot is also too small and unable to melt down the increasingly diverse ingredients."[45] Huntington confirms a Chinese nationalist vision of America declining while China rises.

Such efforts to contrast a good China with an evil West are not confined to elite academic discourse, but inform popular culture as well.

The 1993 mainland Chinese television series *A Beijinger in New York* depicted the trials and tribulations of Chinese businessman Wang Qiming (played by Jiang Wen, China's most popular and virile actor of the time) as he made his way in the dog-eat-dog world of New York City. The series was perhaps most astonishing for its repeated racist depictions of America. At one point, for instance, Wang yells, "Fuck them! They were still monkeys up in the trees while we were already human beings. Look at how hairy they are, they're not as evolved as us."[46] At another crescendo in the action, Wang hires a buxom blond prostitute and has his way with her with a vengeance. The series was a hit. Less sensationally, but perhaps more significantly, the show was notable for its repeated efforts to construct a positive Chinese national identity at America's expense. America is depicted as a place of mean-spirited conflict and self-interest; China, in contrast, is seen as a land of harmony and warm-hearted beneficence. David McCarthy, Wang's chief American rival in business and love, epitomizes American avarice and ruthlessness. By the end of the Wang-McCarthy Sino-American contest, however, Wang has succeeded in business and love. McCarthy affirms Wang's victory and Chinese superiority by heading off to China to teach English.[47]

The Sino-Western encounter also ends with Chinese victory in Mo Yan's 1995 *Large Breasts and Full Hips*—but the Westerner emerges from the encounter dead. Author of *Red Sorghum* (which director Zhang Yimou later made into a hit movie), Mo Yan tells a complex and dark tale of rape, humiliation, and suicide. The story centers upon a Western missionary's affair with a Chinese woman—and the affront this represents to male Chinese pride. China is redeemed, however, when a Chinese bandit calls the priest a "monkey"—"you're a bastard from a screwing between a man and a chimp"—shoots the priest in the legs, and forces him to watch as he rapes the Chinese woman. The priest, humiliated, then commits suicide.[48] Humiliated by past Western aggressions, China turns the tables, humiliating the West and getting its revenge. Both *A Beijinger* and *Large Breasts* thus depict the Sino-Western encounter as a violent contest over female bodies. Female suffering is secondary to the authors' primary concern: regaining face for male Chinese at the West's expense. China's self-image is forged within a "clash of civilizations," a dialogic process of comparison with and distinction from other nations—and China always wins.

CHAPTER 3

A "Century
of Humiliation"

*"Wipe away the national
humiliation!"*

"The sleeping lion has awoken, erasing the national humiliation," reads the calligraphy above Xia Ziyi's 1996 painting *The Awakened Lion*. Painted in anticipation of Hong Kong's 1997 "return to the Motherland," Xia's roaring lion, with bared fangs and angry eyes, does not seem humiliated or ashamed. What is the relationship between the humiliation discussed in the calligraphy and the rage of the lion? Although Marxists as diverse as Kautsky, Luxembourg, and Lenin viewed nationalism as an instrument utilized by the ruling classes to divide and conquer the working classes, Karl Marx himself used psychology to explain it: "Shame is a kind of anger turned in on itself. And if a whole nation were to feel ashamed it would be like a lion recoiling in order to spring."[1] China's past "national humiliation" at the hands of Western imperialism, Xia seems to argue, can be "erased" with an angry roar.

Why does Xia choose a lion, rather than the usual dragon, to symbolize China? He is not alone in doing so. Today's Chinese nationalists

FIGURE 7. "The sleeping lion has awoken!" "Big noses" are scared, confirming China's rise. Source: *The Cartoon Sayings of Deng Xiaoping*, 1996.

frequently depict China as a lion. The editors of the 1996 *Cartoon Sayings of Deng Xiaoping* show China as a lion in a cartoon illustrating one of Deng's sayings on the importance of independence and self-reliance. Dwarfed by a giant lion, frightened Westerners with top hats and big noses declare, "The sleeping lion has awoken!" and run for their lives. Xi Yongjun and Ma Zaizhun's 1996 *Surpassing the USA* suggests an answer to the puzzle. In chapter 7, "The Sleeping Lion Has Been Infuriated," they write: "The French hero Napoleon long ago said, 'Asia's China is a sleeping lion. Once it awakes, it will shake the entire world.' The sleeping lion of the East has already awoken to an obsessively ambitious America, and has roared."[2] By choosing to represent China as a lion, Xi, Ma, and perhaps Xia and the *Deng Sayings* cartoonists have chosen to recall Napoleon's famous view of China. Why do they go out of their way to appropriate a foreigner's view of China? Why not assert China's resurgence in their own terms and images? I suggest that the views of respected Westerners like Samuel Huntington and Napoleon are central to Chinese views of themselves. And Napoleon's image of China as a sleeping lion allows Chinese nationalists to put the past to good use: because sleeping lions do not sleep forever, Chinese can be confident that China will be strong and prosperous again.

The Weight of the Past

In addition to evolving to cope with the demands of present-day Sino-American and Sino-Japanese relations, Chinese national identity evolves to cope with the burden of the past. The crucial national narrative of the "Century of Humiliation" *(bainian guochi)* from the mid-nineteenth century to the mid-twentieth century is central to Chinese nationalism today. What is the relationship between the past and the nationalisms of the present? One view holds that the past determines the present. The Kosovo conflict was frequently depicted as "intractable" because of Muslim-Christian enmity dating back to the Battle of Kosovo in 1389, when the Muslim Turks defeated the Christian kingdom of Serbia. In his 1992 *The Tyranny of History,* an intensely personal reaction to the Tiananmen massacre, W. J. F. Jenner accounts for Chinese identity using a similar argument: "China is caught in a . . . prison of history."[3] The weight of the past, it seems, is particularly heavy in China. Jenner thus pessimistically predicted, incorrectly, that the "Party is over." According to him, the CCP could not last long.

Another view, held by most scholars of nationalism today, maintains precisely the opposite: that historians writing in the present determine the past.[4] Following in historian Eric Hobsbawm's footsteps, most China scholars have stressed how Chinese historians "invent" histories and traditions to serve contemporary ends.[5] In his fascinating study of the 1900 Boxer Rebellion, historian Paul Cohen discusses how Chinese historians "draw on [the past] to serve the political, ideological, rhetorical, and/or emotional needs of the present." Cohen cites the *People's Daily,* which in 1990 sought to combat post-Tiananmen Western sanctions by commemorating the ninetieth anniversary of the Boxer Rebellion with several articles describing the brutality of the foreign armies that marched on Beijing in 1900.[6] Cultural critic Geremie Barmé even goes so far as to assert that "Every policy shift in recent Chinese history has involved the rehabilitation, re-evaluation and revision of history and historical figures."[7] There is little doubt that China's rulers have long used the past to serve the present.[8] By privileging the present, however, such approaches often end up trivializing the way the weight of the past shapes nationalism today.[9]

The concept of national "narratives" can help us better understand the role of the past in nationalist politics today. Narratives are the stories we tell about our pasts. These stories, psychologists have argued, infuse our identities with unity, meaning, and purpose. We cannot, therefore, radically change them at will. Far from being simple tools of our invention, the stories we tell about the past both constrain and are constrained by what we do in the present.[10] Simply put, the storied nature of social life provides our identities with meaning. "Identities," Stuart Hall notes, "are the names we give to the different ways we are positioned by, and position ourselves in, the narratives of the past."[11] Hall's "positioned by, and position ourselves in" nicely captures the balance of agency and constraint in the relationship between individuals and their constitutive narratives. Thus, whereas the past loses any causal weight of its own when it is depicted as an easily malleable tool in the hands of nationalist historians, and the present becomes a prisoner of the past in deterministic approaches, the concept of narrative allows for an interdependent relationship between past and present in nationalist practice.

In particular, narratives about the "Century of Humiliation" frame the ways that Chinese interact with the West today. This period begins with China's defeat in the First Opium War and the British acquisition of Hong Kong in 1842. The period was marked by major wars between China and

Western powers or Japan: the two Opium Wars of 1839–1842 and 1856–1860, the Sino-Japanese "Jiawu" War of 1894–1895, the Boxer Rebellion of 1900, and the "War of Resistance against Japan" of 1931/1937–1945.[12] Many educated Chinese today are painfully aware of the "unequal treaties" signed with the British at Nanjing in 1842 and the Japanese at Shimoneseki in 1895. Unilateral concessions forced on the Chinese in these treaties, such as indemnities, extraterritoriality, and foreign settlements in the treaty ports, are still perceived as humiliating losses of sovereignty. Other symbols of the period still resonate with today's nationalists. The stone ruins of the Old Summer Palace outside Beijing, looted and burned by Europeans in 1860, are a reminder of the "rape" of China. Lin Zexu, a famous Chinese crusader against opium and British aggression, still stands for Chinese courage and virtue.

The "Century of Humiliation" is neither an objective past that works insidiously in the present nor a mere "invention" of present-day nationalist entrepreneurs. Instead, the "Century" is a continuously reworked narrative about the national past central to the contested and evolving meaning of being "Chinese" today.

Furthermore, the "Century" is a traumatic and foundational moment because it fundamentally challenged Chinese views of the world. In Chinese eyes, earlier invaders became Chinese, while barbarians beyond the border paid humble tribute to "civilization" *(wenming)*. Both practices reinforced a view of Chinese civilization as universal and superior. Early encounters with "big noses," from Marco Polo to pre-nineteenth-century European and American traders and missionaries, did not challenge this view. "Our ancient neighbors," writes one young Chinese nationalist, "found glory in drawing close to Chinese civilization."[13] The violent nineteenth-century encounter with the "West" was different. The "Central Kingdom" was not only defeated militarily, but was also confronted by a civilization with universalist pretensions of its own. "The Western impact," writes Tu Weiming, "fundamentally dislodged Chinese intellectuals from their Confucian haven . . . [creating a] sense of impotence, frustration, and humiliation."[14] The "Western devils" *(yang guizi)* had a civilization of their own that challenged the universality and superiority of Confucian civilization.[15] The traumatic confrontation between East and West fundamentally destabilized Chinese views of the world and their place within it. "Trauma brings about a lapse or rupture in memory that breaks continuity with the past," writes historian Dominick LaCapra in a discussion of the Holocaust. "It unsettles narcissistic investments and desired self-images."[16] Just as the trauma of the Holocaust led many in the postwar West to reexamine their tradition, the "Century" threatened a Chinese identity based upon the idea of a universal and superior civilization.[17] "The Israelis' vision of the Holocaust has shaped their idea of themselves," Tom Segev writes, "just as their changing sense of self has altered their view of the Holocaust and their understanding of its meaning."[18] Since stories about the past both limit and define our national identities in the present, the same is true of the Chinese and the "Century of Humiliation": Chinese visions of the "Century" have shaped their sense of self, and these changes to Chinese identity have altered their views of the "Century."

Today, Chinese struggles to come to terms with this period of trauma are reflected in the emergence of new narratives about the "Century." Under Mao, China's pre-"Liberation" (1949) sufferings were blamed on the feudalism of the Qing Dynasty and Western imperialism, and the antifeudal, anti-imperialist masses were valorized for throwing off their chains and repelling foreign invaders. This "heroic" or "victor" national narrative first served the requirements of Communist revolutionaries seeking to mobilize popular support in the 1930s and 1940s, and later served the nation-building goals of the People's Republic in the 1950s, 1960s, and 1970s. One 1959 movie about the First Opium War, for instance, changed its title from *The Opium War* to *Lin Zexu* to glorify Chinese heroism. New China needed heroes.

During the 1990s, however, the official Maoist "victor narrative" was slowly superseded by a new and popular "victimization narrative" that blames "the West," including Japan, for China's suffering. This "new" storyline actually renews the focus on victimization in pre-Mao Republican-era writings on the "Century."[19] Indeed, the image of China as a raped woman, common in Republican China but unpopular during the Maoist period, has reemerged. In Republican China, playwrights like Xiao Jun used rape in nationalist plays such as *Village in August,* in which Japanese soldiers rape a patriotic peasant woman.[20] The return of the "rape of China" theme may be seen in such bestsellers as Chinese-American Iris Chang's 1997 *The Rape of Nanking,* which I discuss in chapters 5 and 6. This text helped transform the 1937 Nanjing massacre into a "rape." But the image had been revived before 1997 in mainland China. A special 1994 edition of *Rainbow* magazine, "The Secret Records of the Eight-Nation Force's Bestiality," is an early example of the reemerging "rape of China" theme. Late Qing historical records, the editors assert, reveal that two hundred thousand Chinese women were killed after being raped by foreign troops in 1900. However, such fantastic claims are really a disguise for what is actually soft pornography.[21] Young male Chinese readers could thus simultaneously satisfy a righteous anti-Western anger and their prurient desires.

The contrast between "victor" and "victim" national narratives is nicely captured in two Chinese movies about the First Opium War of 1839–1842. *Lin Zexu* (1959), mentioned above, is a story of the Chinese people's heroic anti-imperialist struggle. Named *Lin Zexu* to highlight resistance, it does not focus solely on Commissioner Lin, but emphasizes his close relations with a peasant couple who seek vengeance against Eliot, the evil British trader who had killed the peasant woman's father. Lin and the Chinese people *(renmin)* are one in an upbeat tale of popular defiance. *Opium War* (1997), by contrast, is a dark and depressing tale of past tragedy. It is only at the very end of the movie, with the image of a stone lion and the message that "on July 1, 1997, the Chinese government recovered sovereignty over Hong Kong," that China is redeemed. Director Xie Jin's vision of the past is one of opium addicts and humiliation; his vision of the present and future is one of mighty lions awakening to exact their revenge.[22] A victim in the past, a vengeful China will be a victim no longer.

Nineteen ninety-seven seems to have been a pivotal moment in the reemergence of the victimization narrative in China. The countdown to Hong Kong's "Return to the Motherland" in the spring and summer of 1997 created a strong desire to "wipe away" *(xixue)* the "National Humiliation." And in the fall of 1997, sixtieth-anniversary commemorations of the Nanjing massacre, as well as Iris Chang's book about it, directed Chinese attention to their past suffering as never before. Anticipating closure on the "Humiliation," many Chinese paradoxically reopened a long-festering wound. For many Chinese nationalists, this painful encounter with past trauma was expressed in the language of victimization.

China of 1997 may thus prove to be comparable to 1961 Israel, when Eichmann's trial precipitated a dramatic shift in Israeli attitudes towards the Holocaust. The repression of Holocaust memories in the name of the nation-building (creating a "New Israel") that prevailed in the late 1940s and 1950s gave way to a new identification with victimization in the 1960s. The early postwar Israeli rejection of victimhood is reflected in the evolution of Holocaust Day, which was established only in 1953 and did not become a mandatory national holiday until 1959. Early Holocaust Day commemorations emphasized the "martyrs and heroes" of the ghetto resistance, not the victims of the concentration camps who were memorialized in later tributes.[23] China is now undergoing a similar process, as

long-suppressed memories of past suffering resurface. Chinese nationalism since the 1990s cannot be understood apart from this new encounter
with past trauma.

Despite the new focus on "victimization," heroic narratives about the
"Century of Humiliation" have not disappeared. Narratives of "China as
victor" and "China as victim" coexist in Chinese nationalism today. The
"Century" is arguably both what psychologist Vamik Volkan calls a "chosen glory" and what he calls a "chosen trauma."[24] The publisher's preface to a 1991 series of books entitled "Do not forget the history of national humiliation" is typical, describing the "Century" as both a "history
of the struggle of the *indomitable* Chinese people against imperialism,"
and a "tragic history of suffering, beatings, and extraordinary *humilia-
tions.*"[25] Many Chinese nationalists, it seems, are eager to capitalize on
the moral authority of their past suffering. But there is a downside to the
new "victimization narrative." It entails confronting vulnerability and
weakness. The enduring need for heroism and a "victor narrative" serves,
it seems, to allay the fears of those who are not yet ready to confront directly the trauma of the "Humiliation."

Neither "China as victor" nor "China as victim" has yet to probe the
wound of the "Century" very deeply. The fate of the few Chinese who
have attempted to push beyond the polar and facile explanations of "revolutionary heroism" and "imperialist aggression" and explore the deeper
sources of China's early modern encounters with imperialism is instructive. The popular phrase "backwards/beaten" (*luohou aida*) captures their
plight. Interpreted as "the backwards *will be* beaten" (*luohou jiuyao aida*),
the phrase implies that the former caused the latter: economic and tech-
nological backwardness led to China's defeat at the hands of the West. A
few Chinese have pursued this logic, asking themselves, "Why were we
backwards?" In 1995, for example, historian Mao Haijian criticized Chinese scholarship on the Opium War as a contest to see who could best
vilify the British. He suggested that Chinese should instead seek to learn
from their past mistakes: "Self-criticism of our own history is the only
way to ensure that we avoid going down the same historical path again."[26]
Specifically, Mao questioned whether Lin Zexu was really a hero, whether
Manchu official Qishan was really a "traitor," and even whether the
Treaty of Nanking was really a bad thing for China (he suggested that it
helped China to open up sooner rather than later). Although such probing critiques might have been permissible in the liberal 1980s, they were
not acceptable in the nationalist 1990s: Mao was criticized in internal Party
meetings for "thought problems" (*sixiang wenti*). Mao Haijian's bold reap-

praisal of the Opium War appears to be the exception that proves the rule: "the backwards *will be* beaten" is not yet a palatable public interpretation of China's recent past for many Chinese. "China as victim" proponents, it seems, will not tolerate criticisms of their moral authority.

The more popular interpretation of "backwards/beaten" is "backwards *because* beaten" *(luohou yinwei aida)*. In other words, "Western" (especially Japanese) aggression kept China backwards. During the "Say 'no'!" fervor of 1996–1997, for instance, many Chinese nationalists found it more satisfying to blame the West for China's problems than to reflect upon China's role in them. Attributions of blame frequently led to desires for revenge. As noted above, because the First Opium War marked the beginning of the "Century of Humiliation," many Chinese looked to the return of Hong Kong in the summer of 1997 to "erase" the "Humiliation." A Chinese software company released an Opium War computer game in which modern-day Chinese virtual opium warriors battle invading British forces. But this time they can win. The manual reads: "Let's use our wisdom and courage to exterminate the damned invaders!"[27]

Computer geeks were not the only ones to savor sweet revenge. In the spring of 1997, diplomat Ling Qing recalled in a political journal how he felt in 1985 when Deng said that "If talks [with the British] do not succeed, China will decide how and when to take Hong Kong back." "I was truly moved," Ling wrote. "Compared with the situation one hundred fifty years earlier, it was a great 180-degree reversal of fortunes. . . . Today it is our turn to speak and their turn to listen."[28] Anti-British retribution was particularly noticeable in attacks on Prime Minister Margaret Thatcher and Hong Kong Governor Chris Patten. Chinese nationalists enjoyed retelling a story of how Thatcher emerged from a 1982 meeting with Deng without a smile, lost her balance going down the stairs of the Great Hall of the People, and fell to her knees.[29] The message is clear: the British must kneel down and beg forgiveness from their betters. Patten, however, received the brunt of Chinese ire in 1997. Unofficial sources did not mince words: he was described as "irksome" and "blabbering," and told to "Shut up!" For many Chinese, 1 July 1997 was payback time.

Evolving and contested narratives about the "Century of Humiliation," in sum, both reflect and powerfully shape China's relations with the West today. By invoking the people, events, and symbols of China's early modern encounter with the West, Chinese continually return to this unresolved trauma, hoping to master it. However, the "Century" often appears to have no end. China's 1945 victory over the lowly "Jap devils" *(guizi)* did not satisfy its need for closure. Although Mao is thought to have declared that "China has stood up!" neither Communism's victory over the Nationalist Party in the Civil War nor the declaration of "Liberation" in 1949 appears to have exorcised the past.[30] "Victory" over the "American imperialists" in Korea, as we shall see in the next chapter, was more satisfying. Nevertheless, one of 1997's most widespread official slogans was "Celebrate Hong Kong's return, erase the National Humiliation," suggesting that feelings of humiliation live on. And as the 1999 *People's Daily* editorial about the Belgrade bombing, "This is not 1899 China," suggests, China's early modern traumatic encounter with the West continues to haunt Chinese nationalists today.

The Past in the Present

Narratives about China's past both constrain and enable the nationalist politics of China's present. Young nationalists in China are seeking to come to terms with their personal pasts, defining themselves as "pragmatic" conservatives against narratives of the "romantic" and "pro-Western" 1980s. They have also returned to the pre-"Liberation" narrative of a "Century of Humiliation" during which Chinese were victimized by the West, and this new "victimization" narrative now coexists with the earlier "heroic" version. The reemergence of this victim narrative has had real consequences for Sino-American and Sino-Japanese relations. Today, many Chinese nationalists are primed to view American or Japanese actions as aggressive. Their quick judgments following the Belgrade bombing of 1999 and the spy plane collision of 2001 cannot be understood apart from this reencounter with past trauma.

As we shall see in the next two chapters on recent Chinese "histories" of Sino-American and Sino-Japanese relations, this reworking of the national narrative has raised as many questions as it has answered. Recent popular and official texts on Sino-American relations have largely stuck to the victor narrative. Whether writing about actual combat during the Korean and Vietnam Wars, or about Sino-American diplomatic battles, Chinese nationalists overwhelmingly choose stories of heroic victories. Pride in the past can create confidence in the future, and it may be that anxiety over possible future conflict with the United States in the Taiwan Strait and elsewhere gives the victor narrative an enduring appeal.

Popular writings about Sino-Japanese relations, in contrast, have taken the lead in advancing the new victimization narrative about Chinese suffering. As Chinese begin to confront the Nanjing massacre and other Japanese atrocities, anti-Japanese anger and desires for vengeance are spreading. It may be that with China's impressive economic and military modernization, Chinese no longer really fear Japan; they therefore have the luxury of confronting their past victimization at the hands of the Japanese.

CHAPTER 4

The "Kissinger Complex"

反
对
霸
权
主
义
!!

"Oppose hegemonism!"

As noted in the introduction, former U.S. Secretary of State Henry Kissinger paints a rosy picture of Chinese intentions. Like many realists, he infers intentions from capabilities. "Chinese ground forces," Kissinger argues in *The Washington Post,* "are not suitable for offensive operations." And on the economic front, Kissinger maintains, China's "current growth of about 6 percent barely keeps pace with the growth of the Chinese labor force."[1] China is thus not capable of challenging the United States. Kissinger frequently claims that both his academic and public careers have been driven by a desire to "purge our foreign policy of all sentimentality" in favor of a hard-nosed realpolitik.[2] His work on China, he professes, is no exception. In "No Place for Nostalgia in Our China Dealings," Kissinger laments that "with respect to China, too many in both [political] parties substitute nostalgia for analysis of what our national interest requires." Realpolitik, he has consistently argued, is the cure for what ails us.

Yet Kissinger himself frequently recalls his travels in China with pronounced sentimentality. In *The White House Years,* he fondly recalls his secret 1971 flight from Pakistan to Beijing: "It is not often that one can capture as an adult the quality that in one's youth made time seem to stand still; that gave every event the mystery of novelty; that enabled each experience to be relished. . . . Only some truly extraordinary event, both novel and moving, both unusual and overwhelming, restores the innocence of the years when each day was a precious adventure in the meaning of life. This is how it was for me as the aircraft crossed the snow-capped Himalayas, thrusting toward the heavens in the roseate glow of a rising sun."[3] China clearly means much more to Kissinger than a mere piece in the game of geopolitics. Kissinger seems to have developed a devotion to China and its leaders. Following the Tiananmen massacre of 1989, Kissinger wrote of watching the crackdown "with the pain of a spectator watching the disintegration of a family to whom one has a special attachment."[4] Proud of his role in "opening China" and bedazzled by his Chinese hosts, he seems committed to protecting his legacy in United States–China relations. China has become integral to Kissinger's self-concept.

Kissinger's love affair with China does not go unrequited. Many Chinese nationalists today suffer from a "Kissinger complex" to rival Kissinger's "China complex." Their "Kissinger complex" causes them to praise high-status foreigners who, like Kissinger, trumpet China's rise while downplaying its flaws. Such praise gives Chinese nationalists *face,* bolstering their self-esteem and generating confidence in China's future. If, as I argue in chapter 2, Chinese national identity evolves through China's significant bilateral encounters, and if, as I argue in chapter 3, it is also constituted through the stories Chinese tell about their national past, then Chinese writings about past and future Sino-American and Sino-Japanese relations have much to tell us about Chinese national identity. China's Kissinger complex is thus one aspect of its national identity that draws upon both the points made in chapters 2 and 3.

Chinese national identity, as previously argued, evolves in part through China's interactions with the United States. That process is both limited and enabled by evolving Chinese narratives about past Sino-American encounters. As Chinese nationalists tell stories about China's past encounters with America, they define and revise their sense of self. Such identity construction is particularly evident in Chinese treatments of two events: the Korean War of the early 1950s and the establishment of Sino-American relations in the early 1970s. Specifically, nationalists use Korea to create a vision of China as a "beneficent victor," and their accounts of the establishment of bilateral relations both humiliate Richard Nixon and lionize Henry Kissinger to make China look like a winner in past Sino-American contests.

Such versions of the Sino-American past also make it possible for Chinese writers to depict China as a winner in present and future conflicts with the United States. Several of the histories of Sino-American relations examined in this chapter were written during the Taiwan Strait crisis of 1996, when Chinese needed self-confidence to take on and defeat the United States. If pride is a positive evaluation of one's past actions, confidence is a positive evaluation of one's future actions.[5] When we are proud—when we believe that our claims for *face* are affirmed—we gain confidence for the future. One group of social psychologists found, for instance, that subjects who supported a particular team were more confident in their own abilities after a team victory than after a team loss.[6] Similarly, Chinese nationalists today draw on proud narratives of past "victories" over America to create the confidence they need as Chinese for possible future Sino-American conflicts.

By choosing two events separated by twenty years, I hope to show how narratives of Sino-American relations fit into larger narratives of Chinese national identity. Chinese histories of Sino-American relations are not autobiographies but rather stories about the national self in relationship to the United States. Like autobiographies, however, they seek to present a positive *face* both to their writers and to the world.[7] These Chinese histories are about the past, but they reveal a great deal about Chinese nationalists' evolving views of themselves and the world that they live in today.

Korea and Confidence-Building

Recent Chinese writings about the Korean War portray China as a "beneficent victor." The Chinese name for the war, "Resist America and Aid Korea" *(KangMei YuanChao)*, encapsulates victory and beneficence. To many Chinese, Korea marks the end of the "Century of Humiliation" and the birth of "New China." "Victory" in Korea is thus central to the self-esteem of many Chinese nationalists today.

When did the "Century of Humiliation" end? Official Chinese sources frequently declare that it ended in 1945 with Chinese participation in the Allied victory over Japan. As we will see in the next chapter, however, many Chinese are haunted by the belief that Japanese and Westerners do not acknowledge China's victor status in World War II, assigning victory instead to America, which ended the war by dropping atomic bombs on Hiroshima and Nagasaki. Victory over lowly "Japs" *(wokou)*, in any case, is not very gratifying for those Chinese who maintain a Sinocentric view of Asia. Many official sources declare instead that "Liberation" in 1949 marked the end of the "Century." The Civil War with Chiang Kai-shek and the Nationalist Party was over, foreign influence had been driven from the mainland, and, from an ideological perspective, socialism had defeated capitalism. As noted in chapter 3, Mao Zedong is thought to have declared in Tiananmen Square that "China has stood up!" To many Chinese, however, China's victories in 1949 seem incomplete and unsatisfying. Taiwan and Hong Kong were not yet "liberated"; the country was not united. And although America had backed the Nationalists, the Communist victory over their corrupt political rivals was not particularly glorious. There was nothing unprecedented about Chinese killing Chinese.

Victory over the United States, however, can be construed as something special. Recent Chinese accounts of the Korean War construct America as the best, and China as a victor over America, thus making China "better than the best." *The True Story of the Sino-American Contest,* written in 1996 by members of a State Security Bureau think tank, refers to the American military of the 1950s as the "world's number one military power" and asserts that the Chinese people, "relying on their own strength," defeated it.[8] (Notably, this argument completely dismisses North Korean contributions to the war effort. Chinese nationalism dictates that China win on her own.)

Pride in this Chinese "victory" over America is an important psychological resource which builds self-confidence when tensions with the United States rise. In 1990 the Beijing elite, facing U.S.-led international sanctions following the Tiananmen massacre of 1989, capitalized on the fortieth-anniversary commemorations of the onset of the Korean War to bolster their self-confidence, issuing a barrage of nationalist articles and books on Korea. The role of this war as a psychological resource is often explicit. In his preface to *A Paean to the War to Resist America and Aid Korea,* for instance, veteran Yang Dezhi is blunt: "The psychological riches *[jingshen caifu]* that the War has left me are precious. I am confident that China will prosper."[9] Pride in the past creates confidence in the future.

In 1996, following the deployment of two American aircraft carriers near Taiwan, both state and popular nationalists again used the "victory" in Korea to revive what appears to have been a shaken confidence about conflict with America. Li Peng, the "Butcher of Beijing" widely blamed for the Tiananmen massacre, warned, if you "use force against China, the outcome has already been proven by past experience."[10] In his preface to *The True Story of the Sino-American Contest,* former Chinese ambassador to the United States Chai Zemin issued a warning to America: "Do not forget history." American behavior during the Taiwan Strait crisis, it seems, was "insufferably arrogant and bossy"*(yizhi qishi).*[11] The political commissar of the Chengdu Military Region similarly evoked both Korea and Vietnam: "China has dealt with the U.S. on more than one or two occasions. What was the outcome? The United States was defeated on every occasion."[12] Invoking glorious victories over America in the past, these Chinese officials sought to raise a confidence that they could deploy to meet present-day challenges.

Unlike the 1990 fortieth-anniversary commemorations of the Korean War, when official nationalism largely fell on deaf ears, popular nationalists did respond to official nationalist appeals following the Taiwan Strait crisis of 1996. Like Li Peng and Chai Zemin, they also alluded to Korea to bolster their self-confidence. The cover of the very first issue of the *Shenzhen Panorama Weekly,* for instance, is a photograph of a Korean War veteran sternly waving his finger. It is accompanied by a large caption, warning: "We have 'squared off' before." In other words, "We'll beat you again if we need to." In their 1996 *Surpassing the USA,* popular nationalists Xi Yongjun and Ma Zaizhun explicitly link pride in past victories to confidence in future ones: "On the Taiwan question, Americans have forgotten the enormous losses they bitterly suffered on the Korean battlefield and in . . . Vietnam . . . China is strengthening, and the myth of American invincibility has already been shattered."[13]

"Victory" over America also bolstered Chinese pride during the fiftieth-anniversary commemorations of the Korean War in the year 2000.[14] In an interview with the New China News Agency, eighty-eight-year-old General Yuan Shengping proudly exclaimed that "the Chinese race are tough as nails!" Declaring that they "are not afraid of a strong opponent," Yuan concluded both that Chinese should be "proud" *(jiao'ao)* of having driven America back to the thirty-eighth parallel—and that China had "humiliated" *(chiru)* America.[15] Following the perceived insult of the Belgrade bombing the previous year, this role reversal must have been gratifying.

Chinese writings about the Korean War not only assert China's proud victor status and confidence in the future but also create a positive image of the Chinese people as beneficent. The 1990 *Pictorial History of the War to Resist America and Aid Korea,* which mixes actual photographs with

FIGURE 8. Korea and confidence-building. During the 1996 Taiwan Strait crisis, a Korean War veteran warns America that "We have 'squared off' before!" Source: *Shenzhen Panorama Weekly*.

cartoon drawings to teach the "history" of the war to young Chinese readers, is an arresting example of such attempts to build *face*. The Korean War
Museum, which compiled *A Pictorial History,* establishes American evil
in order to depict Chinese virtue. Frames 54–57, for example, are photographs of the "indescribable crimes committed by American troops": mu-
tilated bodies, killing fields, and an infant looking up from a corpse which
presumably is its parent. Following these photographs is a drawing of Chinese soldiers at the bank of a turbulent river. The caption shouts: "Barbarism! Cruelty! Evil! The furious breakers of the Yalu River surge, condemning the cruelty of the American troops."[16]

It is not enough, however, that in such stories even nature condemns
the Americans. America itself must confirm Chinese claims of American
evil and Chinese goodness. Frame 696 shows a cartoon drawing of a Caucasian singing with a group of Chinese soldiers. The caption reads: "This
American prisoner's name is Larry. The policy of superior treatment of
prisoners quickly dissolved his antagonistic mentality towards us. He
frequently sang: 'Hailalalala, hailalalala. . . . The Chinese and Korean
people's strength is great, and has defeated the American devils!'"[17]
"Larry" thus confirms the Chinese authors' depictions of Chinese beneficence and American evil. As the farfetched cartoon makes clear, our deep-
est desire is for others to accept our *face* claims. So long as the authors
can make their young readers believe that Americans acquiesce to Chinese moral superiority, it does not matter what Americans really think—
the schoolchildren of China will develop confidence in their national
identity.[18]

Although North Koreans are not generally given credit for their contributions to the war effort, Korean gratitude towards Chinese soldiers
also helps confirm Chinese virtue. Frame 1000 of *A Pictorial History* is a
famous photograph of an old Korean woman embracing a Chinese volunteer. The photograph (which also appears in the 1990 *A Paean to the
War*) bears the caption: "An old Korean woman reluctant to part with
[yiyi xibie] a Chinese people's volunteer."[19] This affection confirms Chinese claims to beneficence.

The histories of the Korean War I have discussed in this section make
it very clear that national *face,* the self-concept that Chinese nationalists
have of themselves as virtuous victors, requires confirmation from outsiders. "Larry" and the prototypical "old Korean woman" perform a vital function in these narratives, confirming Chinese claims of victory and
beneficence. It would be easy to dismiss such accounts as fiction, but to
do so would be to obscure the ways such fictions shape reality. Anecdotes

such as these can help us understand how Chinese understand themselves and their roles in the twenty-first-century world.

"Dissing" Dick

A need to verify China's ability to defeat the United States also colors recent Chinese writings about the establishment of diplomatic relations between China and America in the early 1970s. Nationalist writers have focused their gaze on two specific events: the People's Republic of China's (PRC's) 1971 admission into the United Nations and the 1972 handshake between Richard Nixon and Zhou Enlai at Beijing airport. These writers have also highlighted two men: Nixon and Kissinger. Chinese accounts of "victories" over Nixon at the UN and at Beijing airport reveal a strong desire to humiliate America. The "Kissinger complex," by contrast, reveals an equally strong craving for American praise. Both feed Chinese nationalists' appetite for *face*.

Recent Chinese narratives about the PRC's 1971 entry into the United Nations exhibit a longing to gain *face* at America's expense. During the early postwar period, the United States was ambivalent about the UN representation issue. Following China's alliance with the Soviet Union and the outbreak of the Korean War, however, the American government actively supported the Nationalists in Taiwan and opposed the PRC's entry into the UN, blocking debate on the issue throughout the 1950s. With China's first nuclear test in 1964 and the 1968 Soviet invasion of Czechoslovakia dramatically increasing fears about the Soviet threat, American attitudes towards mainland China shifted. In 1970, the American ambassador to the UN declared a desire to see the PRC "play a constructive role in the world system."[20] Such words were linked to action: Nixon first sent Kissinger to China to discuss the establishment of diplomatic relations in April 1971. Indeed, Rosemary Foot has made a persuasive case that the Nixon administration viewed China's October 1971 entry into the UN *favorably*. She quotes a Pakistani delegate who describes America's continued opposition to PRC entry as a "diplomatic charade." Nixon and Kissinger actually desired *rapprochement* with the PRC, but had to formally oppose the PRC to appease domestic American popular opinion. Americans were conflicted—on the one hand supporting PRC entry, but on the other hand remaining loyal to the Nationalist Party in Taiwan. Meanwhile, the PRC sought to enter the United Nations from its inception. In the first several months after "Liberation" in 1949, Beijing sent eighteen telegrams to the UN calling for removal of the Nationalists. By 1971, at the height of their campaign for UN entry, 290 delegations from developing countries were invited to China. Chinese aid to Africa increased dramatically and was successful in garnering African support for PRC entry; eleven of twelve African states receiving Chinese aid supported the PRC's bid.[21]

Two decades of PRC exclusion from the United Nations had both instrumental and psychological costs, however, and many Chinese sought payback. Because China was excluded from the UN, the United States was able to legitimize its position in the Korean conflict, labeling China an "aggressor nation." And America was able to isolate China afterwards. While the UN suffered from China's absence—it could not genuinely claim to represent the nations of the world while excluding a quarter of the world's population—China suffered even more from international isolation. A "sour grapes" mentality pervaded Chinese rhetoric about the UN in the 1950s and 1960s. In 1957, for instance, Mao declared: "We are in no hurry to take our seat in the UN."[22] Such words downplay the truth: with the emerging Sino-Soviet split, Mao desired UN entry. As the Cultural Revolution heated up in 1965, Chinese anger over the issue was revealed in Zhou Enlai's threat: "another UN, a revolutionary one, may well be set up so that rival dramas may be staged in competition with that body."[23] Like Ah Q, China's leaders in this period pursued an official rhetoric of pretending not to want what they could not have.

Recent Chinese accounts of China's 1971 United Nations entry suggest that such anger persists. Desires for retribution are evident in both official and popular narratives about the event. An October 1996 *People's Daily* article, for instance, commemorates the twenty-fifth anniversary of the "restoration" of the PRC's UN seat with the lines: "The resolution was passed by an overwhelming majority . . . and thunderous applause burst out in the assembly hall. . . . Many could not refrain from dancing. . . . Certain people of course felt very embarrassed."[24] Although the "applause" and "dancing" confirm China's virtuous victory, so does the fact that these actions embarrass "certain people." *The True Story of the Sino-American Contest* is both more explicit about who these "certain people" are, and more creative in describing their "embarrassment." A picture at the beginning of volume 1 shows the UN General Assembly scene in October 1971 accompanied by the caption: "delegates applauded heartily, and America was utterly discomfited" *(qiji baihuai)*. Chapter 3, "Feeling Proud and Elated *[yangmei tuqi]* at the UN," elaborates on American impotence, humiliation, and anger. "Impotence" *(wunai)* is conveyed by asserting American opposition to China's entry, and then denying American actors any role in a narrative chronicling the actions of China's "chin up and chest out" *(angshou yanxiong)* delegation. Viewing the vote as a victory, the authors quote then American ambassador to the UN George Bush "despondently" *(aosang)* admitting that "this was a loss of face" for America. American anger at the "defeat," however, is demonstrated by an even more fanciful portrayal of Nixon's reaction to the vote, which he apparently watched, "still hoping for a miracle," on television in the White House library: "The room was perfectly quiet. Nixon burned with anger, and the blue veins on his forehead protruded suddenly. 'Unbelievable . . . to perform so poorly at an international forum!'"[25] The authors of *The True Story of the Sino-American Contest* are researchers at the Chinese Institute of Contemporary International Relations (CICIR), a Beijing think tank under the State Security Bureau, China's equivalent to the FBI. Chai Zemin, former ambassador to the United States, was their "consultant." Despite this pedigree, their detailed description of the 1971 White House scene is less a product of Chinese intelligence-gathering than of the authors' fertile imaginations. They project their view of the situation onto Nixon. Because *face* is a zero-sum game, China's win must be America's loss, and American humiliation at defeat must be represented by Nixon's red-faced fury. The "quotes" from Bush and Nixon confirm the authors' claims of diplomatic victory. Such narratives allow China to gain *face* at America's expense.

Recent Chinese accounts of the UN vote are also notable for their silences. They do not mention the Nixon administration's desire for greater Chinese involvement in world affairs to offset Soviet influence. Nor do they discuss China's similar desire to use the United States against the Soviets. Such accounts ignore geopolitics as well as China's instrumental use of aid to buy African votes. Instead, the events are depicted as a moral drama in which good triumphs over evil. In the 1996 *People's Daily* article mentioned above, casting the United States as a "thief" allows the authors to declare China "proud and just."[26]

Recent Chinese accounts of the 1972 "handshake" between Nixon and Zhou Enlai also depict a glorious Chinese victory in order to gain national *face* at America's expense. In *China Shouldn't Just Say No*, the special 1996 issue of *Love Our China* discussed above, People's Liberation Army writers Yu Shaohua, Feng Sanda, and Chen Neimin revel in humiliating Nixon. Chapter 1 is entitled "Nixon Puts His Hand Out First." The authors explain in their text that Nixon was offering an "apology" *(zhiqian)* for John Foster Dulles's refusal to shake Zhou Enlai's hand in

1954.[27] The triumph locates China in the superior position. A proud, even vain, tone permeates an ensuing discussion of Nixon's humiliation upon discovering that no red carpet or masses awaited him at the Beijing airport: "Nixon had hoped for cheering crowds. This plain and simple welcoming made Nixon think of the American opinion poll which had predicted that he would be ridiculed [*yunong*] and fall into a trap when he visited China."[28] The PLA authors clearly delight in imagining Nixon's chagrin.

Narratives of Nixon's Beijing trip treat the event as a Chinese victory over the United States in "*face*-to-*face*" combat. Chinese diplomats made sure that China would be host *(zhuren)* — in a superior position — for the historic meeting. And they told the world that they did not think highly of Nixon by staging a drab reception that was televised internationally. Furthermore, the Nixon delegation was uninvited. Over twenty-five years later, in 1999, Foreign Ministry interpreter Ji Chaozhu proudly recalled how the Chinese negotiating team succeeded in *not* issuing an "invitation," instead merely granting Nixon's "request" for a visit.[29] Ji thereby creates a temporal continuity between the events of the early 1970s and visions of a pre-modern China in which barbarians humbly paid tribute to a superior Chinese civilization: his account thus restores to China the *face* it had lost during the "Century of Humiliation."

In addition to preparing the stage in these ways, Chinese diplomats also carefully scripted the performance. The Minister of Foreign Affairs in 1971, Huang Hua, gained Kissinger's assurances that Nixon would shake Zhou's hand. Such attention to China's national *face* was seen to gain status for the Chinese Communist Party in the international realm, and bolster the regime's legitimacy at home. The desire to appear superior to the United States coexisted with the elite's self-interest in both domestic and international politics.

Hugging Henry

Whereas nationalists today revel in characterizing Nixon as humiliated to make China look as if it won victories over America at the United Nations in 1971 and in Beijing in 1972, they venerate Kissinger for a similar reason: he confirms Chinese nationalist claims to victor status. In the case of Kissinger, however, China wins not only in the early 1970s, but also in the twenty-first century. Kissinger's praise of China's leadership and his predictions of China's future rise are extremely popular among Chinese nationalists. His glowing descriptions of China's leaders and China's future satisfy nationalists' desires for *face*. A "Kissinger complex" among today's Chinese nationalists arises from their vainglorious delight in words of praise from famous foreigners.

One example of this phenomenon comes from recent Chinese accounts of the establishment of relations between China and the United States. Writers of these histories linger on Kissinger's praise of Mao Zedong and Zhou Enlai. The following 1972 exchange between Kissinger and Mao is frequently cited:

> *Kissinger:* "I have assigned your writings to my students at Harvard."
>
> *Mao:* "Those things that I have written are nothing much."

By suggesting that Mao is his teacher, Kissinger implies that he is Mao's student. The statement is high praise coming from a man many Chinese consider the foremost teacher of international relations of his time. Because Kissinger had established the proper hierarchy in their relationship, with China in the senior "teacher" position, Mao could, as 1996's *China Shouldn't Just Say No* proudly explains, "modestly" *(qianxu)* reply.[30] Mao had no need in this context to assert China's "greatness" *(weida)*, this account implies, because Kissinger had already established Chinese superiority. The authors, in effect, transport their readers back to the mythical "good old days" of a Sinocentric Asian order. In this idealized past, Chinese diplomats could also "modestly" refer to China as "our inferior country" *(biguo)*, fully confident of their actual superiority over tributary nations. As Ji Chaozhu did in describing Nixon's visit to China, the authors of this account thus proudly link their narrative of the events of 1972 to a period of glory preceding China's "Century of Humiliation."

Nationalist narratives also delight in Kissinger's praise of Zhou Enlai. In a 1998 interview with *People's Daily* reporter Li Yunfei, for example, Kissinger reportedly stated: "I cherish deep feelings for Zhou Enlai . . . [he] was a man of noble character who towered above the rest in intelligence and had profound knowledge and extensive learning. He was an outstanding politician. . . . The profundity of Zhou Enlai's understanding of the world situation was amazing."[31] Li's article, written to mark the centenary of Zhou's birth, focused on both Zhou's and Kissinger's fine etiquette. Kissinger is quoted saying that Zhou had "good manners"— "better than most Americans." Kissinger informed Li that he told Zhou in 1972 that "If you came to Washington, I would feel embarrassed," be-

cause Americans are not such good hosts. Li also lingers over the minu-
tiae of Kissinger's etiquette in receiving him: "He hurried over to shake
hands with this reporter, saying sincerely: 'If you were not a reporter from
China, I would not be able to find time to do your interview.' Then, he
showed [me] into his Park Avenue office." In the view of Li and his *People's
Daily* editors, Kissinger, "a world-renowned diplomat," was giving China
face by treating its representative with such great respect.[32]

As was the case in the Chinese texts about the Korean War, not only
does the "Kissinger complex" create pride in China's past diplomatic "victories," but it also creates confidence in the future. Kissinger's recent discussions of international relations have been extremely popular among
Chinese nationalists because they are seen to predict America's imminent
decline and China's imminent rise. Tang Zhengyu, for example, concludes
his section of *China Can Say No* with the question: "Some say that the
nineteenth century was the English century, and that the twentieth century is the American century. What about the twenty-first century?" Tang
supports his prediction—"The 21st century will be China's"—by append-
ing a translation of a speech Kissinger gave in 1996, in which he argued
that America would not be able to contain China.[33] Likewise, *Why Does
China Say No?* quotes a 1996 *New York Times* article in which Kissinger
apparently argued that nothing could stop China's rise.[34] A quote from
Kissinger, predicting America's demise with a reference to Spengler's *Decline of the West,* is featured even more prominently—on the back cover—
of *Surpassing the USA.* He is also cited approvingly in the text itself, in a
passage that warns other Americans that "seeking to contain China is to
risk the nation's fate."[35]

Face claims require confirmation. Many Chinese nationalists enjoy asserting that "China will soon replace *[qudai]* America as the world's number one superpower."[36] These writers can relieve any doubts they might
have about such assertions by seeking Western confirmation for such
claims. High-status Westerners like Kissinger perform this function willingly and ably. But not all Westerners are like Henry Kissinger. Chinese
nationalists' demands for international recognition are not always satisfied,
and the rejections they feel they have suffered can make them angry. When
desires for self-confirmation are not met, humans, as social beings, are
not pleased.[37] Social psychologists have found that perceived criticism of
one's group is likely to threaten an individual's personal self-esteem as well.
Those with high collective self-esteem, furthermore, are more likely to
react to threats to their social identity by belittling outgroups and favor-
ing ingroups.[38] National groups are no different. Since extreme nation-

THE "KISSINGER COMPLEX"   67

alists are high in national self-esteem, they are likely to be more sensitive than others to perceived slights to their nation. Extreme nationalists have a greater stake in the fate of the nation; thus, they are the first to rally around the flag.

Chinese nationalists' anger at being denied international affirmation is perhaps best symbolized by their "Nobel Prize complex": a resentment that Chinese achievements have been denied their rightful confirmation by the West. One Chinese scholar explained that "With Deng's 1992 Southern tour and the new spurt of economic development, Chinese are increasingly proud of their accomplishments. They thus find it increasingly hard to bear the disregard and affronts of others." Nationalists saying "no" to America, he laments, ironically continue to pay slavish attention to the views of Westerners.[39] Many Chinese writers are angry that their work has not been recognized, and many Chinese economists believe that they should be awarded a Nobel Prize for China's "economic miracle."[40] Because Gao Xingjian was living in Paris and seen as a "dissident" writer, his 2000 Nobel Prize for literature only infuriated many Chinese nationalists, who saw it as another Western insult. The recognition, they felt, should go to mainland Chinese. Why weren't they being honored for their many accomplishments? The Scandinavians, they argued, were using Gao to bash China on the human rights issue. Even nationalist Gu Qingsheng, whose section of the 1996 *China Can Say No* includes such headers as "McCarthy Lives!" and "We Don't Want Most Favored Nation (MFN) Status, and in the Future, We Won't Give it to You," agrees that the "Nobel complex" indicates that "we have a psychological problem. . . . Although we say that there is nothing special about foreigners, we are very sensitive [towards their views]."[41] The "Nobel complex" and Chinese nationalists' "Kissinger complex" are two sides of the same coin of desire for Western recognition of Chinese *face* claims. Clearly, inaction can be just as offensive as action.

The "Beautiful Imperialist"

David Shambaugh perfectly captured Chinese ambivalence towards the United States in the title of his fine 1991 study of Chinese views of America during the 1980s, *Beautiful Imperialist*. Under Mao, the emphasis was on Americans as evil "imperialists." However, Shambaugh clearly shows that during the 1980s, many Chinese came to see the West in general, and America in particular, as "beautiful." By the late 1990s, however, many

Chinese had returned to the view of America as a land of evil imperialists. In an emotional 1996 speech entitled "A Declaration to the World,"
nationalist Song Qiang argued that "while 'imperialism' may seem like a
funny word from old war flicks, it is not passé."[42] Chinese postcolonial
theorists concur, maintaining, for instance, that criticisms of Chinese human rights abuses are examples of continuing Western cultural imperialism. In 1998 Rey Chow argued that Western discourse on human rights
is just another example of the "extraterritoriality" that is "internalized in
Western attitudes toward China": "The democracy that the West insists
on making China accept is not in essence different from the opium imposed by Britain in the nineteenth century. . . . *In both cases, Westerners
want cash, and Chinese people get smoke.*"[43]

Chinese anxieties about American imperialism have only increased in
the wake of 11 September 2001, given the American invasions of Afghanistan and Iraq, and the "War on Terror." By creating pride in the past, recent narratives about "victories" over the United States in the Korean War
(1950s) and during the establishment of Sino-American relations (1970s)
seek to bolster Chinese self-confidence about possible confrontations with
a resurgent American "imperialism." Many of these narratives display a
vain obsession with praise from abroad, a "Kissinger complex" that reveals the insecurity many Chinese nationalists feel about China's status
in the rapidly evolving world system. Insecurity about American power
may explain why Chinese writings about Sino-American relations have
clung to the old victor narrative of heroic Chinese resistance. It is in writings about Japan, as the next chapter reveals, that the new victimization
narrative has been more pronounced.

CHAPTER 5

Victors or Victims?

*"The Chinese people cannot
be bullied; the Chinese
race cannot be insulted!"*

War is at once the graveyard of peoples and the birthplace of nations. No true nation is born without war; indeed, nations define themselves through conflict with other nations.[1] Modern China is no exception. The 1931/1937–1945 "War of Resistance against Japan" *(KangRi zhanzheng)* was the birthplace of the People's Republic of China. By mobilizing and leading the peasantry in nationalist resistance against the invading Japanese, the Communist Party gained the mass following it later used to defeat the Nationalist Party during the Civil War of the late 1940s.[2] For over half a century now, "defeating the Japanese and saving the nation" has been a dual legacy at the heart of Chinese Communist claims to nationalist legitimacy.

Stories about the Sino-Japanese Jiawu War of 1894–1895 and the Second World War continue to drive Chinese views of Japan and—more to the point—of themselves. China's wars with Japan have been and continue to be a hot topic. For the first three decades of the People's Republic

69

under Mao, the "War of Resistance" was a "chosen glory."[3] China's self-image, aggressively projected to the world, was that of a "victor." Today, however, many Chinese have come to think about the war in less glorious terms. A self-image of "China as victim" is increasingly vying with "China as victor" in the stories Chinese today tell about past wars with Japan. The debates reveal a great deal about recent changes to Chinese national identity.

An "Extraordinary Humiliation"

Although the atrocities of the Sino-Japanese Jiawu War of 1894–1895 are not mentioned as frequently as World War II atrocities such as the Nanjing massacre, Chinese feelings that the Japanese have been unjust and untrustworthy go back to 1895, not to the 1930s and 1940s. The Jiawu War, named for the year 1894 in the Chinese calendar, turned the world of China's elite upside down. For a millennium, China's leaders had looked down on Japan, treating it either benevolently, as a student or younger brother, or malevolently, as a nation of "Jap pirates" *(wokou)*. China's supremacy was abruptly challenged, however, with its loss to Japan in 1895. Earlier losses in wars with "Western barbarians" *(yang guizi)* were one thing, but losing to an inferior *within* the realm of Sinocentric civilization fundamentally destabilized Chinese worldviews.[4] Many Chinese today see the 1895 loss to Japan and the ensuing Treaty of Shimonoseki as the darkest hour in the "Century of Humiliation."

In Chinese accounts, the shock of 1895 is often represented by the encounter between the Qing Court's Li Hongzhang and Japan's Ito Hirobumi during the postwar treaty negotiations at Shimonoseki.[5] A 1991 history of the Jiawu War, written as part of the multivolume "Do Not Forget the National Humiliation Historical Series," references this encounter both in its title, *The Extraordinary Humiliation at Shimonoseki,* and its first chapter, "Humiliation After Defeat." Strikingly, the authors chose to begin their story at the "humiliating" moment of war's end, only afterward presenting a chronology of the war itself. Their account of the negotiations at Shimonoseki combines anger at Ito and sympathy for Li with anger at Li and the Manchu court. Authors Qiao Haitian and Ma Zongping express outrage at the Japanese assassination attempt on Li that preceded the treaty signing. They declare it "scandalous," and, significantly, justify their outrage by asserting that "international opinion" *(guoji yulun)* was likewise outraged. Qiao and Ma also declare the Japanese demands at Shimonoseki "unreasonable"—"a milestone in evil." Ito and the Japanese side, they insist, "took pleasure in making China lose *face*."[6] It is the public nature of China's loss of *face* before the world that infuriates Qiao and Ma almost a century later. The authors blame Li and the Manchu court for the humiliation, seeking to save face for Han Chinese like themselves.

More recent popular accounts also evince anger at Ito and Japan. The preface to 1997's *Blood Debt,* which focuses on World War II and postwar reparations claims, actually begins with a two-page fictional account of an exchange between Li and Ito in 1895. China is depicted as a "baby lamb" and Japan as an "avaricious" and "evil" wolf:

> Li: Taiwan is already in your grasp. Why are you so anxious about it?
>
> Ito: When something is in your mouth, you hunger to swallow it!

The Treaty of Shimonoseki, according to authors Gao Ping, Tang Yun, and Yang Yu, was China's "greatest humiliation."[7] Another popular 1997 book on reparations, *Why Japan Won't Settle Accounts,* also begins with the Jiawu War, when "China . . . fell off the express train of historical development, and *was looked down upon* as 'Shina' . . . the 'sick man of East Asia [italics added].'"[8] When author Li Zhengtang writes "was looked down upon *[bei ren bishi]*," his use of the passive construction implies that the agent doing the looking was world opinion.[9] The insult, again, seems not so much to be China's defeat, or even the ingratitude of Japan, as a former "student," but the public loss of national *face.*

These two 1997 books demanding war reparations focus on World War II and are full of visceral anger at Japanese wartime atrocities. By beginning with discussions of the injustices of the earlier Jiawu War, however, the authors establish a moral framework for their anger, attempting to elevate it from a lower, visceral anger to a higher, ethical anger. Many Chinese nationalists feel that Japan betrayed China during the Jiawu War: the "student" beat up his "teacher." To add insult to injury, China is perceived by the authors to have lost national *face* at Shimonoseki, something they clearly seethe at as a further injustice done to their nation. Only after presenting these betrayals and injustices can the authors justify their angry demands for war reparations. Otherwise, their reparations claims might appear—to themselves as much as to others—to be self-interested (*zisi,* a pejorative in Chinese) or even vengeful.

By blaming Li Hongzhang and the Qing, and highlighting Han Chinese resistance, many Chinese accounts of the Jiawu War transform defeat into victory with psychological stratagems worthy of the proverbial Ah Q. After arguing that the Treaty of Shimonoseki "lost *face* for China by forfeiting sovereignty" *(sangquan wuguo)*, the authors of 1996's *A Century of Hatred* argue that it was "not China's loss but Li Hongzhang's."[10] Blaming Li and the Manchus for the defeat saves face for Han Chinese, who opposed the treaty, according to the authors, by "fiercely" resisting the Japanese in Taiwan, Shandong, and elsewhere.

The Chinese, many narratives of the Jiawu War insist, were in fact victors. The preface to a 1997 historical romance for teenagers, *Loyal Souls: The Story of the Jiawu War,* highlights China as a victor in the eyes of the world: "The Chinese economy's takeoff today has already attracted the attention of the world *[shiren zhumu]:* 'Shenzhen is similar to Hong Kong,' 'Shanghai is like Japan's Ginza [District],' and 'All of the open cities on China's coast are the world's best places for trade and investment' are phrases used daily in newspaper editorials and articles around the world. The Chinese nation, chin up and chest out *[angshou tingxiong],* and feeling proud and elated *[yangmei tuqi],* is striding towards the twenty-first century."[11] Why do authors Li and Shao feel the need to conjure up this glowing image of China in world opinion? Has their heroic account of Chinese resistance convinced them that China was indeed the victor of the Jiawu War? Or is this projection of a positive Chinese self-image onto world opinion a way to maintain a psychological balance, compensating for the loss of self-esteem that resulted from writing about what they actually deem a humiliating defeat?

Defeat in the Jiawu War and the Treaty of Shimonoseki was, and continues to be, a direct assault on Chinese visions of themselves. "Little brother" Japan beat up "big brother" China. The "student" punched the "teacher." For many Chinese, the treaty publicly instituted China's humiliation before the world. The loss of national *face* was even worse than defeat itself. Because Japan is depicted as having caused the public loss of national *face,* anger directed against Japan thus assumes a moral legitimacy and is not just a base desire for revenge.

Victors in the "War of Resistance"

If Chinese feelings that Japan betrayed them have their origins in the Jiawu War and the Treaty of Shimonoseki, it is World War II and atrocities like the Nanjing massacre that arouse the most controversy and passion. Recent Chinese debates about the Second World War show that Chinese

narratives about the war are being revised. While some nationalists ad-
here to the Maoist doctrine that China was the heroic victor of the war,
others are beginning to probe the sensitive thesis that China was a victim
of Japanese atrocities.

Because its success in fighting the "War of Resistance" gave legitimacy
to the Communist Party, victory over Japan has been central to official
postwar histories. Historiography about the war during Mao's reign max-
imized its legitimizing impact. The Communist storyline was simple:
without the Party-led defeat of the Japanese, there would be no New
China. Indeed, under Mao there was little research on the history of Japanese aggression: praising the victorious leadership of Mao and the Communist Party was more important.[12] The newly established People's Republic did not wish to dwell on Chinese suffering.

The "China as victor" view of the war did not disappear with Mao's
death in 1976. On 7 July 1987, the fiftieth anniversary of the Marco Polo
Bridge Incident (when Japan moved south from Manchuria to invade
China proper), a *Liberation Army Daily* editorial reiterated the position
that the war was China's first victory after a century of "resistance" (or,
losses), "wiping away the [national] humiliation with a single stroke *[yiju
xixue chiru]*."[13] In the wake of Western sanctions imposed after the 1989
Tiananmen massacre, the Chinese Communist Party stepped up efforts
to marshal the past to bolster its legitimacy. Chapter 3 describes the ways
in which the ninetieth anniversary of the Joint Expeditionary Force against
the Boxers was utilized in 1990 to attack Western aggression against
China. The Beijing elite also capitalized upon the 1991 sixtieth anniversary
of the Mukden Incident of 1931, which led to the Japanese invasion of Manchuria. Party elder Hu Sheng explained the contemporary relevance of
the "War of Resistance" at a conference commemorating the Mukden Incident: "The PRC . . . is an independent and sovereign nation *[duli zizhu]*
that will not submit to foreign pressure, and will not follow foreign commands. . . . Foreign pressure increases the people's fighting spirit. Of
course . . . China does not view any country as its enemy. . . . But the Chinese people do not fail to see that there are still powers in this world [i.e.,
America] that see China as an enemy."[14] That Chinese can "see" *(kan)* that
Americans "*see* China as an enemy" *(dishi Zhongguo)* justifies the Communist Party's post-Tiananmen hostility towards the West. By projecting
a negative self-image onto Westerners—"they hate us"—the CCP created
a legitimate cause for anger. The post-Tiananmen pronouncements of
Western governments and the Western press, although directed at the
Communist elite, gave the Chinese Communist Party ample evidence to

support their contention. And the CCP largely succeeded in convincing their people that Western sanctions were anti-Chinese, rather than narrowly anti-Communist. The success of the CCP effort helps explain the emergence of popular nationalism in early 1990s China.

As was the case in accounts of the Jiawu War, many discussions of battles during the "War of Resistance" transform defeat into victory using stratagems that divide Chinese victory and victimhood between different groups of Chinese. At the end of their 1997 diatribe *Be Vigilant Against Japanese Militarism!* for instance, Zi Shui and Xiao Shi present "An Exasperating Discussion of Racial Humiliation." The 1931 surrender at Mukden, they argue, should be blamed on the Nationalist Party, not on Chinese in general: "Strictly speaking, Chinese troops were not defeated in battle, *but defeated themselves* through not fighting. . . . It was a shameful day that makes one bear a grudge towards this deceptive world [italics added]." After turning defeat into victory, Zi and Xiao turn shame into pride: "With superhuman strength, the Chinese people have erased the shame of the past, winning respect and glory. . . . The total development of the Chinese race cannot be stopped."[15] China was not defeated at Mukden in 1931; in the end, China won. By deploying this version of Ah Q's "psychological victory technique," Zi and Xiao maintain *face*.

As China opens up to the world, such unilateral assertions of China's status as a victor in World War II are no longer satisfying to many Chinese, especially those insecure about their nation's victor status. The demand that the world recognize China's wartime accomplishments, conferring national *face* upon China, is one of the most passionate themes in recent Chinese scholarship on the war. Zhang Zhuhong's 1995 "The International Influence of the Battle of Taierzhuang," for instance, focuses its attention not so much on what happened at Taierzhuang, the location of a 1938 Chinese victory over Japanese forces, or even on what Chinese think or should think happened. It focuses, rather, on what Zhang asserts that the world thought. Taierzhuang, Zhang argues, *showed the world* that victory was possible at a time of Allied hesitation. The battle "shattered the illusion that the Japanese could not be defeated [italics added]."[16] That Zhang thinks the Allies thought China was a winner is central to how he thinks about himself as a Chinese. In Zhang's narrative of the battle, the Allies confirmed Chinese *face* claims.

Many Chinese are incensed by the belief that Japanese refuse to admit having been defeated by China, failing to confirm Chinese claims to victor status. In his thoughtful 1995 probing of the war, *Wailing at the Heavens,* People's Liberation Army writer Jin Hui maintains that the Japanese are "two-faced" *(liangfu mianrong)* in their attitudes towards Chinese and Westerners. The Showa Emperor, Jin writes, apologized to the United States and Europe, but never to Asia. By maintaining that they lost to the Americans, but not to China, Japanese can feel "more glorious," as if they have "more *face*" *(geng you mianzi)*.[17]

Many Chinese are also angered by the belief that Westerners do not confirm China's victor status. At a 1997 conference commemorating the sixtieth anniversary of the Marco Polo Bridge Incident, the People's Revolutionary Museum's Yuan Jiaxin bitterly complained that the West does not respect China's victor status. Although he did not address why China's role in World War I might earn it the spoils of war, he traced this attitude to the Versailles Conference, where Shantung and other German territories in China were not returned to China, but were instead transferred to Japan. Yuan then argued that since China had "shown the world" its strength during World War II, China's Western allies had to admit China's status, and indeed, they revoked the remaining unequal treaties in 1943, symbolically recognizing China's equality. In the final years of the war, however, the Allies made military decisions without consulting China, revealing that they did not really view China as an equal.[18] The Allies, Yuan deeply felt, did not treat China with respect.

Yuan's belief that the West does not recognize the contributions China made to the Allied victory has motivated a number of Chinese historians. In 1995, Fujian Party historian Lin Qiang wrote: "The War of Resistance was an important part of the anti-fascist war and made a great contribution. . . . But some foreign historians . . . either because of a lack of understanding or prejudice *[pianjian]*, persist in negating the role of the War of Resistance. This is completely wrong." Lin then enumerates China's contributions to the Allied cause: China was the earliest to shoulder the burden of confronting fascism; China protected the Soviet Union's rear from Japan's "northern advance" policy; China aided the British and Americans in battle by bogging down the Japanese in the Chinese interior, thus enabling their "Europe first, then Asia" policy; and China smashed the Axis strategy to rendezvous in the Middle East. Here, significantly, Lin clinches his argument by citing Roosevelt's words of 1942: "If there were no China, think of all the Japanese battalions that could fight elsewhere. They could have immediately taken Australia, India . . . and joined up with Germany in the Middle East." Lin uses Roosevelt's words to claim that China made an indispensable contribution to victory. Indeed, Lin concludes that China played the "determining role" *(juedingxing zuoyong)* in Japan's defeat, and that the "The Chinese War of Resistance was . . . an outstanding contribution that was *the focus of world attention [jushi shumu].*"[19] *Mu,* the final character of the proverb *jushi shumu,* literally means "eye," and even looks like one. The second to last character, *shu,* also contains the "eye" pictograph. Because Chinese is a pictorial language, the effect is to feel the international gaze, or "eyes of the world," in an almost visceral, rather than a coldly cognitive, manner. For Chinese like Lin, it is not enough that Chinese assert claims to victor status: an audience of international opinion must confirm those claims.

The PLA Military Institute historian Luo Huanzhang, however, appears to have written the most defensively and passionately on this subject. In a 1991 article, "The Great Contribution the War of Resistance Against Japan Made to the Defeat of Japanese Imperialism," Luo insists that China's role in defeating Japan was, in fact, greater than America's. "American air and sea victories over the Japanese were important but not decisive," Luo writes, "The Chinese people were *the key determining influence* in defeating Japanese imperialism."[20] Wartime American aid to China presents an awkward complication for Luo. Luo does profess gratitude, "the Chinese people will never forget American aid." But he then cites a proverb from the ancient Chinese philosopher Mencius, "like putting out a large fire with a cup of water" *(beishui chexin),* to argue that American aid was inconsequential: "China's contribution to the war against fascism was much greater than the Allies' aid to China."[21] This is a rather startling comparison. Why does Luo feel compelled to make it? In a 1995 article on the same subject, Luo's motives become clear: "You cannot say that China could not have fought the Japanese without help."[22] Luo's defensiveness appears to stem from a fear that China is seen as unable to defeat Japan alone. Such a fear might undermine Luo's view of China as a heroic victor, threatening his positive self-image.

As the use of Roosevelt's "If there were no China, think of all the Japanese battalions that could fight elsewhere" reveals, a popular way to counter fears that world opinion does not confirm China's status as victor is to find world opinion that does. Research on the "international friends" of wartime China has long been a popular topic. The Party School of the Chinese Communist Party, for instance, sponsored the translation and 1988 publication of James Bertram's 1939 *Unconquered: A Journal of a Year's Adventures Among the Fighting Peasants of North China.* The subtitle of the Chinese translation is *China's War of Resistance in the Eyes of a Foreigner.* "In the eyes of" again points to the importance of others' views to China's national self-image. An important selling point, the publishers decided, was that this foreigners' view of China was positive: the cover flap declares that Bertram "highly praises" the Chinese people's "un-yielding antifascist spirit."[23] Similarly, at the 1997 conference commemorating the Mukden Incident, the Sichuan Academy of Social Science's Xue Yunfeng made special mention of China's wartime "international friends," like American journalist Edgar Snow and Canadian doctor Norman Bethune, to help prove that China was "in the right" *(shi zhengque de)*.[24] Indeed, research on Edgar Snow was a particularly hot topic during the fiftieth-anniversary commemorations of the war in 1995. Zhao Wenli, for instance, argues that by influencing international opinion, Snow gave the Chinese Communist Party great encouragement. The result, Zhao explains, was that Chinese felt supported, rather than isolated.[25] As Chinese nationalists' "Kissinger complex" shows, interest in such "international friends" has not faded.[26] The world's response to Chinese claims for national *face,* whether imagined to be positive or negative, is central to Chinese perceptions of themselves as victors in the "War of Resistance."

World opinion is also central to the claim that the Chinese were *beneficent* victors. Like the Chinese writings about the Korean War discussed in the last chapter, Chinese narratives about the "War of Resistance" seek to construct an image of China as a "beneficent victor." As they attempt to present a magnanimous face to the world, many narratives suppress desires for revenge.[27] *Awakening: A Record of the Educating and Reforming of Japanese War Criminals,* a 1991 pictorial history of China's postwar "reeducation" of Japanese POWs, presents a fascinating example of this dynamic. Both the content and format of *Awakening* reveal that, while its topic is Japanese war criminals, its goal is to create a positive Chinese self-image. Party elder Bo Yibo writes in the preface that "Chinese would have been justified in settling accounts with the Japanese criminals . . . in undertaking racial revenge, but instead we have chosen humanitarianism." *Awakening* focuses on Bo's argument that though Chinese are entitled to revenge, their magnanimous nature led them to treat Japanese POWs with courtesy.[28] The first section of the book, "Frenzied Aggression, Innumerable Crimes," contains photographs documenting Japanese atrocities—skulls, twisted bodies, massacre sites, mass graves—and thus sets up a foil of Japanese evil against which the authors may construct a narrative of Chinese goodness.

Awakening's second section, "Education and Remolding, Repentance and Awakening," documents the Chinese army's "lenient treatment" of Japanese POWs during the war, and the comfortable life in one POW camp, the Fushun Administration of War Criminals, after the war. One two-page pictorial spread is devoted to the excellent medical treatment the Japanese prisoners received, accompanied by the explanation that "following . . . the instructions given by premier Zhou Enlai, the staff . . . treated the war criminals in a humanitarian way. They respected their personalities and never beat, scolded or abused them." Two-page pictorial spreads depict prisoners bathing, playing games, participating in athletics, performing in a camp theater, and enjoying banquets. Six pages are devoted to family visits and travel in China. This section is prefaced by the caption, "Many war criminals said gratefully: 'The Chinese government is so kind that it allows us to travel while we are still in custody. This generosity is unprecedented in world history.'" A picture of one group of Japanese prisoners visiting the Anshan Iron and Steel Works is accompanied by the caption, "The war criminals . . . all declared, 'A miracle!'"[29] Whether Japanese POWs actually said such things is not likely something the compilers, working almost four decades later, could prove. It is telling that even at this historical remove they chose to put these words into Japanese mouths.

The third section of *Awakening,* "Impartial Trial and Lenient Treatment," documents courtroom proceedings and the evidence used to try dozens of Japanese war criminals. It concludes with pictures of Japanese prisoners crying in gratitude upon a court decision to release them, and a photo of the prisoners waving as the ship carrying them home departs. The latter is accompanied by the explanation that they were bidding farewell to the Chinese people "with mixed feelings of joy and sorrow" *(beixi jiaojia).* The Japanese POWs, the compilers assert, were grateful to their Chinese jailers. The final section, "Safeguard Peace and Maintain Friendship Between Japan and China," documents the efforts of the returned prisoners in Japan to promote Sino-Japanese friendship and expose Japanese atrocities during the War.[30]

The book's goal of establishing Chinese beneficence is revealed in its format as well as its content. The title page is printed in three languages: Chinese, Japanese, and English. It appears that the compilers originally intended to print the entire volume in three languages but then chose only to print in Chinese and English.[31] Why choose English over Japanese? English was probably chosen because the Chinese compilers of the volume were more concerned about Western opinion than they were about Japanese opinion. The book is a claim for national *face* that must be confirmed by a third-party audience. That audience, preferably, should be as high in status as possible. English, the Chinese compilers decided, would be preferable to Japanese, or any other language, for that matter.

Despite the ways that some Chinese writers try to gain face for China by portraying happy Japanese prisoners of war, depictions of the war years can become problematic when they open the possibility of friendship on equal terms between "victor" and "defeated," or between China as "teacher" and Japan as "student." The resilience of the "China as victor" narrative was recently revealed when the Bureau of Film and Television censored the winner of the Grand Prix prize at the 2000 Cannes film festival, *Devils on the Doorstep (Guizi laile)*. The film is a moving wartime tale of the friendship that develops between a Japanese prisoner and a group of Chinese villagers. The Film Censorship Committee, however, complained that the "Chinese civilians [in the movie] don't hate the Japanese [prisoner]," but instead are "as close as brothers" *(qin ru xiongdi)* with him.[32] Director Jiang Wen's exploration of the two sides' common humanity clearly threatened the censors' vision of heroic Chinese resistance against the hated Japanese. The Maoist heroic narrative of "China as victor" in the "War of Resistance" continues to thrive in today's China. However, proponents of this view are not satisfied with their own unilateral declarations, but require international confirmation of their claims for China's victor status and beneficence. And the affirmation of Westerners is what they most desire.

Victims of the "Rape of Nanking"

Following the death of Mao Zedong, the prevailing "China as victor" narrative has been challenged by a new interpretation. Many Chinese have come to focus less on heroic "resistance" during the war, and more on Chinese victimization.[33] Symptomatic of this shift, the trope of wartime China as a raped woman, first utilized by nationalist writers during the 1930s but suppressed under Mao, is resurgent. Why have so many Chinese come to think about themselves as victims? I ask this question not to cast doubt upon the undeniable suffering of the Chinese people during World War II, but to better understand the evolution of Chinese national identity. Public debates between Chinese and Japanese over past atrocities like the Nanjing massacre, for instance, are very much about what it means to *be* Chinese or Japanese in the twenty-first century.

The new victimization narrative obsesses about two subjects: quantifying Chinese suffering and presenting the Chinese case to the world. Indian historian Sudipta Kaviraj has noted the tendency of nationalists to count everything they *possess*. Nationalism, he writes, involves a "re-

lentless project of enumeration—the endless counting of its citizens, territories, resources. . . . It counts, it appears, every conceivable quanti-
fiable thing." The statement of the tremendous numbers included in the
imagined "we," Kaviraj argues, acts as a source of great psychological
strength.[34] China is no exception. Enumerating "China"—its vast geo-
graphic and demographic size—has long been central to the modern Chinese nationalist project of creating the psychological strength necessary
to mobilize the Chinese people.[35]

Moreover, recent Chinese accounts of World War II reveal that nationalists also obsessively count everything they have *lost*. The back cover
of 1997's *Blood Debt*, for example, has the line "35 million" splashed across
a photo of a pile of skulls. In addition to this death toll, it also lists economic damages from the war.[36] Less sensational and more scholarly is the
1995 *Losses in the War of Resistance and the Full Story of Postwar Reparations
Efforts*. Following its title, the book has a straightforward organization,
beginning with six chapters documenting different categories of Chinese
damages, followed by a ten-page "Table of Losses" that meticulously translates the prose into numbers. The final three chapters chronicle the history of Chinese reparation claims.[37] Quantifying wartime losses literally
becomes the basis for postwar entitlement claims.

The marked rise in the numbers of war casualties that appear in Chinese assessments of the war reflects the emergence of the victimization
narrative. Immediately following the war, Chiang Kai-shek's Nationalist
Party announced that Japan had killed 1.75 million Chinese. After it came
to power in 1949, the Chinese Communist Party declared that 9.32 million Chinese had been killed. That figure stood for many years, reflecting
the Maoist suppression of victim-speak in favor of a heroic narrative. In
1995, however, Jiang Zemin raised the casualty estimate to 35 million, the
current official Chinese figure.[38] China's early postwar political elite had
needed heroes, not victims; many Chinese today have different needs.

Documenting the Nanjing massacre has been one of the most passionate projects of narrators of victimization, and controversy rages about
the death toll. Many Chinese now argue that at least 300,000 Chinese
died in Nanjing, while many Japanese, especially those on the political
right, argue that the total could not have been so high. The number
"300,000" is etched in stone at the entrance to the Nanjing Massacre Museum in Nanjing, and has acquired symbolic importance for many Chinese. Iris Chang, the Chinese-American author of *The Rape of Nanking*,
has been a vocal advocate of this figure. On a 1998 *NewsHour*, she explained
the importance of the number to David Gergen: "Three hundred thou-

sand, please keep in mind, is more than the death toll at Hiroshima and Nagasaki combined."[39] Peter Novick has used the phrase "victimization Olympics" in a recent discussion of the uses of the Holocaust today. Winners of such competitions gain moral authority.[40] Because close to 300,000 Japanese died from the A-bombs dropped at Hiroshima and Nagasaki in 1945, for many ethnic Chinese like Chang, the toll of 300,000 deaths at Nanjing sets Chinese suffering in the war above that of the Japanese. Combined with the fact that Japan was the aggressor in the war, this figure helps establish China's moral authority over Japan.

Indeed, because the establishment of moral authority requires complex assessments of relative status and power, the number of deaths at Nanjing has become much more than a historical question. For example, a 1997 conference at Princeton University commemorating the sixtieth anniversary of the Nanjing massacre witnessed a stunning flare-up of Chinese passions over the death toll. Two Japanese historians spoke on the subject. Utsunomiya University's Kasahara Tokushi ritualistically confirmed the Chinese 300,000 figure, was deemed sufficiently repentant, and was applauded by the largely Chinese audience. Nihon University's Ikuhiko Hata met a different fate. Claiming to be a moderate historian attacked by both progressive and conservative forces in Japan, Hata argued that his own investigations and calculations revealed that the number of casualties was actually lower. During the question-and-answer session that followed, Iris Chang demanded to know why Hata would not accept the casualty figures Japanese POWs gave their Chinese jailers. Hata replied that "circumstances" (that is, possible torture and coercion) made such figures unreliable. Many in the largely Chinese audience immediately began screaming at Hata—"Stop!" "He lies!" "Enough!" Furious, Chang stormed out of the Princeton conference hall. Panel moderator and prominent Sinologist Perry Link was barely able to control the situation. The numbers debate had clearly situated the two Japanese scholars on a continuum of contrition. By questioning the claim to 300,000 Chinese casualties, Hata did not exhibit enough repentance for his Chinese audience.[41] By insulting him publicly, Chang and many Chinese in the audience sought to make him lose face.[42]

The numbers debate does not occur in an international void. As events at the Princeton conference suggest, quantifying one nation's pain is meaningless unless this effort is performed on the world stage. One of the most fascinating aspects of the Nanjing massacre controversy is that the Chinese and Japanese combatants have their eyes on world opinion more than on each other. Each battle is carefully choreographed for the benefit of

Western audiences.[43] The Iris Chang phenomenon, in which Chinese around the world promoted *The Rape of Nanking*, provides numerous examples of how the Nanjing massacre controversy is staged for Western audiences. At the end of her book, Chang argues that a "second rape" of Nanjing has occurred, because Japanese have suppressed and even denied what happened. Chang claims that "When it comes to expressing remorse for its own wartime actions before the bar of world opinion, Japan remains to this day a renegade nation." The result, she fears, is that the Nanjing massacre has vanished from the "world's collective memory." International opinion, furthermore, is an accomplice to this Japanese crime: "the world is still acting as a passive spectator to the second Japanese rape—the refusal of the Japanese to apologize." Chang is incensed, for example, that American students learn more about Hiroshima than about Nanjing in their school books. Americans, she laments, remember Auschwitz and Hiroshima, but have forgotten Nanjing.[44]

Chang's "second rape" argument is both Sinocentric *and* Western-centric. It is Sinocentric to argue that Americans should learn more about Nanjing than about Hiroshima, even though it was Americans who dropped the A-bomb, but not Americans who sacked Nanjing. America would be better served if American school children did more—rather than less—reflecting on their country's decision to drop the A-bomb on Japanese civilians. But Chang is also Western-centric in asserting, that because American history textbooks say little or nothing about Nanjing, the "world" has forgotten about the massacre. Chinese have certainly not forgotten about it: the Nanjing massacre has been a hot topic in China for years. Chang is Western-centric to exclude China from her "world," instead conflating "the world" with the West.[45]

Chang's main motivation for writing and publicizing *The Rape of Nanking* seems to have been to build Western opinion against Japan. Chang seems driven by a genuine anger that seeks relief through humiliating Japanese. As David Kennedy perceptively noted in an *Atlantic Monthly* review: "Accusation and outrage, rather than analysis and understanding, are this book's dominant motifs. . . . To what purpose is Chang's outrage directed? Nothing less than hauling Japan 'before the bar of world opinion' and forcing it to acknowledge its war crimes."[46] At a 1998 Nanjing massacre conference held at the University of California, Berkeley, I asked Chang if she worried about committing a "third rape" by reprinting graphic pictures of naked Chinese women in her book, thereby subjecting them to further indignity. Her answer was thoughtful. She said that as a woman she had concerns about the pictures and had discussed the issue with her publishers, but had decided that rectifying the "second rape" (Western ignorance of the Nanjing massacre) justified the risk of a "third rape." If her desire to turn Western opinion against Japan overrode such heartfelt concerns, it must have been intense.

Chang was spectacularly successful in realizing her goal. *The Rape of Nanking* was on the *New York Times* bestseller list for over twenty weeks, and it received overwhelmingly favorable reviews from the Western media and academia. Numerous Western print and television journalists, unfamiliar with the Asian politics at stake, accepted the book uncritically. "Few non-Chinese," wrote the *Washington Post*'s Ken Ringle, "remember that sixty years ago . . . the Japanese Imperial Army ran riot in . . . Nanjing, hacking apart in eight weeks between 260,000 and 350,000 people—far more than died in Hiroshima and Nagasaki combined."[47] The *Associated Press*'s Sau Chan goes beyond uncritical acceptance to actively champion Chang's cause, writing: "Much has been written about the Holocaust in Europe . . . and about the atomic bombings of Japan, which killed about 140,000 in Hiroshima and about 70,000 in Nagasaki. . . . But the Japanese death toll falls short of the estimated 260,000 to 350,000 Chinese killed in Nanjing."[48] The Western print media largely either accepted Chang's account uncritically, or even actively advocated her thesis.[49]

The Western visual media was even more sympathetic. Chang encountered favorably inclined interviewers on the *NewsHour with Jim Lehrer, Good Morning America,* and *Nightline. NewsHour* interviewer David Gergen, for instance, appropriated Chang's claims as facts in his questions, saying, for example, "Let me ask you about another mystery surrounding Nanking . . . there were more people killed in Nanking than in Hiroshima and Nagasaki combined. And yet, after all the debates about Nagasaki and Hiroshima, we have amnesia about Nanking. Why?"[50] Gergen thus helps Chang present her account as historical fact.[51]

Despite the angry tone and subjective use of facts displayed throughout *The Rape of Nanking,* academic reviews were also largely positive, especially those written by China scholars. Two Sinologists at the University of California, Berkeley, for example, wrote glowingly about Chang's book. Historian Frederic Wakeman endorsed the book on its back cover: "Iris Chang's *The Rape of Nanking* is an utterly compelling book. . . . Many Japanese have denied that these events ever took place, substituting amnesia for guilt, but Iris Chang's heartbreaking account will make such evasion impossible in the future for all but the most diehard right-wing Japanese extremists." In a lengthy *New York Times* review, Orville Schell, Dean of Berkeley's School of Journalism, also joined Chang in her criticism of Japan. Schell declares, for instance, that all Japanese are in denial about the war, unwilling to confront their "shame or loss of face."[52]

A few American Japan scholars, aware that Chang knows very little of the actual state of Japanese research and education about the Nanjing massacre, have objected to this dominant view. Historian Joshua Fogel, for instance, has argued that "Iris Chang's book is seriously flawed. . . . It is full of misinformation and harebrained explanations."[53] His Berkeley colleague Andrew Barshay concurs, challenging Orville Schell's *New York Times* review of *Rape* as "doubly flawed" in its misrepresentations of Japan.[54] Indeed, these Japan scholars were not alone. Contrary to Wakeman's prediction, *The Rape of Nanking* created controversy rather than settling it. Chang's disdain for the historical record[55] exposed her findings to attack from reputable Japanese scholars, and even helped build popular Japanese support for right-wing revisionists. In April 1998, for example, the Japanese ambassador to the United States, Kunihiko Saito, publicly criticized the book as "one-sided" and "erroneous," and in June 1998 a group of conservative Japanese scholars held a press conference in Tokyo to attack *The Rape of Nanking* as historically inaccurate. Japanese criticisms of Chang's scholarship were largely unsuccessful, however, falling on deaf Western ears. Chang's counterattacks, meanwhile, won a sympathetic hearing from the Western press. The *NewsHour with Jim Lehrer* set up a debate between Chang and Saito, and *Newsweek* ran an article Chang wrote to plug her book and refute Saito and the Tokyo conservatives.[56]

My purpose here is not to point out flaws in Chang's argument. Chang never claims to be an historian; she is a sincere young woman enraged by what she has learned about the atrocities of December 1937. My purpose, instead, has been to show that like "China as victor," the new "China as victim" storyline requires foreign validation. National identities evolve through public contestation, and are based upon recognition from both opponents and neutral parties. The *Rape of Nanking* sensation provided an opportunity for a public contest between Chinese and Japanese narratives of the past before a jury of Western opinion. Thus, two projects are intertwined in victimization narratives: quantifying the pain and presenting the Chinese case to the world.

War Stories

To many Chinese, the modern Sino-Japanese encounter has been highly traumatic. Seen as an inferior for over a millennium, in 1895 the "younger brother" beat up his "older brother," first militarily, in the Jiawu War, and then legally, in the Treaty of Shimonoseki. The strongly felt injustice of these "ungrateful" acts is the origin of the ethical anger Chinese today feel about Japanese atrocities during World War II.

Under Mao, official narratives of the "War of Resistance" sought to utilize China's "victory" both to legitimize the Communist Party and to build a "New China." And many Chinese still cling to this "heroic narrative" about the war, enraged by the view that Japanese and Westerners do not acknowledge China's contributions to the Allied victory. In the 1990s, however, a new "victimization narrative" emerged to challenge the heroism thesis. During and after the fiftieth-anniversary commemorations of World War II in 1995 and the sixtieth-anniversary commemorations of the "Rape of Nanking" in 1997, Chinese paid new attention to their World War II sufferings.

For many, this painful encounter with wartime atrocities has generated a visceral anger towards Japan. Few have moved beyond what sociologist Thomas Scheff calls a "humiliated fury."[57] Japan bashing is ascendant and unquestioned. People's Liberation Army writer Jin Hui's moving *Wailing at the Heavens* may be the exception that proves the rule. Unlike most other commemorative volumes published in 1995, *Wailing* does not stop at either valorizing Chinese victories or agonizing over Japanese atrocities. Instead, Jin engages in sincere soul-searching, asking, for example, why so many Chinese were "as meek as lambs at the slaughterhouse" *(ren ren xing ge)* during the war: "Men are not lambs. But it seems like many of those slaughtered were even more obedient than lambs. . . . Why didn't they resist when faced with death?" This inquiry leads Jin into a probing examination of why the Chinese, like a "sheet of loose sand" *(yipan sansha),* lacked courage and unity in fighting the Japanese.[58] To my knowledge, *Wailing* is the only recent Chinese volume on World War II that asks such heart-wrenching questions, raising the issue of whether national identity can withstand Jin's style of critical inquiry. When faced with the trauma of past atrocities, most Chinese writers instead seek to relieve their pain by bashing Japan. *The Rape of Nanking* was typical, lambasting the entire Japanese race as "sadistic 'conformists.'"[59] And Chang's book was a great success in both China and America.

CHAPTER 6

China's Apology Diplomacy

血
债
要
用
血
来
还
!!

*"The blood debt must
be repaid in blood!"*

In 1996, the Year of the Rat, researchers at the Beijing Asia-Pacific Economic Relations Center issued a two-volume work comparing the modernizations of China and Japan. Part of a series on national affairs that earnestly seeks the "Holy Grail" (*zhenli:* literally, 'truth') of a "rich people and a strong state" (*fumin qiangguo*), *A Century of Hatred* opens with a section entitled "Sino-Japanese Relations During Eight Years of the Rat." The section delimits the scope of the study: it is a brief history of the last century of Sino-Japanese relations, focusing on the Years of the Rat in each twelve-year cycle of the Chinese zodiac. The focus on these years leads the authors to contemplate how the rat became the first sign in the Chinese zodiac. The authors recount a traditional folktale about a race, in which the rat craftily persuaded the cat not to compete, and then rode on the back of the cow most of the way, only to dismount and sprint past it to the finish line. Having told their parable, the authors then assert that China is like the cat (agile but naïve) or cow (honest but foolish), and was beaten by Japan, the cunning rat.[1] As the authors' use of the folktale suggests, complex and multiple motivations, including a variety of emotions and material goals, drive Chinese nationalists. Calling Japan a "rat" clearly satisfied the authors' desire to insult Japan.[2] Yet the goal of their book is largely instrumental: to learn from Japan's successful modernization experience. The image of China presented in the anecdote is also mixed: China has the good qualities of being agile and honest, but also the bad qualities of being naïve and foolish. China deserved to be first but was deceived by Japan. Japan thus humiliated China.

How should Chinese react? The authors, like many contemporary Chinese confronting their perceived "humiliation" at Japanese hands, alternate between self-criticism and anger at their rival. They criticize Chinese for their "great nation complex": "it is hard for us to truly admit to ourselves that we are more backwards than others." But they also devote a lengthy chapter to a comparison of the "mighty" Chinese and "trifling" Japanese national characters. Even though they thus display obvious bias, the authors argue for the need to balance reason and emotion in scholarship: "Some say that most post-Liberation research on modern Chinese history still stagnates at the level of emotional outpourings condemning foreign aggressors. This trivializes the reasoned nature of our research. . . . Neither reason nor emotion should be overemphasized at the expense of the other."[3] Despite these good intentions, however, their title—*A Century of Hatred*—suggests that the authors have difficulty practicing what they preach. Chinese hatred of the Japanese still runs too deep.

Arguing that elites "use" nationalism as a "tool" to bolster their legitimacy, Western scholars today have largely dismissed emotions as irrelevant to nationalist politics. Such analysts can therefore do little to help us understand such nationalist passions.[4] In the China field, the "elites use nationalism" view translates into a powerful "party propaganda" consensus on the genesis of Chinese nationalism: with the decline of Communism, the Party elite fosters and uses anti-foreign sentiment in an attempt to retain power. This "party propaganda" explanation of Chinese nationalism blinds us to the critical roles that the people and the passions play in it. Both the Party elite and popular nationalists participate in nationalist politics, and both emotional and instrumental concerns drive their behavior. Regime legitimacy and the very meaning of being Chinese are at stake. To understand Chinese nationalism, therefore, it is crucial to overcome this juxtaposition of elites against the masses and sense against sensibility. This chapter focuses on the issue of motivation, whereas the next chapter turns to the role of the people in Chinese nationalism.

Despite compelling neurological evidence to the contrary, there is a strong tendency in the liberal West to view emotion and reason as locked into a zero-sum relationship in which any gain for one is a loss for the other.[5] In other words, becoming more emotional entails becoming less rational, and vice versa. Studies of Chinese nationalism are no exception, pitting reason against the emotions. Optimistic pundits tend to downplay the role of the passions in Chinese nationalism. They acknowledge the role of Chinese national feelings, but then assert that the rational pursuit of China's national interest will win the day. In a review of Sino-American relations, for example, one American scholar notes the danger that Beijing and Washington elites may push disagreements for domestic purposes, but cites the Chinese proverb "loud thunder, but little rain" *(leisheng da, yudian xiao)* to conclude optimistically that interests will triumph over the passions.[6] Former president of the National Committee on U.S.–China Relations, Mike Lampton similarly recognizes Chinese fears of Westernization, but then concludes that China pursues its interests "just like other countries."[7] He thus implies that in "normal" countries, emotions like fear do not influence those who make decisions about foreign policy. Optimistic accounts of Sino-Japanese relations also dismiss emotion as secondary.[8] A recent examination of the Sino-Japanese Diaoyu Islands controversy asserts that economic performance is more important than nationalism (that is, interests will trump passions) and thus can reach a conclusion about the controversy marked by "cautious optimism."[9] From this rationalist point of view, the Party will be able to control nationalist sentiments and pursue China's national interest.

More pessimistic pundits, by contrast, lament that reason is impotent when confronted with the passions. David Shambaugh's 1991 *Beautiful Imperialist,* discussed in chapter 4, is a prominent example of the irrationalist view of China's America policy. Shambaugh argues that passion and ideology distort Chinese perceptions of America, concluding that "the vast majority of America watchers in China do not understand the U.S. very well." Because of China's history of victimization at the hands of Western imperialists, "Chinese leaders simply do not trust American motives."[10] Chinese emotions thus impede the development of harmonious Sino-American relations. Pessimistic accounts of Sino-Japanese relations are also less than confident about the triumph of reason. In his 1989 *China Eyes Japan,* Allen Whiting suggests that reason is powerless before the passions: negative images of Japan have thwarted China's interest in closer relations with its Asian neighbor.[11] Arguments over the nature and future direction of Chinese nationalism thus often tell us more about the optimism or pessimism of their proponents—whether they follow in the "rational" or "irrational" traditions—than they do about China.[12]

The idea of *face* can help us overcome the reason vs. emotion dualism that hobbles studies of nationalist motivation. People are emotionally attached to the self-image they present to the world. If a person's *face* is assaulted, his or her feelings are hurt. But *face* also provides people with real power. He who "loses face" loses status and the ability to pursue material goals. As international relations theorist Robert Jervis put it over three decades ago, "prestige and saving face are . . . aspects of a state's image that greatly contribute to its pursuit of other goals."[13] Both passion and reason are intimately intertwined in nationalist politics.

To understand the complex and multiple motives that drive China's nationalists, this chapter explores three recent examples of Sino-Japanese and Sino-American "apology diplomacy": the failed Japanese attempt to apologize for World War II in 1998, the 1999 Belgrade bombing, and the 2001 spy plane collision. Apologies are about power relations. Offenses to the social order threaten established hierarchies, and one way that the aggrieved can regain social position is vengeance. As sociologist J. M. Barbalet writes, "Vengefulness is an emotion of power relations. It functions to correct imbalanced or disjointed power relationships. Vengefulness is concerned with restoring social actors to their rightful place in relationships."[14] Apologies are another means of restoring threatened social hierarchies. The form an apology takes depends critically upon the relative status of the parties involved. The kind of apology necessary to rectify an offense an inferior commits against a superior is greater than that required of an offense committed between equals. For instance, a son who insults his father publicly must give an extended and public apology. Privately insulting one's brother, however, requires a lesser kind of apology. An apology may not be possible, therefore, if there is disagreement over the relative status of the parties involved. If both parties claim to be the superior in a hierarchical relationship with each other, there can be no agreement on the extent of the apology necessary to rectify the offense.

However, the politics of apology is not just about relative status and material power, it is also about equally powerful passions. A public offense causes the injured party to lose face and is, therefore, far more offensive than one made in private.[15] Vengeance and apologies not only help reestablish power relations, they also restore self-esteem. As sociologist Barrington Moore writes: "Vengeance means retaliation. It also means a reassertion of human dignity or worth, after injury or damage. Both are basic sentiments behind moral anger and the sense of injustice."[16]

Social psychologists have convincingly demonstrated that belittling the offender can restore the collective self-esteem of the offended. In one compelling experiment, women who were shown a clip from an altered *Rocky IV*, in which the American boxer (played by Sylvester Stallone) loses to the Russian, lost national self-esteem. Self-esteem was restored, however, when the subjects were subsequently allowed to denigrate Russians.[17] By righting a wrong, apologies can similarly restore the self-esteem of the aggrieved. If an offense is felt to be too hurtful, however, no apology can suffice.

"Deep Remorse" in Tokyo: Sino-Japanese Apology Diplomacy, 1998

In October 1998, Japanese Prime Minister Keizo Obuchi and visiting South Korean President Kim Dae-Jung issued a joint statement in Tokyo. Obuchi expressed his "heartfelt apologies" to the Korean people for their suffering under Japanese colonial rule, and Kim responded with "sincere acceptance." It was the first written apology for the atrocities of World War II that Japan had issued to any country. In a speech before the Japanese Diet, Kim focused on reconciliation, forgiving Japan for its past misdeeds and speaking of their past and future partnership. When he finished his speech, the Diet gave Kim a standing ovation.[18]

Things did not go nearly as well during Chinese President Jiang Zemin's visit to Tokyo the next month. Kim's successful trip had raised Chinese expectations. An editorial in Hong Kong's *South China Morning Post* declared that "China should get an apology every bit as profuse as Korea's."[19] In an oral statement, Prime Minister Obuchi expressed his "heartfelt apologies" to the Chinese people. While Emperor Akihito toasted Jiang at a state dinner, however, Chinese and Japanese diplomats engaged in last-minute haggling over the wording of their joint declaration. Yet in the end, Japan expressed only "deep remorse" rather than "heartfelt apologies" in the written document. Neither Obuchi nor Jiang was willing to sign the document, and the signing ceremony was cancelled.

Why did the Japan-Korea apology succeed, while a similar Japan-China effort failed just a month later? Western pundits have largely laid the blame for the Japan-China apology failure on the Japanese "psyche": the Japanese people, it seems, suffer from an "apology complex." In a high-profile *Foreign Affairs* article, *New York Times* journalist Nicholas Kristof presented a typical explanation: "Japanese people are famously polite, apologizing at the start and end of every conversation and many times in between—which makes the reluctance to apologize for the war even more remarkable. If the Japanese regularly apologize for being a nuisance, even when they are not, why will they not show regret for the slaughter of millions?"[20] Directed at any other ethnic group, such stereotyping of an entire people would be considered taboo by *Foreign Affairs*'s audience. But wartime propaganda about the "Japs" still resonates in the West, and Japan bashing continues to be socially acceptable in the United States.

A minority counterargument, however, holds that China's elite was also to blame for the failure of the Japan-China apology. According to this view, the Chinese Communist Party is more interested in *using* Japan's past misdeeds than in *resolving* them. Significantly, Kristof also advanced this argument. In "an effort to push the guilt button and gain more concessions," he wrote in the *New York Times*, "Jiang's behavior has been impolite and calculating. . . . China's leaders have been less interested in healing the wounds of history than in reminding everyone of their existence." The Chinese Communist Party, Kristof contends, "derives its legitimacy in part from the spirited resistance it led against Japanese invaders, and whenever it wants something from Tokyo it thunders about Japanese war brutality."[21] The Party elite, it seems, puts the past to use in both its foreign and domestic policies.

Both of these arguments are problematic. If the fault lies with the Japanese national character, then how can we account for the fact that the two apologies had such different outcomes? In other words, if the Japanese suffer from some sort of "apology pathology" as Kristof suggests, then how could they successfully apologize to Kim and Korea, but not to China? And if Jiang simply sought to continue using the past as a tool in the bilateral relationship, why would he travel to Tokyo seeking to resolve the issue in the first place? Indeed, his failure only provided ammunition for his critics.[22] It is the past, arguably, that got the better of Jiang—not the other way around. Both of Kristof's arguments advance extreme views of human motivation: either the Japanese are irrationally unable to apologize, or the Chinese are cold and calculating. The politics of apology, however, actually involve a complex interplay of *both* emotions and interests. Apologies implicate both the self-esteem and the relative status of the parties involved. The challenge is to show how considerations of both passion and power affect the process of apologizing.

There were significant differences in the contexts behind the Japan-Korea and Japan-China apologies, differences that help explain the success of one and the failure of the other. Whereas Japan and Korea had achieved general agreement concerning their relative status and, therefore, the necessary extent of the apology, the same cannot be said of Japan and China, who are still far from reaching consensus about their relative positions. They are less likely, therefore, to agree on the degree of apology required to restore proper power relations. Furthermore, where Koreans have been confronting their past suffering under Japanese colonialism for decades, Chinese have only recently begun to face their victimization during the "War of Resistance." The wounds of war are still too fresh for many Chinese to seriously entertain an apology. Considerations of both power and passion suggest, therefore, that talk of genuine Sino-Japanese reconciliation is premature.

As I noted in chapter 2, the prevalence of teacher/student and older brother/younger brother metaphors in Chinese writings about Sino-Japanese relations suggests that many Chinese nationalists today see themselves as superior to Japan. For instance, in the popular 1996 anti-Japanese diatribe *China Can Still Say No,* Song Qiang and his colleagues write, "Sun Yat-sen said that 'China and Japan are brothers: China is the older brother, and Japan is the younger brother.' Unfortunately, this 'younger brother' . . . does not treat his older brother like a human."[23] From this Chinese perspective, Japanese aggression against China during the Jiawu War and World War II is the almost unthinkable act of a student insulting his teacher, or a younger brother beating up his older brother. Such actions threaten Chinese views of a Sinocentric Asia. Violations of this kind can only be corrected by the inferior's *profound and repetitive* public prostrations before the superior. And the kowtowing can only stop when the superior is satisfied that status has been restored. In this Chinese view, only this kind of abject apology can reconstruct the proper hierarchical relationship between China and Japan.

China's instrumental concerns about relative status are compounded by deep emotions. Chinese anger about Japanese wartime atrocities still runs too deep for an apology to heal the wound to Chinese self-esteem. As leading China scholar Kokubun Ryosei has recently noted, the last two decades of Sino-Japanese relations have been marked by increased contact and mutual dependence, but also by growing antipathy.[24] The anger has both visceral and ethical dimensions. Visceral anger may be emotionally pleasing: "A man in a rage does not want to get out of it," wrote sociologist Charles Cooley a century ago. Ethical or righteous anger, however, may have a positive social function: "The higher function of hostility is to put down wrong."[25] Recent Chinese narratives about Japan are full of examples of both lower, visceral and higher, ethical forms of anger.

In *China Can Still Say No,* Song Qiang and his coauthors reveal a visceral anger towards Japan with lines like "We have probably made a mistake . . . you can only be humane towards humans; towards beasts you can only be bestial." They clearly delight in insulting Japan. In a section entitled "Japan Should Beat Itself," for instance, they state: "Japan is an immoral neighbor. . . . Immoral in the past, immoral in the present. Immoral in politics, immoral in economics. . . ."[26]

Even Chinese scholars who have engaged in sincere soul-searching about World War II cannot but express a visceral anger at Japanese atrocities. As noted in chapter 5, PLA writer Jin Hui's thoughtful 1995 *Wailing at the Heavens* is exceptional among Chinese writings on the war because it asks heart-wrenching questions about China's own failures. But Jin's research also forced him to confront evidence of Japanese atrocities, a process which brought forth some troubling emotions: "Skimming these records of violence today, we still frequently curse them in our hearts as 'devils.'" Other "devils," like "Western devils," "British devils," and so forth, must be further specified. Chinese, Jin explains, view the Japanese as the worst of all their early modern oppressors, reserving the term "devils" (*guizi*) just for them. Jin says that thinking about the "devils" led him to consider the issue of retribution very carefully: "I do not seek to arouse a desire for revenge. . . . It is not in the Chinese character to harbor a grudge, and excessively fierce feelings of vengeance can only corrode our hearts. . . . We should be vigilant about the monsters around us, and even more vigilant that we ourselves not become monsters." Despite self-conscious efforts such as these to overcome his anger, Jin's writing still lapses into snubs like "The greatest Japanese characteristic is that they lack a special characteristic," and even racist comments, such as that all Japanese men are "more bestial than beasts."[27] The visceral component of the anger many Chinese feel towards Japan understandably stems from the brutality of Japan's wartime atrocities.

Such visceral anger is reinforced, however, by a higher or ethical anger based upon a strong sense of injustice. The sensationalist diatribe *Be Vigilant Against Japan!* passionately declares apology and indemnity are called for by "a fierce cry coming from the depths of over a billion Chinese souls."[28] As noted in the last chapter, two 1997 books on the topic of war reparations, *Blood Debt* and *Why Japan Won't Settle Accounts,* framed their demands in the context of the injustice of China's public loss of national *face* in the 1895 Treaty of Shimonoseki, asking, in effect, "How could 'little brother' do this to us?" It is only after presenting the injustice of this Japanese betrayal that the authors can justify, to themselves as much as to others, their angry demands for war reparations. To these authors, ethical anger makes visceral anger socially acceptable.

The anger the Chinese display toward Japan is sometimes completely contrived—designed to secure material goods like Japanese aid—and sometimes pure passion, as is the case in Iris Chang's 1997 *The Rape of Nanking*. However, Chinese nationalists' anger is usually both personal and political. The anger seeks to restore both personal self-respect as a "Chinese" *and* China's proper place as superior in Sino-Japanese relations.

Considerations of both power and passion thus prevent many Chinese today from entertaining any Japanese apology seriously: they cannot agree on the two countries' relative status, and their anger at Japan still runs too deep. During the 1995 fiftieth-anniversary commemorations of the Second World War, for example, Chinese nationalists unanimously rejected a series of Japanese apologies as insufficient. One Chinese scholar argued that Japanese Prime Minister Maruyama's 1995 apology for the war was overshadowed by Liberal Democratic Party politician Hashimoto's concurrent visit to Yasukuni Shrine in Tokyo, where Japanese honor their war dead.[29] A Chinese Academy of Social Sciences researcher has dubbed this phenomenon "two tunes within one government," declaring it "abnormal" and "incomprehensible."[30]

Zi Shui and Xiao Shi elaborate on Chinese problems with Maruyama's apology in their *Be Vigilant Against Japanese Militarism!* In a section entitled "How Deep was Maruyama's 'Apology'?," Zi and Xiao complain about four issues: the apology was given at a press conference rather than at the formal memorial service; Hashimoto visited Yasukuni at the same time as Maruyama gave his apology; a Japanese cabinet member issued "revisionist" remarks but was not forced to resign; and Maruyama did not fault Emperor Hirohito for the war. The authors thus conclude that Maruyama's statement was "only half an apology."[31] Their problems with the apology are more than petty: by suggesting that Maruyama publicly blame the emperor for the war, they suggest that he put not only his political career, but perhaps his very life, on the line for Chinese national pride. (Right-wing Japanese nationalists once physically assaulted the mayor of Nagasaki for suggesting that the emperor was responsible for wartime atrocities.) Given the issues that upset Zi and Xiao, it is likely that no apology could satisfy them. In this, they are not unusual. The 1995 Japanese Diet Resolution on the War, which expressed "deep remorse" for what Japan had done in the past, met similar condemnations from many Chinese. Many Chinese nationalists do not seem ready to seriously entertain any Japanese apology, no matter how profoundly felt or eloquently stated.

Instead, many Chinese nationalists seek to restore their self-esteem by bashing Japan. Because they wish to maintain a positive self-image, however, few will admit to such base desires. *Blood Debt* contains a fascinating example of such barely concealed motives. The first chapter is entitled, "I Want One U.S. Dollar of Indemnity." The title suggests that an indemnity can symbolize an apology. The authors explain that "A U.S. dollar . . . is not an indemnity in an economic sense. . . . It is a confession to those victimized by Japan." Professing a desire for just *one* dollar, the authors construct a magnanimous self-image: "Beneficent and generous Chinese seek only a clearing of this historical debt, not historical revenge."[32]

The currency the authors have chosen, however, suggests other motives. They desire an *American* dollar—not a Chinese yuan or a Japanese yen. The monetary damages listed on the back cover are also given in U.S. dollars. This implies that the indemnity must be made before the bar of Western opinion. The authors desire, it seems, to humiliate Japan publicly: "Recollecting the bitterness of fifteen years of resistance. . . . Hasn't the Chinese race been too understanding? . . . As a lesson to future generations, the [Japanese] should be punished—both a moral and just punishment—and an economic one."[33] Contrary to their earlier ostentatious gesture of magnanimity—just "one U.S. dollar"—the authors here suggest that the size of the economic punishment should represent the size of the crime. Discussions of indemnity figures, like the debates surrounding the number killed during the Nanjing massacre that I discussed in chapter 5, seek to place Japanese on a specific point in a continuum of contrition.

Blood Debt is not an anomaly. Recent Chinese writings about Japan reveal that many Chinese nationalists fantasize about punishing, not forgiving, Japan. Moreover, as was the case with *Blood Debt*'s authors, for many Chinese the amount of the indemnity has come to symbolize the degree of Japanese contrition and subservience. Finally, like *Blood Debt*'s authors, many Chinese nationalists play out their conflict with Japan upon an international stage, frequently referring to foreign condemnation of Japanese actions to justify their refusal to accept Japanese apologies. In a section of their *Be Vigilant Against Japanese Militarism!* entitled "Asian Popular Opinion Is Furious," authors Zi and Xiao justify their indignation by quoting a long list of Asian press reports condemning Hashimoto.[34] One PLA writer turns to Western opinion, citing a *New York Times* article calling the Diet Resolution "a self-justification, not an apology."[35] Likewise, another writer maintains that Hashimoto's "international reputation" was damaged by his visit to Yasukuni.[36] Chinese nationalists thus seek to muster world opinion against Japan.

The martial metaphor is deliberate: Chinese and Japanese are arguably still at war, but on the field of public image, not of battle. They do combat today with words rather than with weapons. Foreigners are often unwitting accomplices in a Chinese project of mustering foreign opinion against Japan. A *NewsHour* piece featuring Iris Chang and the Japanese ambassador to the United States, Kunihiko Saito, is a fascinating example of the American media's unwitting collaboration with Chinese nationalists in their verbal war with Japan. Rather than interviewing Chang and Saito separately, or moderating a debate between them, PBS anchorwoman Elizabeth Farnsworth allowed Chang to attack Saito directly—Farnsworth even joined her in condemning him. Early in the interview Chang argued that an apology must be voluntary to be sincere, saying "I think that the measure really of a true apology is not what a person or a government gives grudgingly under pressure. . . . A true apology is what one feels in his heart when he makes that apology." Nevertheless, she later contradicts herself, attempting to coerce an apology from Saito: "Can the ambassador himself say today on national TV live that he personally is profoundly sorry for the rape of Nanking and other war crimes against China?" Saito responded, "We do recognize that acts of cruelty and violence were committed by members of the Japanese military and we are very sorry for that." Despite this step in the right direction, Farnsworth and Chang then had the following astonishing exchange:

> *Farnsworth:* Did you hear an apology?
>
> *Chang:* I don't know. Did you hear an apology?[37]

Having just written a book on the Nanjing massacre, Chang, understandably, is still too angry to accept any Japanese apology. The effect of the exchange, whether Farnsworth intended it or not, is that she helped Chang undermine or devalue Saito's attempt to apologize. She thus, perhaps unwittingly, participated in Chang's project of rallying Western opinion against Japan.

The Farnsworth interview also reveals that Chinese displays of anger such as Chang's frequently do not have the desired effect. Although many Chinese nationalists desire that Japan prostrate itself before them in order to restore their national pride, forcing the Japanese into this position does not satisfy them, but only increases their anger.[38] The *NewsHour* interview displays just this dynamic. Chang began by defining an apology as "voluntary." By the end of the interview, however, Chang's anger was so great that she sought to force an apology from Saito. Nothing Saito might have said in response would likely have satisfied Chang, however, because it could no longer be voluntary.

Many Japanese, to be sure, are not passive spectators of this contest; some are active combatants. Nationalists on Japan's far right seek to save face for Japan by discrediting China's Japan bashers. For example, cartoonist Kobayashi Yoshinori has sought to discredit Chinese claims about Japan's wartime atrocities. In his 1998 manga *On the War,* for instance, he devotes an entire chapter to the Nanjing massacre, arguing that much of the photo evidence has been doctored.[39] Kobayashi is outraged that these "fakes" were displayed at the Hiroshima Peace Museum: he frets that they create self-loathing among Japanese schoolchildren attending the exhibition. He is perhaps most indignant, however, that *The Rape of Nanking* had become an international bestseller, and that by playing fast and loose with the facts, Chang was "deceiving Americans" about Japan, causing them to take China's side in episodes of Japan bashing. Rightwing Japanese nationalists like Kobayashi doubtless object to Chinese demands for an abject apology out of an inflated sense of their nation's superiority equal to that maintained by many Chinese nationalists.

The strong sales of *On the War* suggest, however, that increasing numbers of moderate Japanese are also growing frustrated with what they see as incessant and unappeasable Chinese criticism. Many do not believe that China will accept a Japanese apology, and many argue that the Chinese are trying to establish themselves as the moral superiors in a hierarchical relationship with Japan. After Jiang Zemin's 1998 Tokyo trip, Japanese Foreign Minister Masahiko Koumura told reporters, "While President Kim made it clear that he would like to settle past history, that was not necessarily the case" with Jiang.[40] The Liberal Democratic Party's Machimura Nobutaka, the number two man in the Foreign Ministry, was less circumspect during a 1999 event at the University of California, Berkeley, declaring that Jiang's "harsh words" to the Japanese emperor's face were "astonishing—or perhaps not so astonishing." He explained that Japanese like himself have become "irritated" by China's never-ending demands for Japanese apologies. Machimura was blunt: the Chinese seek "moral superiority."[41] Many moderate Japanese likely feel that the apology Japan should give China should be one appropriate to an offense committed between equals: like the apology given to Korea, it should be sincere but also willingly accepted. It should not lower Japan to an inferior status vis-à-vis China. Japanese decision makers may have been unwilling to give a written apology to Jiang in 1998, because they believed that Chinese would be unwilling to accept Japan as an equal.

Westerners are, like it or not, the audience and judge of such Sino-Japanese conflicts over *face* and should avoid taking sides. We would do well, as Laura Hein notes, to "avoid giving aid and comfort to political agendas not [our] own."[42] Instead, the West should try to understand the stakes of the game. Chinese and Japanese are fighting not just over issues of self-esteem, but also over their relative positions in the new Asian order. Americans and Chinese have recently battled over similar issues.

A "Terrorist Attack": The Belgrade Embassy Bombing, 1999

Immediately following the May 1999 bombing of the Chinese embassy in Belgrade, President Bill Clinton issued a public apology to the Chinese people. American ambassador to China James Sasser quickly followed suit, as did NATO Secretary General Javier Solana. As noted in chapter 1, their phone calls to President Jiang and other members of the Chinese leadership went unanswered for several days. Although their apologies were finally published in the Chinese media four days later, the Chinese leadership publicly rejected them. After lengthy negotiations, Beijing and Washington agreed on compensation packages for both sides. When money finally changed hands in January 2001, however, Chinese Foreign Ministry spokesman Zhu Bangzao again demanded that the United States "conduct a comprehensive and thorough investigation into the bombing, severely punish the perpetrators and give satisfactory account of the incident to the Chinese people."[43]

How can we account for the failure of this Sino-American apology diplomacy? I argue that many Chinese could not accept an apology because they viewed the bombing as an assault on China's national dignity. Refusing repeated American apologies was one of the only ways that China's leaders could seek to regain *face* for the Chinese people.

Though clearly not representative, a collection of 281 condolence letters, essays, and poems e-mailed, faxed, and mailed to the *Guangming Daily* newspaper in the hours and days following the May 1999 Belgrade embassy bombing provides a window into Chinese nationalism today.[44] These writings were posted on the paper's Web site, which created a special page commemorating Xu Xinghu and Zhu Ying, the two *Guangming Daily* reporters who were killed in Belgrade. Shanghai's Xiong Junfeng, for instance, sought to correct a matter of diction: "I believe that we should stop calling NATO's bombing of our embassy a 'barbarous act'—a 'terrorist act'

FIGURE 9. Blood debt. Marching on the U.S. embassy in Beijing on 10 May 1999, a protestor yells an anti-American slogan. Smeared with red, his headband says "blood debt." Photo courtesy of AP/Wide World Photos.

would be more appropriate. Something 'barbaric' stems from ignorance, but American-led NATO's despicable act was clearly premeditated. . . . This was a terrorist attack through and through."[45] The letters reveal that the vast majority of Chinese believed that the United States bombed their embassy intentionally. In contrast, no mainstream Western media source initially took issue with NATO's explanation that the bombing was an accident.[46] Indeed, many Western news articles and editorials did not use the word "bombing" without prefacing it with the qualifier "accidental." That the bombing was an accident thus became self-evident.

How can we account for these mutually exclusive views: the Chinese certain that the bombing was intentional; the Americans equally sure that it was an accident? As I noted in chapter 1, the Western media blamed a Chinese misinformation campaign. The Chinese government, it claimed, was not letting the Chinese people know about Serbian atrocities in Kosovo, but was instead calling attention to NATO "interference" in the "internal politics" of the Yugoslav Federation. Furthermore, the Chinese media did not report Clinton's public apologies immediately following the bombing. The *Washington Post* was eloquent on this matter: "The Big Lie is alive and well in Beijing. . . . It should come as no surprise, after weeks of . . . internal propaganda, that many ordinary Chinese now believe the embassy bombing was deliberate."[47] Communist Party propaganda, in this Western view, explains the Chinese people's mistaken belief that the bombing was intentional.

The Chinese government clearly manipulated information about the Kosovo war in general and the embassy bombing in particular. The problem with the misinformation argument, however, is that numerous Chinese who read the Western press coverage of the Kosovo conflict also believed that the bombing was intentional. The Chinese and American disagreement over whether the bombing was an accident is thus best explained, not by the misinformation argument, but by social psychology: the "intergroup attribution bias." Social psychologists have found that all humans, as social beings, consistently favor their ingroups over outgroups when making attributions.[48] Thus, if an ingroup member does something good, we attribute it to his or her goodness. If he or she does something bad, however, we write it off as beyond the member's control. Conversely, if a member of an outgroup does something good, we dismiss it as "luck" or somehow attribute it to the situation, so it does not reflect well on the outgroup. If an outgroup member does something bad, we ascribe it to his or her badness, which then reflects poorly on the entire outgroup. Out of a desire to view our ingroup as good, in short, we give our fellow ingroup members the benefit of the doubt. This charity does not, however, extend to outsiders.

In the context of U.S.-China relations, Americans perceive their leaders as fellow ingroup members. Americans could not, therefore, easily attribute the Belgrade bombing to innate badness; instead, they focused on the situation: it must have been a tragic mistake. Like all peoples, Americans view themselves positively and desire that others also view them that way. As I noted in chapter 1, the *NewsHour*'s Jim Lehrer was so stunned by the Chinese view that America intentionally bombed their embassy that he brought up the issue seven times in an interview with the Chinese ambassador to the United States, Li Zhaoxing.[49]

For Chinese, however, there is no reason to extend charitable attributions to outgroup Americans. Chinese nationalists on the *Guangming Daily* Web site largely assumed that the bombing was intentional, speculating instead about America's precise goals: to foment domestic social chaos, to damage the Chinese economy, to divide China, to test the Chinese government's resolve, and, more fundamentally, to humiliate China. Because the United States "fears a strengthened China," a "young teacher" from Kunming writes, NATO seeks to "foment chaos."[50] Chaos in China would allow America, according to an e-mail from Beijing, to "topple China without fighting."[51] Tian Chengyou from Zhengzhou similarly argues that the timing of the bombing, which coincided with the rise of China's economy, the tenth anniversary of Tiananmen, and approaching American elections, indicates America's goal—inciting domestic chaos. In an essay entitled "America's Plot," Qiu Yingxiong concurs: "Because of defeats in Korea and Vietnam, America is not sure that it can subdue *[chenfu]* China."[52] Qiu thus argues that America seeks to test the Chinese government's resolve.

If the "intergroup attribution bias" helps explain divergent Chinese and American views on the cause of the bombing, why did so many Chinese view the Belgrade bombing as a threat to China's national self-respect? And how should we understand the various angry responses to this threat, such as demands for apologies and explanations, tongue lashings, demonstrations, calls for economic boycotts, and other forms of revenge? Psychological research on self-esteem helps explain Chinese reactions to the Belgrade bombing. To the extent that individuals associate with a certain group, they gain "collective self-esteem" from that group's accomplishments.[53] Therefore, to the extent that individuals identity with their nations their self-esteem is tied to its fate. We have seen that many Chinese berate Japan in an attempt to restore their self-esteem. The anger that many

FIGURE 10. "Fuck your crazy American!!!" This graffiti appeared outside the west entrance to People's University in Beijing in May 1999. Photo courtesy of Scott Kennedy.

Chinese displayed toward America during the bombing protests, similarly, sought to regain *face* for China.

Chinese protestors clearly felt their nation had been dealt an unjust blow. Almost all of the 281 letters sent to the *Guangming Daily* express an ethical "outrage" or "indignation" (*fennu, fenkai, qifen*). None speaks of more visceral forms of anger, like being "irritated" or "ticked off" (e.g., *shengqi*). Such righteous anger is "designed to rectify injustice"; it seeks, one group of psychologists writes, "to reassert power or status, to frighten the offending person into compliance, to restore a desired state of affairs."[54] Indeed, during the Belgrade bombing protests, many popular nationalists demanded that their government take a tough stand and "restore justice" *(taohui gongdao)*.

Moreover, several of the letters detail specific requests and demands, which often extend well beyond securing a mere apology from NATO. According to some writers, the government should obtain a satisfactory explanation and demand monetary compensation. Yan Cui from Guangzhou wrote a letter to the U.S. president, asking, "Even more infuriating [than the bombing itself] is that after the tragedy, you have been arrogant and impolite, not only failing to offer an apology, but actually resorting to sophistry *[qiangci duoli]*. How can the Chinese people accept such an explanation?"[55] To this writer, Clinton's apologies sound hollow without a convincing account of the bombing. Monetary compensation would offer some satisfaction for a writer from Shanghai, who urges the *Guangming Daily* editors to "sue America, Clinton and NATO in Chinese courts, according to Penal Law Codes 6, 8, 15 and 120, and to seek indemnity under Code 36. . . . Protect the Chinese people's proper rights!"[56] As was the case with *Blood Debt*'s demand for just "one U.S. dollar," indemnities seem important to this writer not simply as monetary compensation, but also as a public punishment that symbolically restores China to its proper status.

Other writers urge a different kind of economic retaliation—boycotts. A poem from Shenyang in China's Northeast extols this form of ingroup loyalty:

When we are wearing Pierre Cardin and Nike . . .
When we are driving Cadillacs, Lincolns, and going to KFC
    and McDonalds . . .
Do we have a clear conscience?
No!!!

As our fishing boats are stopped and searched unreasonably.
As our compatriots lose their lives in the sea protecting the Diaoyu Islands
    [from Japan] . . .

Can we still sit in front of our Sony televisions?
No!!!

Koreans are proud to use their own national products . . .
Can we still find glory by using foreign products?
No!!!

Let's resolve to produce and use national products![57]

This was a popular cry. An employee at the Shenzhen Labour Bureau e-mailed the *Guangming Daily* a copy of a letter he had sent to the Jinshan Corporation, a Beijing competitor of Microsoft: "American products bring us pleasure—and bombs and disaster. And the West uses the profits from its sales in China to build weapons and target the Chinese people. . . . How can Chinese be happy about this? I have long been a nationalist and have never used Japanese goods. . . . Now I will not buy American goods either. I urge your company to seize this precious turning point of broad nationalist mobilization to promote national products, earning *face* for the nation and bringing credit to China."[58] Several information technology companies wrote in pledging sales boycotts. Fujian United Information Services, for instance, promised the *Guangming Daily* that it would cease selling IBM, Lotus and other American products.[59]

To restore their personal self-esteem, some writers vilified America and NATO. Bill Clinton, who embodied America, was a popular object of derision. For instance, Beijing's Chen Jie abuses Clinton as a "bad person" who "cannot even govern his own country," which is "plagued by guns and drugs." NATO faces similar derision. X. F. Liu, from the Stone Computer Group in Beijing, declares NATO a "mad dog,"[60] while Zhou Shaogeng, of the China Railroad Foreign Services Company, composed a lengthy song as a "battle cry to arouse the people." Each stanza begins with a new insult:

NATO is a group of thieves . . .
that use the blood and flesh of others as bricks and tiles
to build their own safe and happy den.
NATO is a group of madmen . . .
whose hearts have been blackened by the smoke of gunpowder . . .
NATO is a group of fools . . .
who close their eyes and refuse to look back.
What is NATO?
NATO is the nemesis of peace . . .[61]

Angered by America's "gunboat diplomacy," nationalist writer Zhang Zhaozhong of China's National Defense University similarly sought to

FIGURE 11. Nazi America. Protestors carry placards in Nanjing. On the left, the USA is equated with the Nazi SS. The characters held by the man on the right say "Blood Debt." Photo courtesy of Hein Thorsten.

save face for China by mocking America as "supercilious" and "over-weening" in his 2000 diatribe *Who Is the Next Target?*[62]

Many letters stress the importance of protecting China from further humiliation by transforming it into a more powerful country. An e-mail from Beijing puts the consensus view succinctly: "We will only avoid being insulted if we strengthen ourselves."[63] The phrase "turn grief into strength" *(hua beitong wei liliang)* is a continuous thread throughout the writings. Many students who wrote to the *Guangming Daily* vowed to study hard to empower China. The radiology majors at Harbin Medical University, for example, pledge: "We promise the Party and all our countrymen that we will turn grief into strength, studying hard to strengthen our country into a world superpower." The incoming biochemistry class of 1998 at Nankai University similarly writes from Tianjin: "We will study hard to strengthen the motherland . . . so that in the not-so-distant future no hostile force will dare or be able to take military action against China."[64] The dream of a "prosperous country and a strong army" *(fuguo qiangbing)* still inspires Chinese over a century after it was first promoted by late-Qing-dynasty reformers.

Many of the writers reassure themselves about China's ability to fortify itself against future humiliation by locating power in unity and numbers. For Wu Jing, whose "heart still feels like a large stone is pressed down upon it," a united China is the answer: "Ever since my feelings of grief and outrage passed, I have been wondering what, as a Chinese, I should do. How can we prevent our martyrs' blood from having flowed in vain?" Wu proposes establishing a commemorative fund: "One yuan from every Chinese would not be much money, but it would show the American imperialists Chinese unity. The Chinese people, of one mind and one will, will not be insulted."[65] Another letter, a poem written out of "great pain and fury" by an undergraduate from Central China Industrial University, finds strength in China's massive population:

> 1.2 billion people shout together:
> The Chinese race will not be insulted!
> The giant dragon has woken to take off in the Orient,
> How can your kind of paper tiger resist?[66]

The boycott efforts mentioned above were also attempts to find strength in unity and numbers.

Other writers turn their attention outward, appealing to "international society" (guoji shehui) to take China's side in a battle for global popular opinion. An e-mail from Shandong is concise: "We must fully utilize the power of popular opinion to attack the American aggressors."[67] Zhang Qian from Beijing has a concrete plan: setting up three counters on the *Guangming Daily* website that would count the days that pass without an American apology:

- Since May 8th there have been XX days, and China has yet to receive a formal apology.
- Since May 8th there have been XX days, and China has yet to receive compensation.
- Since May 8th there have been XX days, and the troublemaking murderers have yet to be punished.

The passing of every additional day, he argued, would bring shame upon NATO. Zhang has a powerful vision of cyber-nationalism: "The Internet is Western, but . . . we Chinese can use it to tell the people of the world that China cannot be insulted!"[68] The editors of the *Guangming Daily* similarly seek to shame America by posting at the top of their condolences Web site two English-language translations of letters to Bill Clinton written by the parents of the deceased. Zhu Fulai and Guo Guiqi write: "We

FIGURE 12. Popular passions. Canton students protest the
Belgrade embassy bombing in May 1999. Photo courtesy
of Du Jiang and the *People's Daily.*

had a happy family . . . a perfect family. How happy we were! . . . We wish
you, your wife, and your daughter a happy life!"[69]

Taking power in numbers to one logical conclusion, several letters speak
emotionally of revenge. The last lines of a poem sent in by Wang Shuke
of Shanxi Province read:

> The countless masses work together,
> and plan revenge in ten years.
> This is the hatred of our race-nation.[70]

Other letters and poems echo this threatening tone, often using the menacing proverb, "undergoing hardships and strengthening one's resolve to wipe away the national humiliation [wo xin chang dan]."[71] Blood is an even more pervasive theme. Many write cryptically that the martyrs' blood will not have been shed in vain, while others demand a cashing in on the "blood debt" (xuezhai). R. X. Liu, for instance, writes from Inner Mongolia: "The blood debt must be repaid with blood! . . . 1.2 billion Chinese will persist in fighting American imperialism to the end. We will not be as meek as lambs at the slaughterhouse."[72] Indeed, for some writers, the restoration of Chinese dignity justifies militarization. An e-mail from Shenyang proposes that everyone contribute money to buy an aircraft carrier: "When we have a strong and modern military, we'll see who still dares to bully us!"[73] A writer from Guangzhou also raises the specter of violence: "Chinese love peace and seek economic development. But . . . we do not fear war. China's youth should unite . . . shoulder to shoulder, and shout at the imperialists: 'The Chinese people cannot be insulted!'"[74] Several letters, notably, invoke pride in past military "victories" over America in Korea and Vietnam. As argued in chapter 4, this pride creates the confidence necessary for a possible future military encounter with the United States.[75]

Despite the ferocity of much of this nationalist rhetoric, it must be understood in the context of the transient threat that the Belgrade bombing represented to Chinese national self-esteem. Whether throwing bricks at the U.S. embassy, hurling invective at the U.S. president, or fantasizing about military retaliation, many Chinese found solace in various forms of "outgroup denigration." Such psychological tactics restored their healthy sense of self-respect. The response of the Belgrade bombing protestors was not simply a calculating way to pursue China's national interests. Because the bombing damaged not just the embassy, but also the cherished identifications of individual Chinese with their nation, their response was deeply passionate.

The Two "Very Sorrys": The Spy Plane Fiasco, 2001

Following the plane collision of April 2001, in which an American EP-3 surveillance aircraft and a Chinese F-8 jet fighter collided over the South China Sea, killing the Chinese pilot and forcing the Americans to make an emergency landing on China's Hainan Island, Chinese and American diplomats in Beijing and Washington engaged in over a week of intensive diplomacy. The focus of the negotiations was the wording of a letter the Americans would send to the Chinese government. The agreed-upon wording came to be known as "The two 'very sorry's": "Please convey to the Chinese people and to the family of pilot Wang Wei that we are *very sorry* for their loss. . . . We are *very sorry* the entering of China's airspace and the landing did not have verbal clearance."[76]

American commentary on the spy place standoff frequently resorted to attributing "culture" to Chinese behavior. What role did culture actually play in Sino-American "apology diplomacy"? Samuel Huntington has asserted that the post–Cold War world is divided into civilizations marked by fundamental cultural difference.[77] A number of Western analysts followed Huntington in suggesting that the fallout from the plane collision confirms that China is both different and dangerous. The Chinese, in this view, are obsessed with saving face. "Beijing's false accusation of U.S. responsibility," Jim Hoagland wrote in the *Washington Post,* is a "a reflexive act of pride." Jiang, it seems, was "getting personal" by drawing a "line in the sand" with Bush.[78] This irrational emotionalism, some Western pundits asserted, is rooted in Chinese tradition. Writing in the *New York Times,* Fox Butterfield located the cultural roots of China's demand for an American apology in "Chinese child-rearing practices" and the "old Confucian tradition of conformity."[79] A cruel Confucian culture, it seems, lies at the heart of Communist tyranny.

Other Western pundits, in contrast, have denied that culture played any role in Chinese behavior, depicting Beijing's response as purely rational and goal-oriented. The *Financial Times*'s James Kynge focused on foreign policy. Jiang Zemin, he wrote, "seized on the incident to demand a halt to U.S. air surveillance missions near the Chinese coastline."[80] On the *NewsHour,* former American ambassador to China Winston Lord highlighted Beijing's domestic objectives: it is "extremely tempting for [Beijing] . . . to use foreign devils and invoke nationalism to distract the populace."[81] Beijing, in this view, was simply cold and calculating, using the incident for domestic and foreign political purposes.

Arguments about Chinese culture thus reproduce the problematic sense/sensibility dichotomy: either the Chinese are rational, or they are irrational. Such arguments also iterate an equally problematic East/West dualism: either we are different, or we are the same.

Culture does matter: cultural differences clearly played a major role in the Sino-American apology diplomacy of April 2001. But Chinese and Americans do not differ in kind: we are all, after all, human beings. The trick is to capture the ways both cultural differences and cultural com-

monalities work together to shape international relations. Recent experimental findings in cross-cultural psychology have revealed significant
East-West differences both in reasoning about causes and about assessing responsibility.[82] These are differences of degree, not kind, but they
can help account for some of the disparate Chinese and American responses to the plane collision.

Cross-cultural psychologists juxtapose Western analytic and Eastern
holistic reasoning. Western reasoning tends to focus on objects and categories and is driven by formal logic; in the East, by contrast, reasoning
embraces contradictions among objects in a yin-yang field of constant
change.[83] In the case of the plane collision, Western analysts, searching
for "the" (one and only) cause of the accident, have focused on the pilots
and their planes. There was much talk in the Western press, therefore,
about the Chinese and American pilots and the lumbering EP-3 and the
speedy F-8. Analytic reasoning led many Westerners to blame Chinese pilot Wang Wei and his F-8 fighter.

This search for a single "cause" of the accident struck many Chinese as
odd. They tended to look instead to the bigger picture. And the circum-
stantial evidence, as they saw it, was damning. The accident occurred off
the Chinese coast, at a time when America was increasing the frequency
of its surveillance flights. Furthermore, the new Bush administration was
pursuing a National Missile Defense (NMD) initiative that has the potential to undermine China's national security. The Bush team had also
embraced Cold War rhetoric, repudiating Clinton's policy of "engagement," and labeling China America's "competitor." (To make things
worse, there is no Chinese notion of "friendly competition" akin to
sportsmanship; instead, a "competitor" is a rival to be vanquished.) Following on the heels of the 1999 American bombing of the Chinese embassy in Belgrade, the plane collision appeared as yet another example of
American bullying. Both the Belgrade bombing and the plane collision
fit perfectly into the emerging "victimization narrative" of Chinese suffering at the hands of the West that I discuss in chapters 3 and 5. In sum,
when all aspects of the political and historic context of the plane collision
are taken into account, it becomes clear why American behavior looked
so belligerent to many Chinese.

Cross-cultural psychologists have also found significant differences in
the ways that Westerners and Easterners assess responsibility. The former
concentrate more on culpability, while the latter highlight consequences.
The distinction is comparable to that between states like Ohio, where po-
lice and insurers use a fault standard to determine who is responsible for
a car accident, and Michigan, a "no fault" state. Michigan lawmakers

notwithstanding, Americans tend to focus on the issue of fault, seeking to get "inside the minds" *(mens rea)* of those involved. Hence our legal focus on "premeditation" and the distinction between " first-degree" and "second-degree" crimes. This also helps account for the American focus on the personalities of the two pilots: the "hotshot maverick" Wang Wei ("China's Tom Cruise") and the stalwart Nebraskan Shane Osborn. Because Americans see Wang as the one who intentionally created a dangerous situation, they will not apologize.

Chinese, by contrast, tend towards Michigan lawmakers' reasoning on auto accidents: they have a more pragmatic, consequence-oriented view of responsibility. Regardless of who was at fault in the plane collision, a Chinese citizen was dead. A sincere American apology was therefore needed to restore the Sino-American relationship. Chinese were angered less by the accident, or even by Wang's death, than they were by the American refusal to apologize. Initial American declarations (from Bush to Powell and down the line) that America was "not responsible"—and demands for the return of the American crew—were seen as highly offensive. A *People's Daily* commentary, for instance, maintained that "U.S. officials' rhetoric about Chinese culpability is more dangerous than the collision itself."[84] By refusing to apologize, America appeared extremely arrogant. A similar cultural misunderstanding had occurred after the Belgrade bombing two years earlier. Americans, focusing on the question of intent, were upset by Chinese skepticism that the bombing was an accident. Chinese, focusing on consequences, were upset because three Chinese were dead and American apologies were not seen as sufficient to restore the relationship.

Chinese and American reactions to the spy plane incident also exhibited a number of cultural commonalities. As noted above, social psychologists have demonstrated that outgroups do not get the benefit of the doubt and that ingroup members seek to maintain collective self-esteem. This work helps explain significant similarities in the Chinese and American responses. In diplomatic contexts, Chinese and Americans tend to view each other as outgroups; after the plane collision, therefore, there was a strong tendency to ascribe hostile intent to "them." Both sides gave the benefit of the doubt to their compatriots and argued that the other had revealed its "true nature," whether as an "imperialist aggressor" or as a "Communist tyrant." The "intergroup attribution bias" thus helps explain the radical divergence between Chinese and American understandings of what happened. Each blamed the other; each sought to save face for their nation at the other's expense.[85]

Psychological research on collective self-esteem can also shed light upon

Chinese and American reactions to the plane collision. As noted above, to the extent that we identify with a group, our self-esteem is tied to the group's fate. Both Chinese and Americans viewed the events of early April 2001 as a threat to their self-esteem. In China, many perceived American callousness towards the fate of Wang Wei as a humiliating loss of *face*. Similarly, in the conservative *Weekly Standard,* Robert Kagan and William Kristol declared the Bush administration's handling of the affair "A National Humiliation": Bush's "groveling" was a degrading "loss of face."[86] The public image of one's nation is clearly not a uniquely "Oriental" concern.

Some Chinese and Americans responded to the mutual identity threat by denying its existence. Although the incident was clearly a disaster for the bilateral relationship, many on both sides quickly claimed victory— a clear sign of denial. Gloating that "We won!" allowed many Chinese and American nationalists to save face. In Beijing, many boasted that President Jiang had planned America's humiliation from the start, and had "taught Bush Jr. a lesson." Qinghua University's Yan Xuetong, for instance, declared that "China stuck to principle" and "did a better job of dealing with the incident."[87] In Washington, meanwhile, Bush was widely praised for having handled the situation masterfully, winning the day. For instance, the "Nelson Report" circulated a parody of the American "we're sorry" letter: "We're sorry the world is now seeing your leaders as the xenophobic, clueless thugs that they really are. We're sorry you are losing so much face over this."[88]

Others responded to the threat to their self-esteem not with denial but by venting a rage designed to restore national self-respect—to regain face. For instance, by publicly calling Bush a "coward" (in a letter from Wang Wei's wife), Beijing sought to gain *face* for China at Washington's expense. And with the release of the American crew on 11 April, American hawks quickly began screaming for vengeance. Secretary of Defense Donald Rumsfeld, who had been muzzled during the sensitive negotiations, immediately held a Pentagon news conference to present additional incriminating evidence against Wang Wei. Nationalists on both sides of the Pacific thus sought to restore face for their nation by denigrating the other.

The idea that cultures can be so different that understanding one another is impossible is extremely pernicious. There is much that all humans share, including pride. But Chinese and American policymakers and pundits do need to be aware of cultural differences. In this case, they needed the open-mindedness to try to understand not just what an apology meant to them, but also what it meant to the other side. We must, in other words, learn to embrace both cultural differences and our common humanity.

The specific language of apology varies across cultures, but, as social beings, we all care greatly about it.

Olympian Apologies

As Team China entered the stadium during the opening ceremony of the 1996 Olympics in Atlanta, NBC sportscaster Bob Costas commented:

The People's Republic of China, one fifth of the world's population, with an economy growing at a rate of about ten percent a year. . . . But of course, there are problems with human rights, copyright disputes, and the threat posed to Taiwan. And within the Olympics . . . they've excelled athletically and built into a power, but amidst suspicions, Dick [Enberg], especially concerning their track athletes and their female swimmers possibly using performance enhancing drugs. None caught in Barcelona, but since those games of 1992, several have been caught.[89]

Costas' impolitic remarks quickly created a furor among Chinese living in the United States. Students and scholars at Harvard and Berkeley led the way, "strongly demanding a public apology from Mr. Costas or NBC!" Chinese activists utilized e-mail networks to gather donations to fund protest advertisements, one of the first of which appeared in the *Washington Post* on 14 August: "NBC commentator Mr. Bob Costas' hostile comments against many international athletes, including Team China, had [sic] badly contaminated the spirit of the Olympics and deeply offended countless viewers worldwide. Mr. Costas and NBC should have the courage to publicly apologize for their ignominious prejudice and inhospitality."[90]

Very likely under pressure from its parent company, General Electric, which does substantial business in China, NBC's Vice President for Sports, Ed Markey, wrote the Chinese students the next day: "Mr. Costas did not intend any disrespect to the People's Republic of China or its citizens. The comments made were not based on NBC beliefs. Nobody at NBC intended to offend anyone, and we regret that this apparently happened. We apologize for any resulting hurt feelings and we sincerely hope this puts the matter to rest." Markey's hope was quickly dashed, as student leader Chen Kai promptly rejected this private apology and demanded a public, prime-time television apology. When Markey responded instead with a public news conference, the students determined to raise funds for yet another anti-NBC advertisement, which they later ran in the *New York Times*.[91] Costas' words were appalling—condemning all Chinese for the transgressions of a few coaches and swimmers is arguably even racist—but the impassioned nationalism of the Chinese activists was also shocking. How should it be understood?

In this chapter I have argued that nationalism involves a combination of both sense and sensibility, a combination captured by the concept of *face*. Like all peoples, Chinese are emotionally bound to visions of their proper *face*. Martin Yang defines *face* largely in terms of affect: "When we say that a man wants a face, we mean that he wants to be given honor, prestige, praise, flattery, or concession, whether or not these are merited. Face is really a psychological satisfaction, a social esteem accorded by others."[92] *Face* is also, however, an instrumental issue. Nanjing University sociologist Cheng Boqing defines *face* as an "individual's credit," which can be stored in a "social bank." Losing face is thus like going socially "bankrupt."[93] Ambrose King similarly writes that "the social aspect of *face* . . . is like the credit card. Having *face* is like having good credit, so that one has a lot of purchasing power."[94]

Saving national face is thus no mere emotional matter: it has instrumental implications for the individual. In Chinese, the phrase "to lose face for . . . " *(gei . . . diulian)* points to the responsibility Chinese have to maintain the *face* of the groups to which they belong. In international contexts, that group is the race-nation *(minzu)*. Responsible for China's national *face*, many Chinese abroad feel a heavy pressure to maintain appearances.[95] In his thoughtful 1996 book *Studying in the USA*, Qian Ning explains, "Life abroad naturally fosters a patriotism that is always deeper than that cultivated by domestic 'patriotic' thought education. . . . The reason is simple: China's image in the world *[shijieshang de xingxiang]* is intimately connected to the position of overseas Chinese abroad."[96] Nationalism is not only about an irrational emotionalism, but also about position—and hence, power.[97] Fearing that Costas had caused China to lose face, Chinese student leaders felt the responsibility—especially strong as intellectuals—to regain it through winning an apology from NBC.

Chinese generally approve of such efforts to maintain the *face* of the group. While winning glory for oneself *(zhengqi)* has a displeasing ring to it, the phrase *zhengguang* and the proverb *guang zong yao zu*, which refer to winning honor or glory for the group, are admirable. Indeed, Chinese press coverage was very supportive of the protestors' claims.[98] The next summer, similarly, one popular Canton monthly proclaimed that Hong Kong had "earned glory for the Chinese race" *(wei Zhonghua minzu zheng le guang)*.[99] The accomplishments of a member of a group are seen to increase the group's face before other groups. CCTV coverage of the Hong Kong handover ceremonies highlighted international celebrations of China's accomplishment.[100] The handover in this sense resembled a debutante ball: China stepped out into international society and demanded *face* in the form of recognition from other national groups.

Problems arise, however, when excessive concerns for *face* lead to nationalist excess. Unwilling to negotiate with NBC and bent on vengeance — publicly humiliating Costas — Chinese protest organizers like Chen Kai appeared unappeasable to American audiences.[101] Seeking to redress a legitimate grievance and regain *face* for China, they only ended up making China lose more face before their intended audience. As Lu Xun and numerous other Chinese observers have noted, excessive concerns for *face* can be self-defeating, making those who harbor them appear as foolish as Ah Q.

CHAPTER 7

Popular Nationalism
and the Fate
of the Nation

*"1.2 billion Chinese
are outraged!"*

Following the 1999 bombing of the Chinese embassy in Belgrade, Zhou Yi, a high school student from Wuhan, joined a demonstration. He later wrote:

I entered the group [of protestors] because I wanted to march with them, to shout out my outrage with them. . . . As a high school student among college students, I thought I would feel lonely, but I felt that I belonged. There were no divisions between male and female, old and young: we were all one family! . . . We were all Chinese boys and girls, sons and grandsons of the Yan and Huang Emperors. . . . Because we are Chinese . . . we cannot be silent. . . . We must scream, we must proclaim our outrage to the world, and we must defend our compatriots, our sovereignty, and our self-respect.[1]

Did Zhou Yi act spontaneously, or was he just a plaything in the hands of Communist puppeteers? Chinese and Western observers of Chinese nationalism have long disagreed over who the agents of Chinese nationalism are. Chinese pundits ascribe agency to the masses; Westerners point to the elites.

Twentieth-century Chinese commentators have tended to describe Chinese nationalism as a "mass" or "popular" movement. At the turn of the last century, for example, many Chinese nationalists embraced Western Orientalist rhetoric about the Asian masses. After traveling to California and witnessing the lowly position of Chinese there, the renowned Japanologist Huang Zunxian returned to China and jubilantly exclaimed, "Now the Whites are afraid of the 'Yellow Peril' . . . It is we, we Asians! We! We! We!"[2] Nationalist pride could be found in the power of the Asian masses.

It was with the arrival of Marxism, however, that popular nationalism arguments in twentieth-century China became standard. Impersonal social forces—the working and peasant "masses"—became the agents of Chinese history. In the communist worldview, the masses were, by their very definition, an anti-imperialist social force. Chinese Communist Party founder Chen Duxiu's evolving views of the Boxer Rebellion of 1900 shed light on this phenomenon. As a liberal enlightenment intellectual in 1918, Chen vilified the Boxers as superstitious and backwards; as a confirmed Marxist in 1924, he praised the Boxers as patriotic anti-imperialists.[3] Although his view of the Boxers changed radically, Chen consistently depicted them as a bottom-up "mass" phenomenon.

With "Liberation" in 1949, the view of mass nationalism became even more predominant in mainland China, but it also evolved. PRC histories of the "Century of Humiliation" highlighted "spontaneous" anti-imperialist uprisings: mass nationalism. However, while Communist ideology prescribed that the masses be given agency in leading the revolution, the dictates of nationalist politics demanded that such assertions be qualified by the ubiquitous "under the leadership of the Party" *(zai Dang de lingdao zhi xia)*. By arguing that the Communist Party was a "party of the people," propagandists could accommodate the Party's role in leading the nationalist revolution with a Marxist view of mass nationalism. In the "victor narrative" of China's pre-"Liberation" encounter with the West, the Party and the people became fused into one heroic entity.

Western observers, in contrast, have long espoused top-down views of Chinese nationalism. John Fitzgerald has presented the "state nationalism" thesis most eloquently.[4] Reasoning inductively from observation of the European experience, Western theorists have largely explained nationalism as a product of the nation's desire to become a state.[5] Fitzgerald argues that Chinese nationalism has evolved according to precisely the opposite dynamic; that is, China as a state in search of its nation.[6] He writes, "the Chinese nation has been created and recreated in the struggle for state power, and it has ultimately been defined by the state as a reward of victory." In the twentieth century, the two principal actors in this struggle were the Nationalist and Communist Parties. The Nationalists, Fitzgerald argues, gave birth to the modern Chinese nation: "In the Chinese revolution, the state was not just midwife at the birth of the nation but in fact its sire. So the founder of the Nationalist Party, Sun Yat-sen, is appropriately remembered as the 'father of the country [guofu].'"[7] Later, however, the Communists contested the Nationalists' version of "China." During the December Ninth Movement of 1935, for instance, Nationalist educators and Communist activists on university campuses in Beijing competed to convince the student body of their different visions of both "China" and "the Chinese."[8] With victory in the Civil War, the Communist Party won the argument, becoming custodian of the Chinese nation. One China scholar even suggests that the "real" nationalist revolution in China only occurred *after* "Liberation," with the development of the infrastructure of communications and transportation necessary for top-down mass mobilization.[9]

The West's view that Chinese nationalism begins and ends with the Communist Party has its origins in both the China studies and nationalism literatures. In China studies, dismissals of CCP declarations about "anti-imperialist masses" in favor of a focus on the political elite have their basis in pervasive Western assumptions about the relationship between state and society in China. Likely influenced by classical liberalism's fear of the state, Western observers have long viewed Chinese politics as a simple matter of coercion. The "brutes of Beijing" impose their will upon a submissive people. Europeans fighting absolutism first constructed the foil of "Oriental despotism" to preach the virtues of liberty to their compatriots. Montesquieu, for instance, depicted Asia—in contradistinction to Liberal England—as the natural home of slavery.[10] To extol the virtues of liberty, Western pundits depicted the "Oriental state" as omnipotent and arbitrary, and Asian populations as impotent and passive.

This Western view of Asian state dominance continued in the postwar period, with the only difference being that China was fit into a "totalitarian" rather than "Oriental" template.[11] With the collapse of the Soviet Union and the Eastern Bloc, Beijing has become, in the eyes of many Americans, the last major bastion of communist tyranny against which America might shine as the "land of the free." The 1989 image of a solitary Chinese man standing before an advancing PLA tank in Tiananmen

Square has revitalized this "state dominates society" view of Chinese politics. Americans continue to construct their "liberal myth" in opposition to perceived Chinese tyranny.[12] Indeed, many Western China experts continue to focus on government repression, dismissing popular opinion as irrelevant both to Chinese politics in general, and to Chinese nationalism in particular.[13]

Recent trends in nationalism theory also underlie the West's state-centric view of Chinese nationalism. Early Western approaches to nationalism emphasized its mass basis. At the turn of the nineteenth century, sociologist Emile Durkheim argued that uprooted and "anomic" individuals are drawn to the feeling of community provided by nationalist movements.[14] In the early post–World War II period, major nationalism theorists continued in this bottom-up tradition, arguing that nationalism fills the "unnatural" religious void modernization has created in the hearts of the people.[15] In the last twenty years, however, the constructivist and rational choice revolutions that have swept the social sciences have synergized in studies of nationalism. Nationalist elites, Benedict Anderson and Eric Hobsbawm have taught us, construct nations and their traditions.[16] This new orthodoxy has shifted attention up and away from the masses to the elite level.[17] Like the "Oriental" and totalitarian views of Chinese politics, therefore, the elitism of current nationalism theory contributes to the dominance of the top-down, "Party affair" view of Chinese nationalism.

Where Chinese analysts have tended to describe Chinese nationalism as a bottom-up or mass movement, Western analysts have tended to the polar opposite view: Chinese nationalism as top-down Party propaganda.

The Party, the People, and the Fate of the Nation

Nationalism, like all social movements, involves both leaders *and* followers. Focusing on one group at the expense of the other, therefore, dangerously distorts our understanding of nationalist politics. Because regime legitimacy is at stake, a better understanding of how the Chinese Communist Party and the Chinese people interact in Chinese nationalism is urgently needed.[18] Today, Chinese nationalist politics exhibits the claim-response dynamic central to the negotiation of legitimacy in all political systems.[19] Popular nationalists both support and challenge the state's claims to legitimacy—and issue their own rival nationalist claims. And the Party both suppresses and responds to challenges to its nationalist credentials. The suppression of legitimate nationalist claims, however, makes the Party lose face and authority before the Chinese people. If the Party represses such claims, it appears to revert to coercive forms of power, a move that undermines regime stability. If the Party responds successfully to popular nationalist demands, in contrast, it gains *face* before nationalist audiences, and solidifies regime legitimacy.

The "fourth-generation" producers of popular Chinese nationalist discourse currently in their thirties may support or challenge the state's foreign policies. For instance, in the 1997 bestseller *The Plot to Demonize China,* Penn State's Liu Kang asserts that the U.S. government, big business, and the media conspire to make China lose face before world opinion. Liu's text clearly seeks to support the Party, and he is said to have high-level connections among the Party elite. The 1996 hit *China Can Say No* also supported the Party's America policy. Other products of popular nationalism, however, challenge the Party's legitimacy, claiming it has failed to maintain China's national *face*. In an open letter sent to the Party leadership in February 1998, for instance, Chinese dissident Lin Xinshu argued that Li Peng should not be given Qiao Shi's job as Chairman of the National People's Congress. His argument, significantly, was not just Li's "incompetence," but also that Li, tainted by his role in the Tiananmen massacre, would be a blight on "China's image in the world."[20] In other words, Li would be unable to maintain *face* for China.

The Communist elite both suppresses and responds to such assaults on its status. Following the 2001 plane collision, for example, the *People's Daily* sought to suppress extreme nationalist postings on its Strong Country Forum *(qiangguo luntan)* online chatroom. Many Chinese cybernationalists responded by moving to chatrooms at private sites like Sina.com, where they fervently decried the state's suppression of their nationalist views. But the story does not, as the Western media so frequently suggests, end with state repression. The elite also responds to popular nationalists by seeking to gain *face* for China. For instance, it has begun an active campaign of promoting Chinese culture abroad. In 1998 the New China News Agency announced an official Web site to promote China's cultural image: the new Web site will "introduce China's 5,000-year-old culture on the Internet, promoting commercial performances and exhibitions. . . . Cultural activities that might degrade the country's dignity, however, will be banned."[21] Similarly, responding to *The Plot to Demonize China* and other popular nationalists' concerns that the American media makes China lose face before international opinion, in September 2000 the Chinese government organized a nine-city tour of the United States to introduce Chinese culture to ordinary Americans.[22] Their real audience, however, was on the other side of the Pacific. By promoting Chinese culture and upholding China's dignity, the Party made a claim to nationalist legitimacy. Such actions demonstrate the Party's belief that crude repression is not enough: the Party must gain *face* for China before "international society" (*guoji shehui*) to earn the support of nationalist audiences at home.

The interactions between the Chinese people and the Communist Party are thus central to nationalist politics today. Regime legitimacy hinges on the combination of strategies that each side chooses during their encounters—and how these strategies evolve over time. This chapter explores three separate waves of nationalism in late-1990s China—the Diaoyu Islands protests of 1996, the *China Can Say No* sensation of 1996–1997, and the Belgrade bombing protests of May 1999—and argues that the Party responded to each with a different combination of suppression and co-optation. The Party suppressed Diaoyu protestors, for the most part. It tried to co-opt and use the *China Can Say No* fever for its own ends, but it had difficulty simply responding to the angry demands of Belgrade bombing demonstrators and wound up having to accommodate them. The Party's movement away from suppression and towards co-optation or acquiescence suggests that a popular nationalism is now emerging in China that increasingly challenges the Party-state. Struggling just to keep up with popular nationalist demands, the Party is slowly losing its hegemony over Chinese nationalism.

State Suppression: The Diaoyu Islands Protests, 1996

The Diaoyu, or Senkaku, Islands comprise an archipelago of eight desolate rocks lying in the East China Sea between Taiwan and Okinawa. The islands are claimed by China, Taiwan, and Japan. "Diaoyu" and "Senkaku" are the Chinese and Japanese names for the islands, respectively. Each name implicitly embodies a sovereignty claim.[23] The dispute over who may claim the islands is long and complex. Chinese claims (made by both the mainland and Taiwan) are based upon historical records dating back to the Ming dynasty (1368–1644), the 1943 Cairo Declaration stipulation that Japan return all Chinese territory it had annexed, and a "natural prolongation" of the continental-shelf argument in international maritime law. Japan's claims are based on the 1895 Treaty of Shimonoseki, which formally ceded Taiwan "and its surrounding islands" to Japan, the U.S.

return of "administrative rights" over the islands to Japan along with Okinawa in 1972, and a "median line" division of the continental-shelf argument in international maritime law.

The first major protests over the islands occurred in 1971, after a September 1970 incident in which the Japanese navy evicted reporters raising the flag of Taiwan on one of the islands. Large, vocal anti-Japanese protests were organized in Hong Kong, Taiwan, and among Chinese in the United States. Normalization of relations between China and Japan in 1972, however, included an agreement between Beijing and Tokyo to shelve the dispute for future resolution. The latest major flare-up in the controversy developed in the summer and fall of 1996. On 14 July, a group of nationalists from the Japan Youth Federation erected a lighthouse on the islands to bolster Japanese sovereignty claims. On 28 August 1996, Japanese Foreign Minister Ikeda Yukihiko reasserted Japan's position: "The Senkaku Islands have always been Japan's territory; Japan already effectively governs the islands, so the territorial issue does not exist." Chinese Ministry of Foreign Affairs spokesman Shen Guofan promptly condemned Ikeda's comments as "irresponsible." On 3 September, Shen stated at a press conference that, "as far as the issue of sovereignty is concerned, the Chinese government cannot make any compromise."[24] As a result, anti-Japanese demonstrations in Hong Kong and Taiwan gained momentum in September of 1996. On 24 September, Chinese Foreign Minister Qian Qichen met with Japanese Foreign Minister Ikeda at the United Nations in New York, seeking to prevent nationalists from escalating the dispute. Two days later, however, Hong Kong national David Chan drowned during an attempt to land on one of the islands. Chan's death spurred even larger demonstrations in Hong Kong and Taiwan.

Meanwhile, authorities in mainland China suppressed anti-Japanese demonstrations in the streets, but protests about the islands were expressed in print and cyberspace. Mainland Chinese protests from the 1996 episode thus have to be read, and because they are usually in Chinese, are less accessible. It is perhaps for this reason that Western journalists and academics have tended to discount their significance in comparison to the publicly performed, easily visible demonstrations that occurred in Hong Kong and Taiwan. A reading of these mainland Chinese writings, however, reveals the existence of a dynamic discourse that challenged the Communist Party's control over nationalism.

Numerous popular mainland books and articles discuss the Diaoyu Islands controversy. The authors of *China Can Say No,* which was published in the summer of 1996, issued a sequel in the fall of that year entitled *China*

Can Still Say No. They explain this decision as follows: "Quite a few Chinese took issue with *Say No* . . . saying 'Why were you so polite to Japan? . . . Don't you see that Japan is even more wicked than America?'" Although the authors made public their resolve to attack Japan in their new book, they do not appear to have required much encouragement. Maintaining that "China has been too warm and accommodating towards Japan," the authors itch for a fight: "To the majority of contemporary Chinese, the mission of containing Japan has already begun; the final battle of the Western Pacific—Protecting Diaoyu—has already become imminent." They have few qualms about preaching spite: "Chinese 'hatred of Japan' is not necessarily a bad thing." The authors advocate a more forceful Japan policy and implicitly condemn the government for suppressing popular anti-Japanese protests.[25]

Be Vigilant Against Japanese Militarism! of 1997 also contains a chapter on the Diaoyu Islands controversy. Authors Zi Shui and Xiao Shi have a sinister view of Japanese intentions: "Japan does not seek to 'return to Asia' as an equal partner *[pingdeng huoban]*, but seeks to become the master *[jiazhang]*. . . . Confronted by the Japan threat, China cannot give an inch." Their message to Party policymakers is equally blunt: "No Chinese should be willing or dare to relinquish sovereignty over Chinese territory, leaving a name to be cursed for generations *[wanshi maming]*."[26] If the Party does not take a firm enough stand against Japan, Zi and Xiao imply, the Chinese people will revolt. Indeed, some writers explicitly disassociate their anti-Japanese nationalism from state-sponsored patriotism. Reviewing the histories of Hong Kong's Diaoyu and democracy movements, Hou Sijie argues that the two are "mutually reinforcing": "nationalism and the struggle for human rights and democracy are not in opposition."[27] Hou is, in effect, arguing against Beijing's illiberal state nationalism in favor of a liberal populist nationalism.

In addition to the print media, e-mail networks and the World Wide Web were a second major arena for popular Diaoyu activism. One Web site, "Defend Diaoyutai," described the rise of "virtual" protest: "Chinese web sites everywhere started spontaneously posting news, forming alliances, and propagating emotions about Diaoyutai. Everyday *[sic]* new Bao Diao [Protect Diaoyu] web pages sprouted up by the hundreds, and they were almost always the spontaneous acts of some outraged individuals."[28] Students also utilized e-mail networks to propagate Diaoyu news not covered by the mainland press.

The Communist Party sought both to suppress and to co-opt popular Diaoyu activism. The framework for suppression was contained within a National Educational Commission circular. According to Hong Kong's *Xin Bao,* the circular contained the following points:

- Patriotic actions require guidance.
- The public must be dissuaded and prevented from organizing spontaneous meetings, demonstrations and protests.
- The publicizing of activities by . . . printing or distributing documents, or using various means of communication is prohibited.

The Vice Minister of Foreign Affairs even went to Beijing University personally to ensure that students remained calm.[29] *China Can Still Say No,* which had been critical of the Ministry of Foreign Affairs' Japan policy, was banned only a month after its release. By contrast, the authors' first book, *China Can Say No,* had supported the Party's America policy and remained in bookstalls for years. Virtual protest within mainland China was also suppressed. The Party denied students Web access for ten days, and banished a prominent online activist to Qinghai in China's far northwest.[30] On a small scale, such crude coercion could be a highly effective policy tool.

But the Communist Party also responded to the claims of popular nationalism by attempting to co-opt it. The propaganda apparatus utilized Chinese- and English-language print media to publish arguments for Chinese sovereignty and condemnations of Japanese actions. Liu Jiangyong of the International Relations Institute published a lengthy study of Chinese historical records documenting Chinese sovereignty claims in the Chinese Academy of Social Sciences publication *Japanese Studies.* Predictably, the study concluded that the islands were China's. More interestingly, it also argued that the issue "be handled through cool government-to-government deliberations."[31] Popular nationalists, in other words, should cool it. The *People's Daily* had earlier published a scathing front-page editorial condemning Japanese actions entitled "Japan, Do Not Do Stupid Things." The editorial clearly sought to champion anti-Japanese anger. The adoption of the phrase "Do not do stupid things" by several popular anti-Japanese books suggests that the editorial was largely successful in co-opting popular sentiments.[32] Lengthy English-language articles in *The China Daily* and *The Beijing Review* also made the case for Chinese sovereignty over the islands. Their purpose was likely twofold: to marshal Western opinion against Japan, and, more importantly, to assuage domestic critics by appearing to champion Chinese nationalism on

the international stage. Clearly, even when it chooses a strategy of suppression, the Chinese state does not have the monopoly over nationalism that Western accounts suggest. And because popular nationalism can
threaten the Party's legitimacy, it is an increasingly significant constraint
on China's Japan policy.

Co-optation and Control:
The *China Can Say No* Sensation, 1996–1997

The role of popular nationalists is even more apparent in the 1996–1997
China Can Say No sensation. If books like *China Can Say No* were simply "propaganda tracts," as former American Ambassador to China James
Lilley and numerous Western journalists have asserted,[33] why did the Party
need to do a public "about face" on the issue? The Party first praised *China
Can Say No* as "fully reflecting popular opinion," but then criticized the
book as an "irresponsible" interference with the state's conduct of for-
eign policy.[34] Conversely, if the "say no" fever was purely popular, as the
Party initially claimed, how could it have been so widely endorsed by
Chinese newspapers tightly controlled by the Party's own Propaganda
Department?

The "say no" sensation involved a complex interplay between Party and
popular actors. The Chinese state sought to use "say no" nationalists, but
"say no" authors also used the Chinese state. Although the content of
official and popular anti-Americanism was largely the same, regime legitimacy was jeopardized as the state lost control of nationalist writings.[35]
The hyphen in "nation-state" lost its strength because popular nationalist writings, unlike official discourse, did not link the fate of the nation
to the fate of the Party-state. When the Party realized that it was being
marginalized in popular writings, it promptly curbed the circulation of
the popular "say no" books.

Before they did so, however, the Party elite clearly sought to use popular "say no" nationalism. Beijing "free writer" Wang Lixiong correctly
blames both Beijing and the Western media for inflaming "say no" nationalism, arguing that in "playing with fire" *(wanhuo)* Beijing undermined
the national interest. Wang faults the Ministry of Foreign Affairs's en-
dorsement of *China Can Say No* at a press conference. After stating that
the book was "popular," and did not represent the official view, a Chinese
spokesman added the line: "It is because the American government is op-
posing China that the Chinese people have expressed their righteous in-

dignation *[fenkai]*." Beijing, Wang explains, sought to utilize Chinese popular opinion as a "bargaining chip" *(chouma)* in its America policy, spark-
ing the nationalist fire. Wang also, however, directs his ire at the Western
press, which, fed by "self-created delusional fears" *(beigong sheying)*, mis-
took appearances for reality and "made a watermelon out of a sesame seed"
(ba zhima dangcheng xigua). The resultant snowball effect of media attention, Wang laments, made China lose face on the international stage.[36]

The producers of "say no" discourse were no mere pawns of the state,
however; they had goals of their own and utilized the state to achieve
them. At a personal level, "say no" nationalists sought to vent their anger,
curry favor with the Party elite, and make a buck. They successfully used
the Party's propaganda apparatus to achieve these goals. *Guangming Daily*
journalist Chen Xiyan explains how the "commoners" *(xiao renwu)* who
wrote "say no" texts "manipulated" *(caozong)* China's official media. By
writing in a vulgar street slang designed to arouse the interest of their readers, *China Can Say No*'s authors received sufficient popular attention to
attract official notice. Because the substance of their argument helped the
state's interests, both as a way to advance foreign policy and as a way to
redirect domestic discontent away from the Party, the state was bound to
endorse it. Once the Foreign Ministry and the New China News Agency
did so, other news organizations felt safe in disseminating "say no" stories nationally. The commercial success of *China Can Say No* was then
assured: "Once grasped," Chen writes, "the strict rules of the official media . . . can be used to convert tiny costs into huge profits."[37]

Having secured official approval and, in effect, put the Party's censorship apparatus to work for them, "say no" authors were able to dominate
popular nationalist discourse. While glowing reviews were published
widely in mainland China during the height of the "say no" fever, critical reviews could only be published in places like Hong Kong and Taiwan.[38] For instance, a sharply critical *Readers Daily* review of *China Can
Say No* was replaced with one that defended it.[39] Similarly, a magazine
editor asked journalist Chen Xiyan to review *China Can Say No* for a special issue criticizing it, but the project was aborted two weeks later.[40]

"Mutual exploitation," to borrow a phrase from Chen, was thus clearly
at play in the "say no" sensation. The Party sought to use "popular opinion," and "say no" authors sought to make money. But regime legitimacy
was also at stake. As "say no" authors staked a claim to "popular opinion," the state's hegemony over nationalist discourse was challenged.

The Chinese Communist Party has long rooted its legitimacy in its nationalist credentials. In 1996, however, popular "say no" nationalists is-

sued a rival claim: they were the true representatives of Chinese popular opinion. Accused by their critics of being Party pawns, "say no" writers and their defenders proclaimed their independence from the state. One glowing review, for instance, declared *China Can Say No* a "pure individual action," written from the authors' own volition.[41] "Say no" authors also argued that they—not the Party—represented genuine popular opinion. In the emotional and grandiose speech "A Declaration to the World," mentioned in chapter 4, Song Qiang defended *China Can Say No* against its critics: "We're respecting popular opinion, not misleading it." Song attempts to submerge himself and his coauthors within popular opinion, arguing that "Some say we have aroused popular opinion. It would be better to say that popular opinion aroused us."[42] In their follow-up tract, *China Can Still Say No,* Song and his coauthors contend that the state should not seek to suppress popular nationalists like himself: "The primary responsibility of diplomacy is to protect national interests . . . mass movements should be seen as normal, and protected, 'people's diplomacy.' "[43] They also, notably, insinuate that the state is failing to protect the national interest.[44]

The Party responded to the "naysayers" with both suppression and persuasion.[45] At the sixth plenary session of the Fourteenth CCP Central Committee in December 1996, participants decided that *China Can Say No* had violated the Party policy that foreign policy is not to be arbitrarily criticized.[46] Fearing that it was losing control over nationalist discourse, the Party clamped down on "say no" writings, quickly banning the more critical *China Can Still Say No* and other new books and writings. Party elites realized that "say no" discourse was not receiving good press abroad, and that the Party stood accused of making China lose national *face* before international audiences because it had allowed "say no" discourse to proliferate. The CCP's "about face" on the "say no" sensation reflected their effort to maintain face before domestic audiences.

But the Party also responded by co-opting popular nationalism, seeking both to moderate extreme views and to persuade the people to let the Party maintain its leading role in Chinese nationalism. For instance, Shen Jiru's 1998 *China Should Not Play "Mr. No"* seeks to counter the parochial nationalism of the "say no" sensation with a more moderate nationalism. Shen is a researcher at the Chinese Academy of Social Sciences (CASS) Institute of World Economics and Politics, and CASS Vice President Liu Ji wrote the foreword to his book. *China Should Not Play "Mr. No"* is arguably an official response to the popular *China Can Say No* books.[47] Shen is clearly a nationalist—"As a great nation, China should participate in constructing a new post–Cold War order"—and he praises the "righteous anger" *(yifen)* of "fourth-generation" popular nationalists. But he rejects the extremism of many naysayers in favor of a more mature attitude towards foreign policy: "China's twenty-first-century international strategy must not be a parochial, nationalist, uncooperative stream of 'nos' . . . twenty-first-century China and the world require understanding, reconciliation, and cooperation—not antagonism." Shen raises the specter of the former Soviet Union as an admonition against those who advocate confrontation: "The Soviets were nicknamed 'Mr. No' for using their veto in the UN Security Council all the time. We do not need to play a second 'Mr. No.'" He then asks, "Is the only way that Chinese can prove their independence and strength by daring to say 'no'?" Shen admonishes popular nationalists that "emotion cannot substitute for policy." It is the elite, in other words, who must coolly construct China's foreign policy. But that elite, Shen recognizes, must also be sensitive to popular opinion: "Those who lose the support of the people will fall from power *[Shi ren xinzhe, shi tianxia]*."[48] Just a year later, Beijing leadership would carefully heed Shen's words.

Crashing the Party: The Belgrade Bombing Protests, 1999

During the Belgrade bombing protests, the Western media repeatedly hammered home the argument that the Beijing elite was manipulating protestors to its own ends. In "Calculating Beijing Seeks to Harness Popular Outrage," the *Financial Times*'s James Kynge paints a top-down picture of the protests: "Beijing [by which he means the Communist elite] has succeeded in converting popular outrage at NATO's bombing of the Chinese embassy in Belgrade into a swelling tide of nationalism." Kynge describes the "cool realpolitik" driving the Beijing elite's "delicately calibrated" reactions to the bombing: "the fuelling of nationalism provides a unifying force at a time when China's communist ideology is dying."[49]

This top-down "party propaganda" spin on the protests tells us more about ourselves (for example, about our fears of communist "tyranny," or our denial that common Chinese might be genuinely angry with us) than it does about what actually happened in China in May 1999. The protests were actually an overwhelmingly bottom-up phenomenon; the Party had its hands full simply responding to the demands of popular nationalists. Like the Diaoyu Islands and *China Can Say No* sensations of 1996–1997, the way the Belgrade bombing protests played out in China involved a complex interplay of top-down and bottom-up pressures. In 1999, however, the CCP was forced to make a pronounced strategic shift from suppression to accommodation. Far from coolly manipulating the protestors, the Party was on the ride of its life. As Minister Wei Zhen famously said to Tang dynasty Emperor Li Shiming over a millennium ago, "Water can support a boat, but it can also flip it" *(shui ke zai zhou, yi ke fu zhou).*

The "party propaganda" spin on the protests also fails to account for the outrage expressed by overseas Chinese. Although they were exposed to the Western press, Chinese students demonstrated across the United States and Europe. In a letter sent to the *Guangming Daily,* North Carolina State University's Wang Wei angrily denounced the "farce" of the so-called "freedom of the press" in the United States. Wang laments that the Western media was "swindling" "ordinary Americans" about what was going on in the Balkans.[50] Moreover, mainland Chinese are not easy dupes: many of them also have access to the Western press and radio broadcasts to China, and are savvy interpreters of media sources. An e-mail from Beijing notes that the Chinese media "clearly sympathizes with the heroic Serbian resistance," while CNN focuses on atrocities in Kosovo. This self-described "pained and thoughtful Chinese" has no doubt, however, that the bombing was *not* a "tragic mistake."[51]

During the Belgrade bombing protests, popular nationalists gradually shifted from supporting the CCP to making demands of it. For instance, in "An Open Letter from a Chinese University Student to Premier Zhu" posted on the Web page of the Chinese electronic journal *China and the World,* He Yu of the Computer Department at China Engineering College asks, "How could they dare to bomb our embassy?" He Yu's sarcastic response reveals his frustration: "The [Americans] know that our government policy is one of merely lodging 'fierce protests *[qianglie kangyi]*.'" He then warns: "Premier Zhu. . . . Our government's weak stance has created a distance between itself and the people. . . . You are so capable . . . and we need you. . . . But without the 'people's confidence *[minxin]*,' how can you lead China's economic construction!"[52] Although he supports Zhu Rongji and the PRC government, He Yu clearly fears that the government's weak response to the bombing is undermining its legitimacy.

A recognition of the breadth of contemporary Chinese popular opinion serves as a vital counterweight to the usual Western assertions that Chinese nationalism be dismissed as top-down propaganda. The Belgrade bombing protests were remarkably widespread. There were street demonstrations in over one hundred Chinese cities, and Chinese of all generations and walks of life participated in protest activities. The collection of 281 condolence letters, essays, and poems e-mailed, faxed, and mailed to

FIGURE 13. Protestors and PLA. Students confront the authorities outside the U.S. embassy in Beijing, 9 May 1999. Photo courtesy of AP/Wide World Photos.

the *Guangming Daily* newspaper discussed in chapter 6 reveals the diversity of the protestors. The *Guangming Daily* letters represent genuine Chinese popular opinion and should not be dismissed as mere propaganda. The geographical distribution of the sample is impressive: letters came from at least twenty-six of China's thirty-one provinces, autonomous regions, and municipalities.[53] Students and teachers wrote in from thirty-five universities: three in the United States, one in Canada, two at National Singapore University, and the rest distributed throughout China, from the Zhejiang Industrial University to the Jilin Arts Academy. The media, the Party-state, and the information technology industry were also well represented. Thirteen letters arrived from people working within the Party-state, and seven individuals from the information technology industry wrote in, mostly describing how they used their Web sites to publicize "May 8th" (that is, the 8 May bombing) or to advocate economic boycotts of American products. Letters also came from journalists and editors at fourteen regional newspapers (from Xinjiang's *Shihezi News* to the *Three Gorges Daily*), three television stations in Henan, Hebei, and Canton, and *People's Daily, Guangming Daily,* and *New China* reporters stationed in Poland, Pakistan, and Tokyo, respectively.[54]

Like He Yu, many of the writers who sent letters to the *Guangming*

Daily clearly wanted their government to take a tougher stand on the bombing. In a letter signed by thirty-five "hot-blooded youth from Hunan," the line "We support the Chinese government's just stand!!!" reads more like a demand than acceptance of CCP leadership. An e-mail from Wuxi, Jiangsu Province, similarly places a burden upon the Party-state: "I hope that the Chinese government will take the necessary measures to show the world that China will not be insulted."[55] As the phrases "we support" and "I hope" suggest, the decision to support the government is perceived to be voluntary, not coerced. Furthermore, the support of the letter writers clearly depends upon the government fulfilling its nationalist obligation to "restore justice" for the Chinese people.

Unable to suppress the protestors, authorities were forced to plead with them for calm. In a nationally televised speech on 9 May, then Vice President Hu Jintao urged workers to work, and students to study. The Propaganda Department then set out to persuade the people of the wisdom of Hu's words. The *People's Daily* issued a photograph entitled "Beijing Workers Study Hu Jintao's Speech" with the caption: "The workers expressed a desire to work hard, promote economic development, and increase our national strength."[56] A New China News Agency report on the same subject, "Workers Turning Anger into Motivation," began, "For the last few days, workers in all localities have resolutely supported the important televised speech delivered by Comrade Hu Jintao." It concluded with an example: "Gu Yongmei, a female worker at the third steel-melting workshop of Xining Special Steel Group, said that we must turn the righteous indignation into power, do our own jobs well, and exert ourselves for the prosperity and strength of the motherland."[57] The next day the New China News Agency issued a similar report—"Students Turn Indignation into Motivation": "All the classrooms at Beijing University were filled with students craving knowledge. . . . Jian Yi, a student of the International Relations Institute, said . . . 'Although I am still filled with indignation, I think the best way to love my country is by getting back to the classroom.'"[58]

Pleading with protestors to go back to work was a risky strategy. Judging from history, they might not listen. During the 1930s, Nationalist Party officials repeatedly urged students to study calmly in order to "strengthen the nation," while Communist activists urged them to take to the streets. The Communists eventually won that argument, when large numbers of students joined the revolution. It is thus ironic that the Communist elite was now trying a tactic similar to one whose failure caused their ascendancy. The Party elite's choice of Vice President Hu Jintao to deliver the

FIGURE 14. "Blood for blood!" Protestors carry the national flag in Nanjing.
Photo courtesy of Hein Thorsten.

state's televised reaction to the bombing reveals that they were well aware
of the risks that they were taking. Jiang Zemin, Zhu Rongji, Li Peng, and
other high leaders were not willing to issue a message pleading for re-
straint. Jiang had been criticized after the bombing for being too weak
with his "constructive, strategic partnership" approach to American policy, and Zhu was under attack for giving away too much with regard to
the World Trade Organization (WTO) entry negotiations during a recent
trip to the United States. Seeking to co-opt popular nationalism on the
one hand, but appealing for calm on the other, would be no easy task.
The senior leaders thus decided to pass this hot potato to Hu Jintao, who
could take the fall if the Chinese people perceived the CCP's response to
be too weak. As it turns out, Hu passed the test and is now China's president and chairman of the CCP.

The Party also sought to co-opt popular nationalism by championing
the Chinese cause. Besides repeatedly and eloquently condemning the
bombing, the Propaganda Department sought to convey to domestic nationalists the impression that "international opinion" was on China's side.
As I noted in chapter 1, the China Internet Information Center, an English language government Web site, organized an extensive Belgrade
bombing site, which included a page entitled "International Community
Responses." It contained links to 159 documents in which prominent foreigners were said to condemn the bombing. Although the site was in En-

glish and sought to shame America and NATO, its primary audience was probably nationalists back home. The Party, it suggested, was winning the battle for international popular opinion, gaining *face* for China at America's expense.

The Belgrade bombing protests were largely a bottom-up movement; they were not, as most Western observers insisted, a top-down Party affair. Given an understanding of the recent Chinese past as one of victimization at the hands of Western aggression, and the universal social psychological tendency not to give outgroups the benefit of the doubt, it is little wonder that Chinese across the globe were outraged by what they perceived to be an intentional provocation.[59] The Western press's insistence that a diabolical Communist elite manipulated the Chinese protestors tells us more about ourselves than about what actually happened in May 1999.

Two Chinas

The CCP is losing its control over nationalist discourse. Under Mao, the Party claimed that because it led the revolutionary masses, the Party and the nation were fused into an inseparable whole. Only communists, in other words, could be genuine Chinese nationalists. Under Deng and especially under Jiang and now Hu, however, the CCP's nationalist claims are increasingly falling on deaf ears. Popular nationalists now regularly speak of the "motherland" *(zuguo)* and the "Chinese race" *(Zhonghua minzu)* without reference to the Party. And this separation of the Party-state from the nation is not occurring only in marginal popular publications. PLA writer Jin Hui's *Wailing at the Heavens* is a fascinating example. Published in 1995 as part of an official series commemorating the fiftieth anniversary of the "War of Resistance," it underwent rigorous editing at the People's Liberation Army Literature and Arts Press. General Zhang Zhen wrote the book's preface, further granting the book official status. General Zhang cites Deng Xiaoping on how "Only socialism can save China" to make the standard official argument that "In modern China, patriotism is tied to socialism." In the book itself, however, Jin Hui unties that knot, underscoring the "separation of the Chinese concepts of state *[guojia]* and motherland *[zuguo]*," and arguing that "there are 'two Chinas': the Chinese people's 'motherland,' and the rulers' 'state.'"[60] Jin's analysis radically undermines the idea that China is dominated by a monolithic "Party-state" with complete power over nationalist discourse.

Because the anti-foreign tenor of popular nationalism is largely the same as that of state nationalism, Western analysts have too frequently dismissed popular nationalists as puppets in the hands of the Communist elite. This view is a grave mistake. In China today, popular networks are challenging the state's hegemony over nationalism, threatening to rupture the Chinese nation-state. And this is occurring at a time when, given the bankruptcy of communist ideology, nationalism has become even more central to state legitimation. Both the Party and the people are recognizing that the people are playing a greater role in Chinese politics. As the theme song from the hit 1996 CCTV series "Hunchbacked Prime Minister Liu" *(Zaixiang Liu luoguo)* put it:

> There is a scale between heaven and earth.
> Its weight
> Is the people.
> Its rod jumps with the affairs of state,
> *Yi ya yi der wei ai.*
> You
> Determine if the scale will be balanced!

Popular nationalists are not just influencing domestic politics; they are also beginning to influence the making of Chinese foreign policy. A pop-up now appears on the main page of the Ministry of Foreign Affairs (MFA) Chinese-language Web site soliciting the opinions of ordinary Chinese. The pop-up links readers to a page where they can e-mail the MFA and read the transcripts of electronic chats now held regularly between senior MFA officials and concerned Chinese "netizens." No such pop-up or link appears on the MFA's English-language site.[61] The MFA, it seems, not only directs its attention at the international community, but also has an eye on the demands of domestic nationalists. The MFA is aware that popular nationalists now command a large following, and is actively seeking to appease them.

During the protests about the 1999 Belgrade bombing and the 2001 spy plane collision, popular nationalists severely restricted the range of political options open to those who make decisions about the Party's foreign policy. John Keefe, who was special assistant to U.S. Ambassador to China Joseph Prueher during the April 2001 spy plane incident, later related that, during the negotiations in Beijing, American diplomats "saw a Chinese government acutely sensitive to Chinese public opinion."[62] Such sensitivities are only likely to increase. Western policymakers ignore how this new factor affects Chinese foreign policy at their own peril.

CHAPTER 8

Chinese Nationalism and U.S.-China Relations in the Twenty-First Century

化
悲
痛
为
力
量
‼

"Turn grief into strength!"

National identity is both dependent upon interactions with other nations, and constituted in part by the stories we tell about our national pasts. Like all forms of identity, national identity does not arise in isolation, but develops and changes in encounters with other groups. Thus, Chinese nationalism cannot be comprehended in isolation; instead, it must be understood as constantly evolving as Chinese interact with other nationalities. In particular, because of the stature of the United States and Japan, Sino-American and Sino-Japanese relations are central to the evolution of Chinese nationalism today.

National identities are also shaped by the narratives we tell about our national pasts. The past does not determine present behavior. Nor is it the mere tool of present-day nationalist entrepreneurs. Narratives about the past can and do change, but only slowly, because they give meaning and coherence to our identities. Chinese nationalists today are particularly concerned with telling and retelling narratives about the "Century of Humiliation" that began with China's defeat in the First Opium War with the British in the mid-nineteenth century and formally ended with China's victory over Japan at the end of World War II. For three decades under Mao, memories of China's suffering at the hands of Western and Japanese imperialism were largely suppressed so that Party historians could construct a New China inspired by a heroic "victor narrative" of China's past. Today, however, Chinese are confronting the pain of what they suffered during the "Century of Humiliation," and constructing a "victimization" narrative about it that challenges the earlier heroic narrative. These debates about the Chinese past have direct impact on Chinese nationalists today. For instance, Chinese anger following the 1999 Belgrade bombing and 2001 spy plane incident cannot be understood apart from the new victimization narrative of Chinese suffering at the hands of Western imperialism.

Awareness of the ways Chinese nationalism engages with other nations and the ways it narrates the past reveals how it is shaped by the passions of the Chinese people. Thus, awareness of these factors forces a revision of the mainstream view that Chinese nationalism is a tool of the elite: that with the slow death of communist ideology, the Communist Party foments nationalism to legitimize its rule. In my discussion of China's apology diplomacy in chapter 6, I addressed the ways nationalism implicates our identities and emotions and argued that it should never be reduced to simply an instrument or tool used to maintain political legitimacy. The ways nationalism emerges out of interaction correspond to the ways we as individuals interact with others. To the extent that we identify with a group, our personal self-esteem is tied to its fate. We want our groups to be seen as good. Perceived slights to our groups are frequently met with anger and resistance. National identities are no different. Nationalists are frequently motivated to save national face or preserve national self-esteem.

Many Chinese understood the 1999 bombing of the Chinese embassy in Belgrade and the 2001 spy plane collision as American assaults on Chinese dignity. Little wonder that they were angry and sought to restore their self-respect as Chinese by denouncing the United States. Such passionate responses account for the increasingly vital role popular nationalists are playing in regime legitimation in China today, as I argued in chapter 7. Hence, Chinese nationalism is not an exclusively elite, top-down phenomenon. The Communist Party has lost its hegemony over Chinese nationalist discourse. Popular nationalists now command a large following and exert tremendous pressure on those who decide the PRC's foreign policy. In fact, the legitimacy of the current regime depends upon its ability to stay on top of popular nationalist demands.

These arguments about Chinese nationalism might help answer the pressing question of what China policy America should pursue at the onset of the twenty-first century. China policy debate in the United States is driven, as political scientist Robert Ross has noted, by "diametrically opposed understandings of Chinese intentions."[1] Conservative hawks and liberal human rights advocates frequently invoke the image of China as the last "Red Menace" to advocate a policy of containment or even confrontation with China. In contrast, conservative business interests seeking increased trade with China and liberals with visions of a "global village" led by America depict China as a status quo power to promote a policy of engagement. In the end, both views tell us more about American politics and ideology than they do about China's own foreign policy goals and motivations.

That China policy debate has become so polarized is potentially disastrous. Rather than taking stock of how those who determine Chinese foreign policy might be affected both by the policies of other states and by emotional investment in the nation, analysts are tempted to infer Chinese intentions from Chinese capabilities alone. China bashers thus rant away, oblivious of the impact that their words and deeds have on Chinese nationalists, who (not surprisingly) respond with equally virulent America bashing. Such diatribes feed off of one another, eroding the trust that binds the U.S.-China relationship. Even more ominously, hard-liners on both sides, seeking to save face, advocate "demonstrations of resolve," increasing the likelihood that the U.S.-China conflict they predict will come to pass.

Dragon Divination

Since intentions are invisible, foreign policy analysts have generally focused on China's material power. Those who infer intent directly from capabilities divide into three camps. The first is represented by the *Washington Times*'s Bill Gertz, author of *The China Threat* and leader of the conservative "Blue Team" on Capitol Hill, who, as noted in chapter 2, points to every Chinese arms acquisition as evidence of Chinese militarism. Members of the second camp include the Brookings Institution's Bates Gill and Michael O'Hanlon, and the late Gerald Segal of the International Institute for Strategic Studies. These writers also infer intent directly from capabilities, but come to the diametrically *opposite* conclusion: China does *not* pose a threat. In articles entitled "China's Hollow Military," "Why China Cannot Conquer Taiwan," and "Does China Matter?," Gill, O'Hanlon, and Segal argue that China, "a middling power," is no threat. In a head-to-head fight, the United States would win hands down.[2] Americans, therefore, can rest easy. The third group also infers Chinese intentions from military capabilities, but rejects head-to-head comparisons. Writing in a 2001 issue of *International Security*, political scientist Thomas Christensen criticizes Gill, O'Hanlon, Segal and others who invoke America's superiority in the balance of power with China to portray China as no military threat. Asymmetric military strategies (waiting until the American military is bogged down elsewhere, undermining America's Asian alliances, information and electronic warfare, etc.) allow China to pose major problems for American security interests without catching up militarily.[3]

But intentions cannot be inferred from power alone, whether relative or asymmetric. Despairing of ever understanding the motives that drive the makers of foreign policy, these policy analysts and scholars focus narrowly on material capabilities. They are ill equipped, therefore, to address the complex issue of intentions. Political scientist Randall Schweller has explored the question of what policy a hegemon like the United States should adopt towards a rising power like China. He does an admirable job of cataloguing potential policy options: preventative war, balancing, bandwagoning, binding, engagement, buckpassing, and so on. In the final analysis, however, Schweller concedes that choosing the appropriate policy hinges on the "accurate recognition of the rising power's true nature." "In the end," Schweller admits, "the best that can be hoped for is that the established powers will properly identify the challengers' long-term goals . . . [to] avoid over-reacting or under-reacting to the developing situation."[4] Because he is a rationalist like Christensen, however, Schweller is poorly equipped to accomplish what he himself calls for.

Christensen and Schweller may be right that states have fixed goals and a "true nature." But they may not. What if intentions are dynamic? I have argued that just as personal identities and intentions change through interactions with others, national identities and goals evolve through international encounters. The American China-policy debate, however, largely treats China in isolation from the international scene, dismissing the role that the actions of other nations play in shaping Chinese behavior. In fact, U.S. China policy has a pronounced influence on Chinese views of the world system. As Chinese analyst Wang Hainan argues, "the major factor affecting Sino-U.S. relations is American China policy."[5] For example, the Chinese government's response to the April 2001 plane collision over the South China Sea cannot be understood without a sense of how the new Bush administration's rhetoric and actions affected Chinese. During the presidential campaign of 2000, Bush repudiated Clinton's policy of "engagement," declaring that China is not America's "partner." In the Chinese view, such words were later put into action when the new administration aggressively pursued a National Missile Defense (NMD) initiative that Chinese see as threatening. Combined with Bush's initial disregard for the life of the missing Chinese pilot, these events contributed to Chinese perceptions of the American response to the collision as both arrogant and belligerent.

In addition to considering China as engaged in dynamic relationship with the rest of the world, students of China must acknowledge the complexity of human motivation if they wish to interpret China's intentions accurately. Analysts must move beyond a narrow rationalism to consider the role that emotions play in foreign-policy decisions.[6] Considerations of both power and passion informed the April 2001 Sino-American apology diplomacy, as explored in chapter 6. Relative power is manifested in apologies: for the same offense, a boy must apologize more profusely to his father than to his brother, because apologies help reestablish hierarchies of power. The diplomatic negotiations that followed the spy plane collision revealed that Beijing and Washington are jockeying for position in the post–Cold War international order.

However, we should not forget that apologies also draw upon and arouse powerful emotions. Both the 1999 American bombing of the Chinese embassy in Belgrade and the April 2001 plane collision fit perfectly into an emerging Chinese "victimization narrative" in which Chinese chronicle a long history of injury at the hands of Western aggressors. Viewed against this historical backdrop, in both the 1999 and the 2001 crises, Chinese saw America humiliating their country yet again. Hoping to restore their self-respect, many Chinese sought to heal these new wounds by insulting America in street protests and online chatrooms. At the same time, many Americans were offended by Chinese imputations that the bombing and collision were intentional. Like their Chinese counterparts, many responded by advocating revenge. Following the return of the American plane crew in April 2001, Kagan and Kristol of the *Weekly Standard* demanded that "China must now pay a price."[7] Thus, these moments of Sino-American apology diplomacy in the recent past have been motivated both by the need to establish relative status, and by the need to maintain *face*. Understanding how the intentions of each nation were manifested in these crises is, therefore, not a simple matter of assessing the national interest of their respective diplomatic strategies. We must also ponder the ways "softer" aspects of national identity—such as pride, anger, and the lust for revenge—influence decision makers on both sides.

Pernicious Polemics

Understanding Chinese intentions requires that analysts broaden the scope of their investigations beyond China's material capabilities. Chinese and American foreign policies are interactive, so the probable effect on Chinese of U.S. words and actions must be incorporated into any analysis of Chinese intentions. Foreign policy decisions cannot be reduced to rational cost-benefit calculations; a variety of emotions also drive those who make them.

Indulging in fits of self-righteous anger, however, America bashers in China and China bashers in the United States seem oblivious to the impact that their polemics have on their foreign counterparts. While blaming others may be emotionally gratifying, it is dangerous, because excessive criticism can create an escalating pattern of abuse, in which criticism begets criticism. As a result, many Chinese and Americans increasingly view Sino-American relations in zero-sum, Manichean, black-and-white terms reminiscent of the Cold War. Such extreme views of each other undermine mutual trust and lay the psychological foundation for violent conflict. As Qin Yaqing, Assistant President of the Foreign Affairs College of China, has recently warned, "worst-caseism" on both sides of the Pacific "could take on a life of its own."[8]

American pessimists have suggested that such a conflict with China is inevitable. Focusing on the material structure of the world system, historian Paul Kennedy has argued that rising powers (like China) and hegemons (like the United States) are destined to fight.[9] Scholars working in the realm of symbolic or identity politics, such as political scientist Samuel Huntington, also argue that an armed conflict is unavoidable.[10] I disagree. Neither the structure of the world system nor the cultural differences between China and America make conflict between China and the United States inevitable.

Experimental work in social psychology helps explain why conflict with China is only a worst-case scenario, not a foregone conclusion. Studies in this field have convincingly demonstrated that individuals extend favor and privilege toward fellow members of the groups with which they associate. However, discriminating in favor of one's fellow ingroup members does not necessitate discriminating against an outgroup.[11] Even though the members of an ingroup will reserve trust and sympathy for their own, and will withhold such positive sentiments from members of the outgroup, they do not necessarily develop *hostile* sentiments toward outsiders. As a prominent social psychologist puts it, "any relationship between ingroup identification and outgroup hostility is progressive and contingent rather than necessary and inevitable."[12] These experimental findings suggest that cultural theorist Edward Said was overly pessimistic when he posited that the mere supposition of difference is perilous.[13] "The recognition of difference," as one anthropologist argues, "does not always or necessarily involve an inferiorization of the Other."[14]

The relations between national groups are no different from other intergroup relations. While all individuals, to varying degrees, assimilate into national groups and favor fellow nationals over foreigners, they do not invariably pit their nations against other nations. International competition and conflict is not the inexorable product of national identity. It only occurs when individuals frame comparisons between their nations and other nations in zero-sum terms. An example of a case in which this kind of zero-sum comparison has led to armed conflict is that of Israeli-Palestinian relations, about which psychologist Herbert Kelman has written extensively. The two national identities, he argues, have become locked into a state of "negative interdependence." "Each perceives the very existence of the other," he argues, "to be a threat to its own existence and status as a nation." Israelis and Palestinians, in Kelman's view, not only compete over material goods like territory and resources, but also engage in a conflict over identity and existence. Such "existential combat" involves a systematic effort to delegitimize the other group by defining it in morally unacceptable ways. Palestinians depict Zionism as "racism," while Israelis label the Palestine Liberation Organization (PLO) as "terrorist."[15] Such rhetoric leads to further polarization: this kind of conflict cannot be resolved until both sides refrain from zero-sum thinking about their relationship.

Unlike Israelis and Palestinians, Chinese and Americans do not compete directly over material resources like land and water. Kelman's research does, however, raise a number of provocative questions: Do Chinese and American nationalists today allow for a Sino-American difference that is non-competitive, a space where Chinese can love China without hating America and where Americans can love America without hating China? Or have nationalist writers locked the identities of China and the United States into a state of existential conflict, a kind of a negative interdependence in which any American gain is seen as China's loss, and vice versa?

It is not only American China bashers who steer their rhetoric into dangerous waters. The writings of parochial Chinese nationalists are equally discouraging. In the 1996 diatribe *Surpassing the USA,* authors Xi Yongjun and Ma Zaizhun amuse themselves with "a few theatrical and rather comical juxtapositions." They begin with clichés. China is the world's richest spiritual civilization, America the most advanced material civilization; China is the collectivist capital, America an individualist's heaven. Xi and Ma then become playful and self-indulgent: America has but two hundred years of history, while China's Tongrentang Pharmacy alone is 388 years old; the American "Declaration of Independence" was a handwritten document of but four thousand words, while China's "great" *(weida)* "Four Books" was printed on the world's first press and contains over three billion characters.[16] The authors clearly intend to establish Chinese superiority at America's expense. Do their characterizations of Sino-American difference promote cooperation, or do they encourage conflict? Their first juxtaposition set China, "the world's richest spiritual civilization," against America, "the most advanced material civilization." The key question is how Xi and Ma frame this difference. Are spiritual and material civilizations viewed as separate, so that America's advanced material civilization does not pose a threat to China's spiritual civilization? Or do Xi and Ma view the material and spiritual in relation to one another, so that any American success comes at China's expense, and vice versa? The larger framework of Xi and Ma's text suggests that they see Sino-American relations as a zero-sum game. Their very title, *Surpassing the USA,* says as much. Moreover, chapter 5 is entitled "The Decline and Death of the Stars and Stripes." "China's rise," they write, "is the sign for America's fall."[17]

Unfortunately, Xi and Ma's view of Sino-American relations as fundamentally conflictual is increasingly prevalent among Chinese nationalists. This view promotes competition and conflict. In a critique of the 1996 "say no" nationalist sensation, one Chinese analyst lamented that "a 'zero-sum' mentality holds that America's gains (or losses) are China's losses (or gains)."[18] Another Chinese scholar explains that the "fourth generation" of nationalists in their thirties has been socialized into a view of the West as China's enemy: "Because of the education they have received, in their subconscious the West, and the U.S. in particular, has always been our enemy, oppressing us, invading our motherland, and even killing our countrymen. . . . To them . . . Oriental culture is superior to Western culture and bound to dominate the world."[19] Such an understanding of the Sino-American relationship allows parochial nationalists to view China as the morally pure victim of American evil.

After the May 1999 American bombing of the Chinese embassy in Bel-

FIGURE 15. Dehumanizing the USA. Beijing, 9 May 1999. The Chinese character translated as "he" is actually "it." The phallic "NATO" bomb is likely a reference to the Monica Lewinski scandal. Photo courtesy of AFP.

grade and the April 2001 plane collision over the South China Sea, a conflictual view of Sino-American relations seems to have gained even greater currency in China. America, in this emerging Chinese view, is not just arrogant but actively seeks to prevent China from prospering and gaining its rightful place at the top of the world system. As Deng Yong has argued in two recent articles, Chinese strategists are increasingly attributing a "highly coherent global strategy bent on power expansion" to American foreign policy.[20] If such views continue to spread, an anti-Western revisionism will become a legitimate foreign policy option for many Chinese. This trend has only continued following the American invasions of Afghanistan and Iraq, with the *People's Daily* arguing that American expansionism has entered its "fourth stage" of seeking "global empire."[21]

During the 1999 Belgrade bombing demonstrations, one protestor held up a drawing of Clinton along with the caption, "He is the war criminal" in English. In the original Chinese characters, however, "he" is actually the inhuman "it." The Chinese version thus implies that Clinton is not just a "war criminal," but is inhuman or even subhuman. A condolence letter sent to the *Guangming Daily* around the same time also engages in existential combat, dehumanizing America: "American scum *[Meiguo lao]* are truly like 'Piggy looking into the mirror'—and they think extremely highly of themselves!"[22] Piggy, a mystical warrior-pig, provides comic relief during the Monkey King's adventures in the Chinese classic *The Journey to the West.* "Piggy looking into the mirror" *(Zhubajie zhao jingzi)* is a famous Chinese *xiehouyu,* or riddle-pun: neither Piggy nor Piggy in the mirror (his reflection) are human *(liwai bushi ren).* America, author Peng Xuewu derisively jokes, is not human; it is just an ugly but vain pig. Human Chinese and inhuman Americans are thus qualitatively different.

The bombing was regularly referred to as "barbaric," and its American and NATO perpetrators were often depicted as demons or beasts. The official *People's Daily* issued a cartoon depicting the United States as a giant gorilla. Similarly, the protest poster I dubbed the "Demon of Liberty" in the introduction altered the symbol of the Statue of Liberty to demonize the United States. A writer from Shandong Province references a well-known fable to the same ends: "The Eight Nation Army invaded a hundred years ago, and the American invasions of Korea and Vietnam were several decades ago. The smoke has cleared, and the fires caused by foreign bombs and rockets have all burned to ashes. The Cold War is long past. The wolf won't eat men any more, right? And the fox will be tamed, right? How can the world have so many things that are black and white? Aren't they all gray? Why did a Chinese write 'Mr. Dongguo and the Wolf'?"[23] Chinese children memorize the story "Mr. Dongguo and the Wolf" *(Dongguo xiansheng he lang)* in elementary school. It is an Aesopian fable about a kind man who helps a wolf escape a hunter. When the danger has passed, however, the wolf turns on his savior. The moral of the story is that one should clearly distinguish good from bad. Our writer's point is that America—the wolf—has a fundamentally evil nature. Chinese, therefore, should not fool themselves into believing that America can become good.

The emergence of existential conflict in Sino-American relations was also evident following the April 2001 plane collision over the South China Sea. As was the case in 1999, many Chinese viewed the incident as a threat to their self-esteem: perceived American callousness towards the fate of pilot Wang Wei was a humiliating loss of *face.* Chinese nationalists thus displayed an anger towards America that sought to restore national self-esteem, as they did in the earlier episode.

Similarly, many Americans are also increasingly viewing U.S.-China relations in zero-sum terms. Americans have long used the image of Chinese tyranny to construct their "liberal myth."[24] This did not end with the Cold War. American ideologues continue to depict China as the last bastion of despotism, in order to better flatter themselves as champions of freedom. Such rhetoric fosters a Manichean vision of U.S.-China relations: America must stand up for democracy, disciplining an evil and despotic China.[25] Indeed, following the 2001 plane collision, many American commentators and policymakers revived Cold War–style rhetoric. For example, the American Enterprise Institute's Arthur Waldron claimed that the crisis had been a "blessing in disguise": by shattering dangerous American illusions about China, the incident revealed the "repression," "assertive nationalism," and most fundamentally, "the continued ugliness of the Chinese regime."[26]

In May 1999 and April 2001, in the heat of the moment, both Chinese and American nationalists sought to save face at each other's expense. However specific those moments were, they do reveal the danger inherent in a Sino-American relationship devoid of mutual trust. Once the "others" cease to be human, the psychological foundation for violence is laid. In *War Without Mercy*, historian John Dower tells a chilling tale about the role that dehumanization played in the brutality of the Pacific theater of World War II. Racial rhetoric and demonization of the "other" set the conflict between the United States and Japan apart from the war in Europe. Americans saw the "Japs" as brutal "monkey-men"; Japanese viewed American GIs as demons and devils. Few prisoners were taken; there were far fewer POW camps in Asia than in Europe.[27] Parochial Chinese and American nationalists today sometimes tell an alarmingly similar tale.

Pride and Deterrence

Because Chinese and American foreign policies influence each other, both sides must avoid incendiary rhetoric and unilateral actions. That those who decide Chinese and American foreign policy frequently act on the basis of strong emotions only adds urgency to this warning. Psychologists and sociologists have demonstrated that emotions like anger often lead to attempts at revenge. And psychologists have found that humans are more willing to take risks to regain what they think they have lost than to let it go and seek a comparable gain. Combined, these findings suggest that the desire to restore *face* after its perceived loss might induce leaders to act on their emotions, taking greater risks than they otherwise would.

Chinese nationalists frequently speak of injustice. In 1997's passionate anti-American bestseller *The Plot to Demonize China*, Xiong Lei writes that "we do not seek to foment hatred of Americans, only to restore justice."[28]

The Chinese who threw bricks at the U.S. embassy in Beijing after the bombing of their embassy in Belgrade in May 1999 were also moved by an ethical anger that sought to right a wrong. They were genuinely angry— not, as Western observers suggested, toys in the hands of a communist puppeteer.[29] Their anger, significantly, had a higher, or ethical, dimension. Chinese protestors sought retributive justice: they wanted to restore China's proper place in international society. When status has been unfairly taken away, a righteous anger can justify violence. Beyond simply being indignant about status loss, individuals are also more willing to take risks to restore it, because losses bring more pain than gains bring pleasure.[30] American and Chinese leaders, therefore, are more likely to take risks to right perceived wrongs than they are likely to accommodate them. This attitude helps to explain Beijing's reckless decision to call Bush a "coward" in response to the April 2001 crisis, and Bush's impetuous declaration a few days later that he would "do whatever it takes" to defend Taiwan. A strong desire to restore their reputations impelled both sides to risk exacerbating Sino-American tensions.

Such emotional desires to save face are frequently rationalized with the language of deterrence. Following the release of the American crew in April 2001, Robert Kagan and William Kristol warned of the dangers of appeasement, writing that "it is the appeasers who wind up leading us into war." They then raised the specter of a Cold War–style domino effect: "American capitulation [to China] will embolden others around the world."[31] While Kagan and Kristol claim to be concerned only with maintaining American credibility and upholding the national interest, they may also have been motivated by desires for vengeance. Dressed up in the language of deterrence, such desires threaten to lead the United States down the same path that led to war with Vietnam. After World War II, American Cold Warriors, haunted by the "lessons of Munich," vowed not to appease future rivals. Traditional deterrence theorists argued that the protection of strategic interests required the maintenance of America's reputation for resolve. Kissinger and other arbiters of American foreign policy used the rhetoric of deterrence theory and the "domino effect" to justify American military interventions across the globe. "If we don't stop the 'Commies' today in Timbuktu," the argument ran, "they'll be in Topeka tomorrow."

In hindsight, it is clear that the propositions of deterrence theory were flawed. The Soviets did not learn the lessons that Americans thought that they were teaching them in the third world, in part because it is impossible to control the ways that others will construe one's actions.[32] What one party intends as a display of resolve may be interpreted by another as anything from bluffing to belligerence. What Americans view as a defensive demonstration of will, Chinese may view as an act of aggression. Moreover, the lessons Americans think we have taught in one situation might not translate to another. As political scientist Jonathan Mercer has convincingly argued, "resolve is not a poker chip that can be stored up or spent in successive hands of international politics."[33] Making China "pay a price" for its April 2001 "hostage-taking," as Kagan and Kristol demand, will not necessarily deter Chinese aggression on other issues driven by different logics, such as Taiwan. The success or failure of deterrence lies in the mind of the potential attacker. Like it or not, because we cannot control the mind of another, deterrence can never assure foolproof security. We can and should have an adequate defense (or, general deterrence), but we must accept a degree of insecurity. Attempts at "preventative" deterrence and posturing such as aggressive rhetoric or provocative military buildups (or drawbacks, such as at the Korean DMZ) may provoke the very aggression they are designed to deter.

In his 1992 film *The Story of Qiu Ju,* Director Zhang Yimou tells a moving tale of a peasant woman's encounter with the law. After the village chief kicks her husband in the groin, Qiu Ju demands an apology. Surprised by a public reproach from a young woman, the village chief refuses. Qiu Ju then turns to China's newly emerging legal system for restitution. In the startling conclusion, the village chief, who is not a bad guy, is sent to jail. Qiu Ju's "apology diplomacy" had led to very unexpected and extreme consequences.[34] A similar desire to "demonstrate resolve" led America to armed conflict with Vietnam in the mid-1960s. In another instance, an urge to "teach 'little brother' a lesson" led China to invade Vietnam in the late 1970s. Both nations paid a heavy price for their arrogance. Let us not repeat past mistakes. Desires to save face must not allow Sino-American relations to spin out of control.

Beyond the "Contact Hypothesis"

When Chinese and Americans perceive their identities to be in a state of "negative interdependence," they will engage in "existential combat," seeking to dehumanize each other. Dehumanization lays the psychological foundation for war. My final question, therefore, is, What can be done?

In his classic *The Nature of Prejudice,* psychologist Gordon Allport proposed that equal status contact would improve intergroup relations.[35] Desegregation and a host of other civil rights policies of the 1960s and 1970s were premised upon this now famous "contact hypothesis." U.S.-China exchange programs funded by numerous American nonprofit organizations are still premised on this belief. According to this logic, if only we had more intercultural contact, there would be fewer misunderstandings and less Sino-American conflict.

Unfortunately, several decades of experimental studies in social psychology have revealed that increased contact will improve intergroup relations only under certain conditions. To wit, the contact must be meaningful, voluntary, extended in duration, varied across contexts, generalized beyond the immediate situation, and must occur among individuals who are similar in all but cultural background. In other words, as two prominent psychologists put it, "what is in people's heads—how they think and feel . . . plays a critical role in determining the outcomes of contact across group boundaries."[36] If the conditions are not right, increased intergroup contact actually *exacerbates* intergroup bias, increasing the likelihood of open conflict.

Indeed, some of the most vociferous nationalists in both America and China have spent extensive time living in the land of their perceived mortal enemies. Penn State faculty member Liu Kang is coauthor of what is arguably the nastiest of the anti-American diatribes of China's late 1990s, *The Plot to Demonize China*. Although he has lived in the United States for over a decade, he can see nothing but evil in his adopted home. He complains that there are "no more Edgar Snows [or, friends of China] in America today."[37] Liu sees American enemies everywhere he looks, and goes to great lengths to defame them. Similarly, a number of prominent American critics of China speak Chinese and have lived in China. Richard Bernstein and Ross Munro, journalists who have lived and traveled extensively in China, are coauthors of the sensationalist *The Coming Conflict with China*, which argues that China is militarizing with expansionist aims.[38] Simply increasing intercultural contact is clearly no panacea for Sino-American relations.

To address the problems caused by the possibility that increased intergroup contact might exacerbate hostility and conflict, social psychologists have explored ideas they call "decategorizing" and "recategorizing" social identities. The "decategorization" of social identities involves an attempt to decrease the salience of a social identity by transforming an intergroup context into an interpersonal one. When people view each other as separate individuals and not as group members, bias does indeed decrease. There are two major problems with the decategorization approach, however. One is that decategorization may decrease bias between individuals from different groups, but it does not necessarily change group stereotypes. For example, an American tourist visiting China may come to view her translator as a nice individual, but that may not have any effect on her stereotypes of "the Chinese" as a group. Generalization to the outgroup as a whole is more likely when group identities are salient, rather than obscured; the "nice" Chinese translator must be seen as Chinese, not simply as an individual, for stereotypes about "the Chinese" to change.[39] The other major problem with attempts at decategorization is that they may be perceived as threats to group distinctiveness. "Die-hard" group members will likely respond to such threats by hardening intergroup boundaries and increasing intergroup bias. The Chinese nationalist imperative to modernize but not Westernize, for example, is likely driven in part by fear that the distinctiveness of Chinese identity will be threatened by increased contact with the West.

"Recategorization" as common members of a single, more inclusive group is a more promising strategy. Rather than shifting down from an intergroup context to an interpersonal one, an intergroup context once framed as "us" versus "them" is shifted up so that each group includes the other in a larger "we."[40] Tian Jing, a student at Sichuan Teachers College, gave a moving example of such recategorization following the 1999 Belgrade bombing. Tian wrote about the experience of going to his English class the day after the bombing, and wondering if his American teacher Abbott would dare to show up for class. According to Tian, Abbott arrived with a long face and profuse apologies: "How are you? I'm very sorry. Although my family stay [sic] here, I don't worry about our safety, I just worry about the relationship between the people of the two nations. . . . " Tian tells how Abbott began to cry, as did all of his Chinese students. "His heart was close to us." Tian then describes Abbott's "warmhearted" and "beautiful" wife Nancy and reminisces about the good times the class had had with the two Americans. "We respect and love them. We were just friends, with no national boundaries! But today, he repeatedly apologized, and our hearts were all pained. Clinton, he's taking responsibility for your crime! You have hurt the Chinese people and a just and good American." Tian concludes that "most Americans are trustworthy as friends," and that "Sino-American friendship is possible."[41] Tian is describing a recategorization of identities. In Tian's eyes, his Chinese classmates, Abbott, Nancy, and himself, have become an inclusive and good "we."

Chinese and Americans should take such stories to heart and resolve to learn to live together, with all their differences. A common ingroup identity can be fostered through the pursuit of common goals. Studying English likely contributed to Tian's inclusion of Abbott within his "we." Similarly, U.S.-China cooperation in pursuit of shared goals can promote the development of common ingroup identities. Clearly, some joint ventures will be more successful than others. Studying English is perhaps not an ideal example of the joint pursuit of common goals, because it creates a hierarchical relationship between teacher and student. American efforts at promoting human rights in China, for example, would not be likely to succeed: America would be seen as acting too much like a teacher. Instead, what is needed are goals like fighting international drug trafficking or pirating, in which Chinese and Americans cooperate as equals. Such activities can create common ingroup identities and help satisfy Chinese desires for international recognition.

Realists are right—there are conflicts of material interests in U.S.-China relations today. A common interest in a stable East Asia likely outweighs any material conflicts, however. The more likely danger to bilateral relations lies in the possible emergence of what Kelman called "existential conflict," or the development of a zero-sum identity competition on both sides of the Pacific. Until Chinese and Americans learn to affirm, rather than threaten, each others' national identities, their mutual benefit from a stable East Asia will not ensure peace in the twenty-first century.

Notes

Introduction: Dragon Slayers and Panda Huggers

1. Eckholm, "China Faults the U.S." The dramatic facial expressions and tone of voice Zhu used to express his righteous indignation evoked Peking opera. Thus, his primary audience may have been the Chinese public, not the U.S. government. I thank Allen Whiting for this insight.

2. Sanger, "Powell Sees No Need for Apology," and "Lieberman: China Played 'Aggressive Game of Aerial Chicken.'"

3. Lam, "Behind the Scenes."

4. Tell, "None Dare Call it Tyranny."

5. "It's Not Over."

6. Derbyshire, "Communist, Nationalist, and Dangerous."

7. Kissinger, "The Folly of Bullying Beijing" and "Storm Clouds Gathering."

8. Church, "Deng Xiaoping Leads Second Revolution."

9. Li Xiguang and Liu Kang, *Yaomohua Zhongguo de beiho (Plot to Demonize China)*, pp. 142–47.

10. Pelosi's Web site is at http://www.house.gov/pelosi/china.htm (accessed 25 March 2003).

11. Schell, *Virtual Tibet.*

12. Kaiser and Mufson, "'Blue Team' Draws Hard Line on Beijing."

13. Patten was persona non grata in Beijing until he returned as a European Union High Commissioner, when his colonial past was forgiven. See Harmsen, "EU's Patten No Longer a 'Thousand-Year Sinner.'" My thanks to Peter Neville-Hadley for this intervention.

14. Iritani, "News Corp Heir Woos China."

15. That is not to say that sentiments directed against Britain, Russia, Korea, or other nations do not play a role in Chinese nationalism today. I choose anti-Japanese and anti-American views both because they are more prominent, and because they are more consequential: they have greater implications for the peace

and stability of the twenty-first century. Random sampling of all cases of Chinese antiforeign sentiment in the mid-1990s, in any case, would create as many problems as it would resolve. On case selection biases, see, for example, Collier and Mahoney, "Insights and Pitfalls."

16. For three fine accounts of the U.S. perspective, see Lampton, *Same Bed, Different Dreams*; Mann, *About Face*; and Tyler, *A Great Wall.*

17. Note that this categorization of Chinese youth generations conflicts with the delineation of generations of political leadership. To distance himself from Mao, leader of the "first generation," Deng declared himself leader of the "second generation," despite the fact that they both participated in the Long March and the War of Resistance. Hence Jiang is of the "third generation," and Hu Jintao leads the new "fourth generation" of technocratic leadership. See Li Cheng, *China's Leaders.*

18. Song Qiang et al., *Disidairen de jingshen (Spirit of the Fourth Generation)*, pp. 206, 202. Unless otherwise noted, all translations from the Chinese are my own.

19. Mannheim, *Essays on the Sociology of Knowledge.* Maurice Halbwachs, father of social memory studies, has similarly argued that "autobiographical memories" of events personally experienced tend to be richer and more meaningful than "historical memories." See Halbwachs, *The Collective Memory.*

20. Xu Ben, "Contesting Memory."

21. See, for example, Gellner, *Nations and Nationalism.* John Fitzgerald, as we shall see in chapter 7, even suggests that twentieth-century China has undergone just the *opposite* process, with states vying to create nations. See Fitzgerald, "Nationless State."

22. Duara cites William Skinner's work on regional systems, which demonstrates the extensive commercial and social networks that linked villages in imperial China. He also cites his and James Watson's essays on popular gods during the Qing Dynasty. Religious and kinship institutions, they argue, fostered a shared cosmology that linked the peasant to Beijing, creating a consciousness of a larger "China." Duara, "Deconstructing the Chinese Nation," p. 21. See Duara, "Superscribing Symbols," and Watson, "Standardizing the Gods." See also William Skinner, "Marketing and Social Structure in Rural China."

23. Mike Szonyi, for example, has challenged Duara and James Watson's separate contentions that popular gods served to unify China more than they accentuated regional differences. See Szonyi, "The Illusion of Standardizing the Gods."

24. See, for example, Metzger and Myers, "Chinese Nationalism and American Policy."

25. See, for instance, Duara, "Nationalists among Transnationals."

26. Lei Yi, "Xiandai de 'Huaxia zhongxinguan' yu 'minzu zhuyi' [Modern 'Sinocentrism' and 'Nationalism']," pp. 49–50.

27. Xiao Gongqing, "Cong minzuzhuyi zhong jiequ guojia ningjuli de xinziyuan [Deriving from Nationalism a New Resource that Congeals the State]," p. 21.

28. "Women you zui youxiu de rennao [We have the best brains]," p. 30.

29. Sautman, "Racial Nationalism and China's External Behavior," p. 79.

30. Kedourie, *Nationalism,* p. 141.

31. I thus follow Henri Tajfel, who defined social identity as "that part of an individual's self-concept which derives from his knowledge of his membership in a social group ... together with the value and emotional significance attached to that membership." Tajfel, *Human Groups and Social Categories*, p. 255.

32. Like Liah Greenfeld, I use "nationalism" loosely as an "umbrella term" covering national identity/nationality, national consciousness, nations, and their ideologies. Greenfeld, *Nationalism: Five Roads to Modernity*, p. 3.

33. See, for example, Wang Bin, *Jinshu, wenziyu (Censorship and Imprisonment)*.

34. I owe the term "indirection" to a personal communication with Donald Munro, summer 2000.

35. Proverbs, incidentally, are particularly useful at revealing deeply rooted, if not always realized, ideals that form the basis for Chinese perspectives and behavior.

36. I thus agree with Allen Whiting's assessment in *China Eyes Japan* that negative images of Japan have thwarted China's interest in closer relations with its Asian neighbor.

37. Other foreigners can be "devils" too, but would require specification, as in "Western devils" *(Yang guizi)* or "American devils" *(Meiguo guizi)*. Left unspecified, "devils" is assumed to be short for "Japanese devils" *(Riben guizi)*. For an extended discussion, see the section entitled "How the Chinese Noun 'Devils' Came to Solely Signify the Japanese," in Jin Hui, *Tongwen cangzang (Wailing at the Heavens)*, pp. 146–58.

38. I borrow this translation, which suggests the racial element of much of Chinese nationalist discourse, from Geremie Barmé. See *In the Red*, p. xiii.

39. For instance, Zhang Zangzang tells a fantastic story in the 1996 sensation *China Can Say No* about an American named "Mark." A womanizer who preyed upon innocent Chinese women, Mark is said to have prowled Chinese streets and campuses with condoms in his wallet: "His love is like spit, it flows so easily." See Song Qiang, Zhang Zangzang, and Qiao Bian, *Zhongguo keyi shuobu (China Can Say No)*, p. 60. Zhang and other young male Chinese nationalists, furthermore, frequently generalize from such "anecdotes" to make racist remarks about *all* white males.

40. Indeed, University of Chicago sociologist Zhao Dingxin has repeatedly misrepresented my work. In a 2002 *China Quarterly* article he asserts, "Contrary to ... Gries' argument that the [Belgrade] embassy bombing marked a long term negative shift in popular Chinese perceptions of America, th[is] study demonstrates that the anger expressed during the anti-U.S. demonstrations were *[sic]* more a momentary outrage." This is puzzling, given that in the 2001 *China Journal* piece that he cites, I draw on work in social psychology on "collective self-esteem" and "outgroup denigration" to explicitly argue: "Despite the ferocity of much of this nationalist rhetoric, it must be understood in the context of the transient threat that the Belgrade bombing represented to Chinese national self-esteem." Whether "momentary" or "transient," we are making the same point: much of the anti-American anger expressed during the protests was a product of the heat of the moment—not necessarily representative of more enduring attitudes. Zhao also criticizes my article as "not drawn from a representative sample"—

despite the fact that I openly acknowledge in the piece that my sources are "not . . . representative." Zhao Dingxin, "An Angle on Nationalism," pp. 886–87; Peter Hays Gries, "Tears of Rage," pp. 30–39. Zhao's survey-research methodology takes replicability as its standard; my interpretive content-analysis approach takes validity as its standard. Each method has its strengths and weaknesses. For one thing, Zhao has a representative sample of a tiny population (students at three elite Beijing schools); I have a nonrepresentative sample, but it is national in scope and is not limited to students. Although our arguments are similar, I believe that my method positions me to make the argument more persuasively. Utilizing a survey-research methodology, Zhao would need longitudinal data to make any claims about whether the outrage was "momentary" or not. But Zhao lacks such data, having performed surveys just once. My content-analysis approach, in contrast, allows me to interpret the language used by Chinese reacting to the bombing. Drawing on experimental findings in social psychology on collective self-esteem, I argue that by choosing to express an "outrage" or "indignation" (*fennu, fenkai, qifen*) tied to the notion of injustice, rather than more visceral forms of anger, like being "irritated" or "ticked off" (for example, *shengqi*) they were seeking to right a wrong—not expressing an enduring, blind anger.

41. See Shi Zhong (Wang Xiaodong), "Xifangren yanzhongde 'Zhongguo minzuzhuyi' ['Chinese Nationalism' in the Eyes of a Westerner]." For Barmé's parry, see *In the Red,* p. 369.

42. See de Tocqueville, *Democracy in America.*

43. As the University of California at Davis's Michelle Yeh has cogently argued, "cultural nationalism cannot be an effective critique of Orientalism because it replicates and perpetuates the latter epistemologically." That is, by essentializing difference within a dualistic framework of "East versus West" *(Dong/Xi)* or "China versus America" *(Zhong/Mei),* Chinese postcolonialism replicates Orientalism's view of the world. It also inverts it, by privileging mainland Chinese forms of knowledge as "experiential" or "intuitive." For example, the notion that Asians can understand Shakespeare, but that only Asians—not Westerners—can appreciate the Tang poetry of Tu Fu, has been labeled "reverse Orientalism" (Wixted, "Reverse Orientalism"). The voices of Caucasians like myself and émigré Chinese scholars like Yeh are thus muted by the hierarchy of power implicit within Chinese postcolonialism's Sinocentric "Cultural China" framework. See Yeh, "International Theory and the Transnational Critic," p. 328.

44. In addition, the synchronic methods of literary criticism, French cultural historian Roger Chartier has suggested, can be combined with a diachronic examination of "interpretive communities" of contemporary agents and their evolving interactions with those same texts over time. See Chartier, "Texts, Printing, Readings," pp. 157–58.

45. See, for example, Xiao Tong and Du Li, *Longli (Dragon History).*

46. Another challenge is posed by variations in regional and national identities. Most of my research, conducted in Beijing, the nation's capital, privileges national identity. I can say little about provincial identities or regional variations in Chinese identity. Edward Friedman has written extensively about regional

differences and Chinese national identity in *National Identity and Democratic Prospects.*

47. Department of Defense, *Annual Report.* Viewable at http://www.defenselink .mil/news/Jun2000/china06222000.htm. Accessed 25 March 2003.

48. Waldron does not, however, disclose his sources revealing nefarious Chinese intent. Commissioners Kenneth Lewis and June Teufel Dreyer nonetheless concurred with Waldron's opinion. See U.S.–China Security Review Commission, *Report to Congress.* Viewable at http://www.uscc.gov/anrp02.htm. Accessed 25 March 2003.

1. Saving Face

1. Letter 2.39 on the *Guangming Daily*'s Belgrade bombing Web site, *Xu Xinghu Zhu Ying lieshi yongyuan huozai women de xinzhong! (Martyrs Xu Xinghu and Zhu Ying Will Live Forever in Our Hearts)*, which is currently located at http://www .gmdaily.com.cn/2_zhuanti/jinian/jnzj/jnzj.htm (accessed 25 March 2003). Two hundred eighty-one condolence letters are posted in ten text files linked towards the top of the page. Subsequent references to the Web site in this chapter will be abbreviated as *Martyrs.* I have numbered the letters for easy reference. "Letter 2.39," for instance, is the thirty-ninth letter in the second set.

2. *Martyrs,* letters 8.9, 3.8.

3. On e-mail preparations in Chicago, see CND-U.S. 99–05–11 and 99–05–18 at: http://www.cnd.org/CND-U.S./ (accessed 10 December 1999).

4. "BeiYue zha shiguan [NATO Bombs Their Embassy]."

5. He Yu, "Open Letter to Premier Zhu."

6. The site, no longer viewable online, was located at http://www.china.org.cn/ ChinaEmbassy/Response_e/index.htm.

7. "Apology Without Sincerity." Translated in the Foreign Broadcast Information Service as FBIS-CHI-1999–0512.

8. Han Zhongkun, "Zhongguo, bushi yibajiujiu [This Is Not 1899 China]."

9. For an excellent cultural history of the 1980s, see Wang Jing, *High Culture Fever.*

10. For an English-language review of two of the first "say no" books, see Gries, review of *China Can Say No, China Can Still Say No,* and *Studying in the USA.*

11. As Robert Jervis noted in a discussion of international relations over a quarter century ago, "men are . . . hesitant to believe that actions affecting them and occurring in rapid sequence could have occurred by coincidence." See Jervis, *Perception and Misperception in International Politics,* p. 321.

12. Christensen, "Chinese Realpolitik," p. 37. See also, "A Belgrade Bombing Explodes in Beijing," "China's True Colors," and "Defusing the Crisis with China."

13. Zhao Suisheng, who has written extensively on Chinese nationalism, has presented most explicitly the mainstream "party propaganda" consensus. He argues that two of the key features of today's "pragmatic nationalism" are that it is

"state-led" (read: party) and "instrumental" (read: propaganda). Although he later admits that nationalism is no longer the "sole province of the communist regime," he nonetheless advocates the dominant "statist" view of Chinese nationalism. Similarly, although he recognizes emotions of "deep bitterness at China's humiliation," Zhao nevertheless insists that nationalism in China is "national-interest driven," based upon a "calculation of benefits and costs." See Zhao Suisheng, "Chinese Nationalism and its International Orientations." This party propaganda view of Chinese nationalism lines up the Party elite and reason against the people and the passions. The Chinese Communist Party is depicted as a rational actor constructing and deploying nationalist sentiment for its own instrumental purposes, while the Chinese masses are portrayed as blinded by an irrational anti-foreign hatred.

14. Yan Tao and Liu Ruting, "Zhongguo renmin shi buke zhansheng de! [The Chinese People Cannot Be Defeated!]," *Xinhua*, 11 May 1999, viewable at http://www.peopledaily.com.cn/item/kangyi/199905/12/051252.html (accessed 25 March 2003).

15. Zhang Tianwei, "Jiyi jiushi yizhong xianshi [Memory Is a Type of Present Reality]."

16. Gries, "Tears of Rage."

17. The *Milky Way,* a Chinese cargo ship headed for the Middle East, was intercepted by the U.S. Navy in 1992.

18. *Martyrs,* Letter 8.11.

19. "A Lesson in Diplomacy."

20. Li Zhaoxing, interview by Jim Lehrer.

21. As Michigan psychologist Lloyd Sandelands has recently suggested, "Perhaps what distinguishes West from East is *not* the degree to which people participate in society but the *feelings* they have about that participation. Westerners seem more troubled by impositions on their cherished individuality. A narcissistic self-consciousness keeps them from seeing and accepting the extent of their submission to the group." See Sandelands, *Feeling and Form in Social Life,* p. 55. Italics added.

22. Ho, "On the Concept of Face," p. 882.

23. The late Isaiah Berlin was one of many to challenge the sharp dichotomy between self and society: "My individual self is not something which I can detach from my relationship with others. . . . For what I am is, in large part, determined by what I feel and think; and what I feel and think is determined by the feeling and thought prevailing in the society to which I belong." See Berlin, *Four Essays on Liberty,* pp. 156–57.

24. The 1899 *Oxford English Dictionary (OED),* for example, defined *face* as, among other things, "disguise" or "pretense." Cited by Kipnis, "'Face,'" pp. 120–23.

25. Mann, *About Face,* p. 8.

26. Garver, *Face Off,* pp. 49, 4.

27. Goffman, *Interaction Ritual,* p. 6.

28. "Dissing" is slang for "disrespecting."

29. Berkow, "A Mask for Bad Behavior."

30. Goffman, *Interaction Ritual,* p. 239.

31. Buruma, *Bad Elements,* p. 13.

32. Lipsyte, "Backtalk."

33. Speier, "Honor and Social Structure," pp. 50, 58, and 59. I thank Arlie Hochschild for this reference.

34. Nisbett and Cohen, *Culture of Honor.*

35. When thinking about the Chinese culture of *face,* it is wise to bear in mind, as Andrew Kipnis reminds us, that "translation requires unpacking one's own assumptions as much as describing foreign ones." See Kipnis, *Producing Guanxi,* p. 105. We must, therefore, be wary of the Western tendency to disparage *face.*

36. Hu Hsien-chin, "The Chinese Concepts of 'Face.'" Andrew Kipnis similarly argues that *lian* is of "first order visibility" while *mianzi* is of "second order visibility": the former is "directly knowable" while the latter depends upon a "third party audience." See Kipnis, "'Face,'" p. 126.

37. What Kipnis has called the "third party audience" plays a central role in the negotiation of *face.* See Kipnis, "'Face.'"

38. As a matter of relative ranking, *face* is a zero-sum resource. The problem is one of inflation. If every student received an "A," for example, an "A" would lose its meaning. This makes the quest for greater *face* highly competitive. Manipulating *face,* furthermore, is difficult. Because it is "located" in other people's minds, one's *face* is highly elusive. Changing others' opinions is not a simple matter of might or money. Indeed, attempting to buy *face* or coerce its recognition from others, for instance, is usually self-defeating, reducing one's prestige rather than enhancing it. Instead, *face* must be earned through conformity to social norms and association with institutions or individuals with high status. See Milner, *Status and Sacredness,* pp. 81–83.

39. Zhai Xuewei's 1997 essay "'Mianzi' mianmianguan [The Faces of 'Face']." Zhai's article inspired my own title for this section.

40. Political scientists Niel Diamant and Alastair Iain Johnston have convincingly debunked the myths of harmonious Chinese legal and strategic cultures, respectively. See Diamant, *Revolutionizing the Family,* and Johnston, *Cultural Realism.*

41. Ting-Toomey, *Challenge of Facework,* p. 111.

42. A century ago, sociologist Charles Cooley introduced the idea of a "looking-glass self": "Our ideal self is constructed chiefly out of ideas about us attributed to other people." George H. Mead concurs, noting in 1934 that "the individual experiences himself . . . only indirectly . . . by taking the attitudes of other individuals towards himself." Psychologist Leon Festinger has dubbed such processes "social comparison": when we are uncertain about our beliefs or social standing, we engage in "social reality testing" through comparison with salient reference groups. See Cooley, *Human Nature and the Social Order,* p. 397; Festinger, "Theory of Social Comparison Processes"; and Mead, *Mind, Self and Society,* p. 138.

43. People, social psychologists agree, actively interpret their social environment. We do not see things as they "are," but actively construct our universe. See Kant, *Critique of Pure Reason;* and Taylor, "Social Being in Social Psychology."

44. See Zheng Xinshui, "Lu Xun lun mianzi wenhua [Lu Xun on *mianzi* Culture]."

45. For a perceptive analysis of Ah Q's "psychological victory technique" *(jing-*

shen shenglifa), see Lu Junhua, *Lun Ah Q jingshen shenglifa de zheli he xinli neihan (On Ah Q's Psychological Victory Technique)*.

46. Lu Xun, "True Story of Ah Q," p. 75.

47. More broadly, People's Liberation Army writer Jin Hui laments that Chinese nationalists today suffer from an "Ah Q style blind optimism": "For over one hundred years," Jin writes, "generation after generation of Chinese have been dreaming that since we were once strong, although we are now backwards we will certainly become strong again." Such "illusions," he warns, are "even worse than spiritual opiates." See Jin Hui, *Tongwen cangzang (Wailing at the Heavens)*, pp. 186–87. Social creativity allows people to maintain ingroup positivity, but it may also create overly high expectations.

48. Hu Hsien-chin, "Chinese Concepts of 'Face,'" pp. 50–54.

49. Beck, "No Protester Died in Tiananmen." Sociologist Charles Cooley noted close to a century ago that "few have any compunction in deceiving . . . persons towards whom they feel no obligation." Cooley, *Human Nature and the Social Order,* p. 388.

50. Holdridge, *Crossing the Divide,* pp. 218–221.

51. Li Fang, "Women zhe yidairen de Meiguo qingjie [Our Generation's America Complex]," p. 15.

52. Li Fang, "Chongnianshi de Meiguo xingxiang [Childhood Images of America]," p. 10.

53. Jin Niu, "Zhongguo ruhe shuobu? [How Should China Say No?]," p. 8.

2. Chinese Identity and the "West"

1. Gertz, *China Threat,* pp. xiv, xii, 198, xi, and xiii.

2. Gertz, "China Whistleblower," p. 165.

3. The back cover of *The Plot to Demonize China* features a picture of Li with his *Washington Post* host Bob Kaiser. The accompanying caption asks, "Friends? Enemies?" See Li Xiguang and Liu Kang, *Yaomohua Zhongguo de beiho (The Plot to Demonize China)*.

4. The *People's Daily Online,* for instance, has devoted several articles to refuting Gertz's *Washington Times* articles. See, e.g., "*Washington Times* Carries Article with Sinister Intention." Westerners who merely downplay Chinese capabilities can also become the target of Chinese ire. As the outspoken *Beijing Review* nationalist Li Haibo noted in response to the late Gerald Segal's argument that China is a "middling power": "Chinese feel insulted when their strength is underestimated." See Li Haibo, "China and Its Century," and Segal, "Does China Matter?"

5. Chow, "King Kong in Hong Kong."

6. Madsen, *China and the American Dream.*

7. Cultural theorist Peter van der Veer holds convincingly that, "It would be a serious mistake to deny agency to the colonized in our effort to show the force of colonial discourse." "The Foreign Hand," p. 23. The Orient has never been sim-

ply a docile object of Western discourse. As political scientist James Scott and psychiatrist Frantz Fanon have shown, the oppressed can maintain their agency and dignity through resistance. See Fanon, *Wretched of the Earth,* and Scott, *Weapons of the Weak.*

8. Clark, "Emotions and Micropolitics in Everyday Life," p. 314.

9. See Weinstein and Deutschberger, "Some Dimensions of Altercasting."

10. Chen Xiaomei, *Occidentalism,* p. 39.

11. Zi Zhongyun, "Impact and Clash of Ideologies," p. 531.

12. Song Qiang, Zhang Zangzang, and Qiao Bian, *Zhongguo keyi shuobu (China Can Say No),* pp. 7–10.

13. Li Fang, "Women zhe yidairen de Meiguo qingjie [Our Generation's America Complex]," p. 14. "Complex" is my translation of "*qingjie.*"

14. Wen Ming, "Misguidance in Vain."

15. Guan Shijie, "Cultural Collisions Foster Understanding." Cited by Zhao Suisheng, "Chinese Intellectuals' Quest," p. 725.

16. Xiao Tong and Du Li, *Longli (Dragon History),* pp. 287–88.

17. Such desires to reorder extant hierarchies are certainly not unique to Chinese, but are common to postcolonial nationalisms throughout the third world. Psychiatrist Frantz Fanon has analyzed the native's "impulse to take the settler's place" in the context of the French colonial empire. "The native," he writes, "is an oppressed person whose permanent dream is to become the persecutor." His "minimum demand," Fanon argues, is that "the last shall be first and the first last." Guan Shijie and the authors of *Dragon History* would likely agree. Fanon, *Wretched of the Earth,* pp. 53, 57.

18. Li Fang, "Chongjian Zhongguo youxi guize [Rewriting China's Rules of the Game]," p. 14.

19. Song Qiang, Zhang Zangzang, and Qiao Bian, *Zhongguo keyi shuobu (China Can Say No),* p. 323.

20. Jin Niu, "Zhongguo ruhe shuobu? [How Should China Say No?]," p. 9.

21. Although I borrow from Tanaka's "Japan's Orient" idea, I cannot condone other aspects of his work. Tanaka's Japan bashing, for example, is deplorable. Historian Joshua Fogel is right that Tanaka commits "purposeful misreadings" of his texts to suit his ideological agenda. See Fogel, Review of *Japan's Orient.* Additionally, Tanaka is certainly not the first to note the centrality of China to Japanese identity. In his 1986 *The Fracture of Meaning,* David Pollack presented a "hermeneutics of Japanese culture" for the millennium beginning in the seventh century, when the first extensive Japanese contact with China occurred. Pollack draws on Mencius's metaphor of a frog at the bottom of a well to make his provocative point: "The fundamental meaning of life itself could be expressed only in terms of walls . . . China was Japan's walls, the very terms by which Japan defined its own existence." Harry Harootunian, Tanaka's mentor at the University of Chicago, has similarly investigated the "nativist transformation" in late Tokugawa thought, which involved the "decentering" of China from its privileged position in Japanese discourse. See Harootunian, "The Functions of China in Tokugawa Thought." Donald Keene, dean of Japanese literary studies in the West, has also

shown how Japanese literature and art during the Sino-Japanese War of 1894–1895 sought to arouse nationalist pride, constructing a Japanese identity separate from and superior to China. See Keene, "The Sino-Japanese War of 1894–95." Finally, China continues to be central to Japanese understandings of themselves today. For instance, the enchanting 1997 film *Chugoku no toribito (The Bird People of China)* is a post-materialist *Heart of Darkness/Apocalypse Now*–like tale of two Japanese who go to China in search of jade and wealth, but end up finding themselves.

22. Tanaka, *Japan's Orient*, p. 18.

23. Wang Hailiang, "ZhongRi guanxi 150 nian zhi wojian: Yu Shantian Zhenxiong xiansheng shangquan [My View of 150 Years of Sino-Japanese Relations: A Discussion with Yamada Tatsuo]," pp. 19–23. Historian Joshua Fogel, by contrast, calls Yamada's volume "a model of balance and poise." Personal communication, 1999.

24. Allen Whiting is right that Chinese discussions of "Sino-Japanese friendship" "reflect rhetoric, not reality." Such discussions do, nonetheless, have real functions. See Whiting, *China Eyes Japan*, p. 181.

25. Wang Xiuhua, "Qingtu bujin de ganqing [An Emotion We Just Can't Get Out]."

26. Chen Jian'an, Xu Jingbo, and Hu Lingyun, "Xiandai Zhongguoren de Ribenguan [The Contemporary Chinese View of Japan]," p. 1.

27. They may actually have wanted their Chinese respondents to project a negative self-image onto the Japanese to provide an outlet for their own anger. Rage, sociologist Charles Cooley notes, can be a source of satisfaction. Cooley writes that, "A man in a rage does not want to get out of it. . . . An enduring hatred may also be a source of satisfaction to some minds." See Cooley, *Human Nature and the Social Order*, p. 284.

28. This nationalist imperative is embedded in political rhetoric like the ubiquitous adjectival phrase, "with Chinese characteristics" *(you Zhongguo tese)*.

29. Gao Zengjie, "ZhongRi guanxizhong wenhua yinsu de yiyi [The Significance of Cultural Factors in Sino-Japanese Relations]," p. 107.

30. Feng Zhaokui, "Xulun [Introduction]," pp. 3, 9, and 22, emphasis added.

31. Buruma, *Bad Elements*, p. 95.

32. Song Qiang et al., *Zhongguo haishi neng shuobu (China Can Still Say No)*, p. 161.

33. Song Qiang et al., *Disidairen de jingshen (The Spirit of the Fourth Generation)*, pp. 247–49.

34. Ge Xin, *ZhongRi youhao shilue (A Brief History of Sino-Japanese Friendship)*, p. 113, emphasis added.

35. On collective self-esteem and "basking in reflected glory," see Cialdini, "Basking in Reflected Glory."

36. Li Zhengtang, *Weishenme Riben bu renzhang (Why Japan Won't Settle Accounts)*, pp. 9, 14.

37. Psychologist David Matsumoto has argued that in Japan, "it is definitely more acceptable for a higher status person to show anger to lower-status others than vice versa." Matsumoto, *Unmasking Japan*, p. 149. I believe the same is true in China.

38. Some Japanese have also used the same brothers metaphor—but to argue for Japanese superiority. In 1937, for example, General Matsue Iwane wrote that, "The struggle between Japan and China was always a fight between brothers within the 'Asian family.' . . . When an elder brother has taken all that he can stand from his ill-behaved younger brother [he] has to chastise him . . . to make him behave properly." See Toshio Iritani, *Group Psychology of the Japanese in Wartime*, p. 290. Iris Chang calls Iwane's use of the brothers metaphor a "self-delusion." See Chang, *Rape of Nanking*, p. 219.

39. Jiang Lifeng et al., *ZhongRi guanxi sanlun (Three Essays on Sino-Japanese Relations)*, pp. 73–75, 215, and 221.

40. Dirlik, "Past Experience, If Not Forgotten, Is a Guide to the Future," p. 71.

41. Howland, *Borders of Chinese Civilization*, p. 249.

42. Dirlik, "Past Experience, If Not Forgotten, Is a Guide to the Future," p. 70.

43. Wang Jisi, "Why Such Strong Reactions?" Translated in FBIS-CHI-95–102, 1 May 1995. Wang was so taken by the Chinese debate over Huntington that he published *Civilizations and International Politics*, a 1995 compilation of twenty-eight essays on the subject. See Wang Jisi, *Wenming yu guoji zhengzhi (Civilizations and International Politics)*.

44. Jin Junhui, "Clash of Civilizations Theory No Accident." Translated in FBIS-CHI-95–102, 1 May 1995.

45. Li Shenzhi, "Fear Under Numerical Superiority." Translated in FBIS-CHI-97–296, 23 October 1997. Like Li, many Chinese juxtapose a racially pure and superior Han China with an inferior, "mongrel" America.

46. Translated by Geremie Barmé. See Barmé, "To Screw Foreigners Is Patriotic," p. 184.

47. See Barmé, *In the Red*, p. 276.

48. Translated in Cai Rong, "Problematizing the Foreign Other," p. 122. For an insightful discussion of how "the sexual transgression in *Fengru feitun [Large Breasts and Full Hips]* turns into a violent and intricate confrontation between the Chinese self and the foreign Other," see Cai Rong, "Problematizing the Foreign Other," p. 109.

3. A "Century of Humiliation"

1. Cited in Scheff, *Bloody Revenge*, p. 105.

2. Xi Yongjun and Ma Zaizhun, *Chaoyue Meiguo (Surpassing the USA)*, p. 228.

3. Jenner, *The Tyranny of History*, p. 2.

4. As Elie Kedourie put it over forty years ago, "Nationalists make use of the past in order to subvert the present." Kedourie, *Nationalism*, p. 70. Sudipta Kaviraj calls this phenomenon the "conceit of the present." See Kaviraj, "Imaginary Institution of India," p. 6.

5. National histories and traditions, Eric Hobsbawn maintains, are mere "inventions." See Hobsbawm and Ranger, *Invention of Tradition*.

6. Cohen, *History in Three Keys,* pp. 213, 221.

7. Barmé, "History for the Masses," p. 260.

8. See Unger, *Using the Past to Serve the Present.*

9. As my use of the qualifier "often" suggests, there are numerous exceptions to this generalization. One of the earliest and most prominent China scholars to point out how the weight of the past affects Chinese nationalism was Benjamin Schwartz. See Schwartz, *In Search of Wealth and Power.* My thanks to Paul Cohen for this suggestion.

10. Because we can both choose among competing narratives and slowly revise those that exist, there is, nevertheless, room for individual will (agency) and change. See McAdams, *The Stories We Live By,* and Singer and Salovey, *The Remembered Self.* Sociologists Anthony Giddens and Margaret Somers have highlighted the ontological quality of narratives. Giddens argues that narratives provide the individual with "ontological security": "The reflexive project of the self . . . consists in the sustaining of coherent, yet continually revised, biographical narratives." See Giddens, *Modernity and Self-Identity,* p. 5. Somers contrasts "representational narratives" (selective descriptions of events) with more foundational "ontological narratives," which are "the stories that social actors use to make sense of—indeed, to act in—their lives. [They] define who we *are;* this in turn can be a precondition for knowing what to *do.*" See Somers, "Narrative Constitution of Identity," p. 618.

11. Cited in Olick and Robbins, "Social Memory Studies," p. 122.

12. When did the "War of Resistance" begin? The Japanese invaded and colonized Manchuria following the Mukden Incident of 1931; however, invasion of the rest of China did not begin until after the Marco Polo Bridge Incident of 1937.

13. Li Fang, "Chongnianshi de Meiguo xingxiang [Childhood Images of America]," p. 23.

14. Tu Wei-ming, "Cultural China," p. 2.

15. Of course, the Chinese encounter with the West extends back centuries before the nineteenth. For a provocative analysis of the East-West encounter during the British Macartney Embassy of 1793 to the Qing court, see Hevia, *Cherishing Men from Afar.*

16. LaCapra, *History and Memory after Auschwitz,* p. 9.

17. The members of the Frankfurt School of cultural critics pioneered attempts to account for the emergence of Nazism out of the Western cultural tradition. The classic Frankfurt School statement is Max Horkheimer and Theodor Adorno's 1944 *Dialectic of Enlightenment.*

18. Segev, *The Seventh Million,* p. 11.

19. Paul Cohen has more to say on Republican Era "national humiliation" writings and also notes a "resona[nce]" between Republican Era writings and those of the 1990s. See Cohen, "Remembering and Forgetting," p. 17.

20. See, for example, Liu, "The Female Body and Nationalist Discourse."

21. Lu Zhong, "Baguo lianjun yexing milu [Secret Records of the Eight Nation Force's Bestiality]." The cover of this magazine contains a photo of a naked woman being molested, and the back cover gives a sneak preview of the con-

tents: "The Japanese general had the [Chinese] women stripped naked and put in a male gray wolf. . . . The American commander drank while watching his soldiers gang rape the women. He then pushed the ham bone he had been eating into a woman's . . . "

22. For an extended comparison of the two movies, see Karl, "The Burdens of History."

23. See Zerubavel, *Recovered Roots*, p. 75. My thanks to Paul Cohen for this reference. My hypothesis linking 1961 Israel and 1997 China was inspired in part by Vera Schwarcz's compelling work on the historical memories of the Chinese and Jewish peoples. See Schwarcz, *Bridge across Broken Time*.

24. See Volkan and Itzkowitz, *Turks and Greeks*, pp. 7–10.

25. "Chuban congshu zongzhi [Series Preface]," p. 1, emphasis added.

26. Mao Haijian, *Tianchao de bengkui (Collapse of the Heavenly Kingdom)*, p. 26.

27. Golden Disc Ltd., *Yapian zhanzheng (The Opium War)*. The British are not the only targets of nationalist ire, however. Before battling the Brits, Chinese cyberwarriors must first trek to Beijing, where they have to secure approval from the Imperial Court. The corruption they encounter is a not-too-veiled critique of present-day Chinese politics.

28. Ling Qing, "Wo xiang Lianheguo dijiao 'ZhongYing lianhe shengming' [I Submitted the 'Sino-British Joint Declaration' to the United Nations]," p. 18.

29. See, for example, Xu Bin, *'97 Xianggang huigui fengyun (Hong Kong's Stormy '97 Return)*, pp. 107–112.

30. Mao apparently never actually declared that "China has stood up!" See Fitzgerald, "China and the Quest for Dignity." That does not, however, change the powerful role of this anecdote in the victor narrative of Chinese nationalist discourse.

4. The "Kissinger Complex"

1. Kissinger, "Storm Clouds Gathering."

2. Kissinger, *White House Years*, p. 191. Cited in Madsen, *China and the American Dream*, p. 66.

3. Kissinger, *White House Years*, p. 742. Cited in Madsen, *China and the American Dream*, p. 69.

4. Kissinger, "Drama in Beijing." Cited in Madsen, *China and the American Dream*, p. 12.

5. Barbalet, *Emotion, Social Theory, and Social Structure*, p. 87.

6. Specifically, the researchers measured assessments of personal efficacy, like the ability to win a date with an attractive member of the opposite sex. Researchers are still exploring the exact relationship between personal and collective self-esteem. But they are clearly interrelated. See Hirt et al., "Costs and Benefits of Allegiance."

7. See Singer and Salovey, *The Remembered Self*.

8. Chen Feng, Huang Zhaoyu, and Chai Zemin, *ZhongMei jiaoliang daxie-*

xhen (True Story of the Sino-American Contest), p. 69. A notion of racial hierarchy also underlies such arguments. Defeating "racially superior" whites, the logic runs, is more glorious than defeating yellow Japanese and Nationalist Chinese.

9. Yang Dezhi, "Qianyan [Preface]," p. 3. Yang's confidence stems in part from his belief that the salient "world" at the time—the third world—viewed China as a victor: "Our victory inspired the people of the third world in their anti-colonial struggles." Yang Dezhi, "Qianyan [Preface]," p. 1.

10. Garver, *Face Off,* pp. 107–8.

11. Chai Zemin, "Daixu [Preface]," pp. i and ii.

12. Garver, *Face Off,* pp. 107–8.

13. Xi Yongjun and Ma Zaizhun, *Chaoyue Meiguo (Surpassing the USA),* p. 232.

14. See, for instance, the *People's Daily's* front page editorial, "*Aiguozhuyi he geming yingxiongzhuyi de buxiu fengpai—jinian Zhongguo renmin zhiyuanjun KangMei YuanChao chuguo zuozhan 50 zhounian* [The Eternal Banner of Patriotism and Revolutionary Heroism: Commemorating the Fiftieth Anniversary of the Chinese People's Volunteers' Setting Off to Do Battle in the War to Resist America and Aid Korea]."

15. "Zhonghua minzu shi yinggutou – Fang Yuan Shengping Jiangjun [The Chinese Race Is Dauntless: An Interview with General Yuan Shengping]."

16. Liang Qianxiang, *KangMei YuanChao zhanzheng huajuan (A Pictorial History),* pp. 29–31.

17. Liang Qianxiang, *KangMei YuanChao zhanzheng huajuan (A Pictorial History),* p. 366.

18. As sociologist Thomas Scheff writes, "When we are accepted as we present ourselves, we usually feel rewarded by the pleasant emotions of pride and fellow feeling" ("Shame and Conformity," p. 396). However, it is our *perceptions* of acceptance, not actual acceptance, that influences us.

19. Liang Qianxiang, *KangMei YuanChao zhanzheng huajuan (A Pictorial History),* p. 524.

20. Foot, *Practice of Power,* p. 47.

21. Foot, *Practice of Power,* pp. 22–51.

22. Foot, *Practice of Power,* p. 22.

23. Foot, *Practice of Power,* p. 28.

24. Fu Hao, "A Ruling Given by History." Translated in FBIS-CHI-96–212, 23 October 1996.

25. Chen Feng, Huang Zhaoyu, and Chai Zemin, *ZhongMei jiaoliang daxiexhen (True Story of the Sino-American Contest)* p. 322.

26. Fu Hao, "A Ruling Given by History."

27. Recent American interpretations of the handshake differ significantly. At the beginning of *A Fragile Relationship,* Harry Harding writes that Nixon extended his hand "to compensate for Dulles' pointed refusal to do so at Geneva." This is a far cry from an apology. John Holdridge, who worked under Kissinger at the National Security Council (NSC) and was present at the handshake, has recently written that the cold reception at the airport was "not seen as a snub." See Harding, *A Fragile Relationship,* p. 1; Holdridge, *Crossing the Divide,* p. 84.

28. Yu Shaohua, Feng Sanda, and Chen Neimin, *Zhongguo qizhi shuobu (China Shouldn't Just Say No)*, p. 12.

29. Dai Xiaohua, "Interview with 'Senior Diplomat' Ji Chaozhu."

30. Yu Shaohua, Feng Sanda, and Chen Neimin, *Zhongguo qizhi shuobu (China Shouldn't Just Say No)*, p. 13.

31. Li Yunfei, "Zhou Enlai Was the Most Outstanding Politician," p. 311.

32. Li and his *People's Daily* editors are not alone in reveling in foreigners' praise of Zhou Enlai, and Kissinger is not the only foreigner who has fawned over him. In 1999, for instance, an entire edited volume, *20 Days that Shook the World: Zhou Enlai's Passing in the Writings of Foreign Reporters,* was devoted to the topic. See Zhu Jiamu and An Jianshe, *Zhenhan shijie de 20 tian (20 Days that Shook the World).* However, Zhou Enlai himself would likely have been displeased with the attention many Chinese lavish on "foreign friends." In 1944 Zhou had astutely advocated "No anti-foreignism, no fear of the foreign, and no fawning to the foreign." It is thus ironic that Li and the editors of *Renmin ribao* fawn over Kissinger's praise of Zhou to construct a vision of Chinese superiority.

33. Song Qiang, Zhang Zangzang, and Qiao Bian, *Zhongguo keyi shuobu (China Can Say No)*, pp. 202-205.

34. Peng Qian, Yang Mingjie, and Xu Deren, *Zhonguo weishenme shuo bu? (Why Does China Say No?)*, p. 16.

35. Xi Yongjun and Ma Zaizhun, *Chaoyue Meiguo (Surpassing the USA)*, p. 228.

36. Peng Qian, Yang Mingjie, and Xu Deren, *Zhonguo weishenme shuo bu? (Why Does China Say No?)*, p. 2.

37. Sociologist Charles Cooley has perceptively deconstructed this dynamic: "We enter . . . into the state of mind of others, or think we do, and if the thoughts we find there are injurious to or uncongenial with the ideas we . . . cherish as a part of our self . . . we feel a movement of anger." Cooley, *Human Nature and the Social Order,* p. 266.

38. Luhtanen and Crocker, "Self-Esteem and Intergroup Comparison."

39. Jin Niu, "Zhongguo ruhe shuobu? [How Should China Say No?]," p. 5.

40. Zhao Suisheng, "Chinese Intellectuals' Quest for National Greatness," p. 731.

41. Song Qiang, Zhang Zangzang, and Qiao Bian, *Zhongguo keyi shuobu (China Can Say No)*, p. 285.

42. Song Qiang et al., *Disidairen de jingshen (Spirit of the Fourth Generation)*, p. 89.

43. Chow, "King Kong in Hong Kong," pp. 98 and 101.

5. Victors or Victims?

1. Howard, *Causes of Wars.*

2. For the classic statement of the "peasant nationalism" thesis, see Johnson, *Peasant Nationalism and Communist Power.*

3. Volkan and Itzkowitz, *Turks and Greeks,* pp. 7-10.

4. The evolving views of late Qing Japanologist Huang Zunxian are indicative of this profound transformation in Chinese views of the world. His late-1870s *Poems on Divers Japanese Affairs* was, according to historian D. R. Howland, "both the first and last text that represented Japan as a prodigal son returned from a long absence and received with much hope for a common future." In Huang's view, Howland argues, China and Japan "would undertake a renovation of Civilization, not only maintaining continuity with the past, but also preserving their moral superiority over the West." Howland notes that in his *Poems* Huang "chooses to comment on those aspects of Chinese culture most visible in Japan." Huang thus establishes China and Japan as the same, and the "West" as a mutual bearer of difference.

That changed dramatically with the 1894–1895 Jiawu War. Howland claims that by the late nineteenth century, for Chinese like Huang "the familiar [Japan] had become foreign." In his monumental turn-of-the-century *Japan Treatise*, Huang depicted Japan not as part of a Sinocentric civilization, but rather as part of an alien Western order of sovereign states. In his famous practice of "brush talks" with Japanese friends, Huang had earlier treated written Japanese as *undifferentiated* from Chinese. In a profound indication of this shift from similarity to difference, Huang began *translating* from Japanese, now viewed as a separate language. See Howland, *Borders of Chinese Civilization*, pp. 232, 116, and 230–39.

5. Although Marxist historiography emphasizes impersonal social forces, the Confucian historiographical tradition, like the *Plutarch's Lives* tradition in the West, views history as a chronicle of the actions of great men. The centrality of figures like Li and Ito to contemporary Chinese accounts of 1895 suggests that the Confucian tradition lives on in contemporary Chinese historiography.

6. Qiao Haitian and Ma Zongping, *Maguan qichi (Extraordinary Humiliation at Shimonoseki)*, pp. 3, 7, 9.

7. Gao Ping, Tang Yun, and Yang Yu, *Xuezhai (Blood Debt)*, pp. 1–3.

8. *"Shina"* is a Japanese word for "China" that eventually replaced the old *"Chugoku,"* which was based on the Chinese *"Zhongguo,"* or "Central Kingdom." Stefan Tanaka cites this transformation as evidence of Japanese Orientalism; Joshua Fogel contests Tanaka's interpretation, arguing that *"Shina"* actually came to Japan from *Chinese* usage. Given Tanaka's political agenda, I am inclined to agree with Fogel. See Tanaka, *Japan's Orient*, pp. 5–7 and 134–41; Fogel, *Cultural Dimension of Sino-Japanese Relations*, pp. 66–76.

9. Li Zhengtang, *Weishenme Riben bu renzhang (Why Japan Won't Settle Accounts)*, p. 94.

10. Xing Xiangyang, ed. *Bainian enchou (A Century of Hatred)*, pp. 345, 348.

11. Li Xiaofei and Shao Longyu, *Zhonghun (Loyal Souls)*, p. 1.

12. See, for example, Jing Zhong, "KangRi zhanzhengshi yanjiu shulue [Research on the History of the War of Resistance against Japan]."

13. Having established China's identity as a victor, the authors then turn to the more clearly practical motives driving their editorial, that past wars legitimize defense spending: "Without a strong national defense, there will be no national independence. . . . We do not hope for war, but we must remain vig-

ilant." See "Wuwang lishi, zhenxing Zhonghua [Do Not Forget History; Arouse China]."

14. Hu Sheng, "Zhonghua minzu de ningjuli [The Chinese Race's Power to Coalesce]," pp. 4, 6–7.

15. Zi Shui and Xiao Shi, *Jingti Riben diguo zhuyi! (Be Vigilant against Japanese Militarism!)*, pp. 302–303.

16. Zhang Zhuhong, "Taierzhuang zhanshe de guoji yinxiang [International Influence of the Battle of Taierzhuang]," p. 33.

17. Jin Hui, *Tongwen cangzan (Wailing at the Heavens)*, pp. 97–99.

18. Yuan Jiaxin, talk given at the Beijing Conference Commemorating the Sixtieth Anniversary of the Marco Polo Bridge Incident, 1997.

19. Lin Qiang, "Zhonghua minzu zouxiang shijie de lishi zhuanzhe [Historical Turn of the Chinese Nation towards the World]," pp. 21, 24, 25, and 29, emphasis added.

20. Luo Huanzhang, "Zhongguo KangRi zhanzheng dui dabai Riben diguo zhuyi de weida gongxian [The Great Contribution the War of Resistance against Japan Made to the Defeat of Japanese Imperialism]," pp. 45 and 47, emphasis added.

21. Luo Huanzhang, "Zhongguo KangRi zhanzheng dui dabai Riben diguo zhuyi de weida gongxian [The Great Contribution the War of Resistance against Japan Made to the Defeat of Japanese Imperialism]," p. 41.

22. Luo Huanzhang, "Zhonguo gongchangdang dui cujin shijie fan faxisi tongyi zhanxian de gongxian [The Contribution the Chinese Communist Party Made to the World Anti-Fascist United Front]," p. 8.

23. Bertram, *Buke zhengfu de renmen (Unconquered)*.

24. Xue Yunfeng, talk given at the Beijing Conference Commemorating the Sixtieth Anniversary of the Marco Polo Bridge Incident, 1997.

25. Zhao Wenli, "Aidejia Sinuo yu Zhongguo Kangzhan [Edgar Snow and the Chinese War of Resistance]," pp. 193, 196.

26. See, for example, Zhang Zhuhong, *Guoji youren yu KangRi zhanzheng (International Friends and the War of Resistance against Japan)*, as well as my discussion in chapter 4.

27. The section on "The Nanjing People's Heroic Struggle" in a 1987 history of the Nanjing massacre seems to be an exception to this rule. In the topic sentence of the third paragraph is the phrase "to ease hatred by killing the enemy *[shadi xuehen]*." See Nanjing Massacre Historical Materials Editorial Committee, *QinHua Rijun Nanjing datusha shigao (History Relating to the Horrible Massacre Committed by the Japanese Troops in Nanjing)*, p. 200.

28. *Awakening* thus has a very similar narrative structure to the *Pictorial History of the War to Resist America and Aid Korea* I discussed in chapter 4.

29. Sun Zhongyi, *Juexing (Awakening)*, pp. 54, 56–57, 58–59, 60–61, 64–65, 70–75, 76–81, 77, 78.

30. Sun Zhongyi, *Juexing (Awakening)*, pp. 117, 126, 128–59.

31. The caption for photograph 2.10, for instance, is mistakenly printed in Chinese and Japanese, rather than in Chinese and English. This suggests that the com-

pilers' original intention was to print in all three languages, or to print another edition in Japanese. It thus seems likely that they made a deliberate choice to print this edition in English rather than Japanese. See Sun Zhongyi, *Juexing (Awakening)*, p. 40.

32. Film Censorship Committee of the Bureau of Film and Television Broadcasting, "Pianzi *Guizi laile* yu pijun lixiang juben zhuyao butong zhichu [Places Where the Film *Devils on the Doorstep* Deviates from the Approved Script]." My thanks to Rebecca MacKinnon for her help in providing me with a copy of this document.

33. The *China Daily* has noted that, "In [Mao's] China . . . not enough was done to study and publicize Japanese war crimes and other atrocities during World War II. Starting from the early 1980s, however . . . the Chinese public has become increasingly aware of the shocking facts of the massacre." See "China Massacre Brought into Focus." CASS historian Zeng Jingzhong concurs, declaring in a review of fiftieth-anniversary scholarship on the war that research on Japanese violence has become a strength of the field. See Zeng Jingzhong, "1995 nian KangRi Zhanzhengshi yanjiu de jinzhan [1995 Developments in Research on the War of Resistance against Japan]," p. 216.

34. Kaviraj, "The Imaginary Institution of India," pp. 30–31.

35. On this topic, see, for example, Gries, "Student Activists and the Politics of Persuasion," pp. 23–24.

36. Gao Ping, Tang Yun, and Yang Yu, *Xuezhai (Blood Debt)*.

37. Meng Guoxiang and Yu Dewen, *Zhongguo Kangzhan sunshi yu zhanhou suopei shimo (Losses in China's War of Resistance and the Full Story of Postwar Reparations Efforts)*.

38. Kristof, "Burying the Past: War Guilt Haunts Japan."

39. Gergen, "Forgotten Holocaust."

40. Novick, *The Holocaust in American Life*.

41. Similarly, when two decades ago, it was suggested that only five million Jews had died in the Holocaust, many Jews across the world were outraged. See Marrus, *The Holocaust in History*. My thanks to Paul Cohen for this reference.

42. "Viewing Nanking: Perspectives from Japan," panel at "Nanjing, 1937: Commemorating the 60th Anniversary of the Nanking Massacre," Princeton University, 22 November 1997. My thanks to the University of California Berkeley's Center for Chinese Studies for funding travel to this conference.

43. Hata, for instance, cited prominent Western scholars Bruce Cumings and Allen Whiting, who have stated that the 300,000 figure is merely symbolic. "Viewing Nanking: Perspectives from Japan" panel.

44. Chang, *Rape of Nanking*, pp. 15, 200, 221.

45. Chang is certainly not alone in excluding China from "the world." The topic of "world history" *(shijie lishi)* in China has long excluded China. My thanks again to Paul Cohen for this comment. The topic of "comparative politics" in America similarly (and inexplicably) excludes American politics.

46. David Kennedy, review of *The Rape of Nanking*, p. 110.

47. Ringle, "You Think You Know What Evil Is, says Iris Chang."

48. Sau Chan, "Nanking Chronicles the 'Forgotten Holocaust.'"

49. Writing in the *Atlantic Monthly* and *Asiaweek*, David Kennedy and Paul Ferguson are important exceptions, presenting balanced reviews that include some criticisms of Chang's disdain for the facts. See Ferguson, "Barbarism under Fire," p. 32; and Kennedy, review of *The Rape of Nanking*.

50. Gergen, "Forgotten Holocaust."

51. My point here is not to question Chang's numbers, but rather to point out how the Western press became complicit in her Japan-bashing project.

52. Schell, "Bearing Witness." Schell also conducted a sympathetic interview with Chang on National Public Radio (NPR) in January 1999.

53. Fogel, review of *The Rape of Nanking*.

54. Barshay, "To the Editor."

55. Chang goes well beyond established facts when she argues that Emperor Hirohito was complicit in the "Rape." Although she concedes that it is "impossible today to prove," she goes on to praise David Bergamini's *Japan's Imperial Conspiracy* as a "riveting narrative" of Hirohito's personal decision to invade Nanjing. She reveals her bias when she then writes, "*Unfortunately*, Bergamini's book was seriously criticized by reputable historians who claimed that he cited sources that simply did not exist." Chang nevertheless feels justified in asserting, on the basis of Bergamini's research, that Hirohito was "exceptionally pleased" by the massacre. See Chang, *Rape of Nanking*, pp. 175–177, emphasis added.

56. Chang, *Rape of Nanking;* Farnsworth, "I'm Sorry?"

57. Scheff, *Bloody Revenge*, p. 61.

58. Jin Hui, *Wailing at the Heavens*, pp. 231, 234.

59. Chang, *Rape of Nanking*, p. 31.

6. China's Apology Diplomacy

1. Xing Xiangyang, *Bainian enchou (A Century of Hatred)*, p. 10.

2. Similarly, calling Bill Clinton a "rat" satisfies "blue team" leaders Edward Timperlake and William Triplett's desires to bash both Democrats and China. See Timperlake and Triplett, *Year of the Rat*.

3. Xing Xiangyang, *Bainian enchou (A Century of Hatred)*, pp. 74, 334, 717–794.

4. John Fitzgerald's fascinating argument that "dignity" is central to Chinese nationalism may be the exception that proves the rule: he is one of the only China scholars to systematically address the role of emotions in Chinese nationalism. See Fitzgerald, "China and the Quest for Dignity." But Fitzgerald is on thin ice when he asserts that *thymos*, the desire for recognition or self-esteem, "compels us not just to 'stand up' and be recognized but also to 'say no' to others." Social psychologists have now convincingly demonstrated that desires for recognition do not necessarily induce hostility towards outgroups. As Marilynn Brewer points out, "outgroup antagonism is not a necessary extension of ingroup positivity and enhancement." See Brewer, "Ingroup Identification and Intergroup Conflict," p. 28.

5. Liberal thought, Roberto Unger argues, is plagued by a fundamental conflict between moralities of reason and desire: "For reason, when it sets itself up as moral

judge, the appetites are blind forces of nature at loose within the self. They must be controlled and if necessary suppressed. For the will, the moral commands of reason are despotic laws that sacrifice life to duty. Each part of the self is condemned to war against the other." See Roberto Unger, *Knowledge and Politics*, p. 55.

Neurologist Antonio Damasio has convincingly argued in his fascinating *Descartes' Error*, however, that this popular zero-sum view is fundamentally flawed. Nonetheless, the "Cartesian split" continues to pit reason against the passions in mainstream Western thought. See also Margrit Eichler's compelling plea in *The Double Standard* that "We must cease to treat rationality and emotionality . . . as two mutually exclusive qualities of actions and must instead treat them as separate continua that vary independently"(p. 121).

6. Levine, "Sino-American Relations," p. 90.

7. Lampton, "A Growing China in a Shrinking World," pp. 121 and 136.

8. Chae-jin Lee, for instance, highlighted economic complementarities and was optimistic about Sino-Japanese relations in books written in the 1970s and 1980s. See Lee, *China and Japan,* and *Japan Faces China.*

9. Downs and Saunders, "Legitimacy and the Limits of Nationalism." This optimistic view that reason will triumph over the passions is rooted in the "rationalist" tradition of philosophers like Hegel and Kant. Indeed, a recent article that sides with the optimists about Chinese nationalism concludes by citing Kant's "spirit of hopeful determination to make the best of history." Metzger and Myers, "Chinese Nationalism and American Policy," p. 37.

10. Shambaugh, *Beautiful Imperialist,* pp. 41 and 301.

11. Whiting, *China Eyes Japan.* In a more recent article, Deng Yong follows in Whiting's footsteps by suggesting that hostility and suspicion impede Sino-Japanese cooperation. See Deng Yong, "Chinese Relations with Japan."

12. Gries, "A 'China Threat'?," p. 67.

13. Jervis, *Logic of Images in International Relations,* p. 7.

14. Barbalet, *Emotion, Social Theory, and Social Structure,* p. 136.

15. In his *Confessions,* for instance, Jean-Jacques Rousseau admits his fear of discovery after falsely accusing a maidservant of theft: "When she appeared my heart was agonized, but the presence of so many people was more powerful than my compunction. I did not fear punishment, but I dreaded shame: I dreaded it more than death. . . . I felt no dread but that of being detected, of being publicly and to my face declared a thief, liar." The emotional intensity of the moment is palpable, and clearly context dependent. Should his secret be exposed *publicly,* Rousseau's social credit among his peers would be depleted. The instrumental stakes of a more private confrontation, however, would not be as great so may not have elicited such strong emotions. Cited by Cooley, *Human Nature and the Social Order,* p. 291.

16. Moore, *Injustice,* p. 17.

17. Branscombe and Wann, "Collective Self-Esteem Consequences of Outgroup Derogation."

18. Sullivan, "Japan Leaders Apologize to Kim."

19. "Beyond Apologies."

20. Kristof, "Problem of Memory," pp. 40–41.

21. Kristof, "Burying the Past."

22. Rennie and Hindell, "Jiang Attacked over War Apology Failure."

23. Song Qiang et al., *Zhongguo haishi neng shuobu (China Can Still Say No)*, p. 102.

24. Kokubun Ryosei, "Beyond Normalization."

25. Cooley, *Human Nature and the Social Order*, pp. 284 and 280.

26. Song Qiang et al., *Zhongguo haishi neng shuobu (China Can Still Say No)*, pp. 161, 88, 122.

27. Jin Hui, *Tongwen cangzan (Wailing at the Heavens)*, pp. 155, 116, 150, and 157–58.

28. Wang Junyan, *Jingti Riben (Be Vigilant against Japan)*, p. 2.

29. Liu Jiangyong, "Riben meihua qinlue lishi de dongxiang ji qi genyuan [What Lies Behind the Japanese Attempt to Beautify Its History of Aggression?]."

30. Feng Ping, "'Xiezui waijiao' yu 'shiyan waijiao' ['Apology Diplomacy' and 'Misstatement Diplomacy']," p. 16.

31. Zi Shui and Xiao Shi, *Jingti Riben diguo zhuyi! (Be Vigilant against Japanese Militarism!)*, pp. 249–50.

32. Gao Ping, Tang Yun, and Yang Yu, *Xuezhai (Blood Debt)*, p. 16.

33. Gao Ping, Tang Yun, and Yang Yu, *Xuezhai (Blood Debt)*, pp. 16–17.

34. Zi Shui and Xiao Shi, *Jingti Riben diguo zhuyi! (Be Vigilant against Japanese Militarism!)*, pp. 261–68.

35. Wu Xinhua, "Kaipian [Introduction]," p. 10; and "Jieshupian [Conclusion]," pp. 123–24.

36. Liu Jiangyong, "Riben meihua qinlue lishi de dongxiang ji qi genyuan [What Lies Behind the Japanese Attempt to Beautify Its History of Aggression?]," p. 3.

37. Farnsworth, "I'm Sorry?"

38. This dynamic seems similar to that of an abusive relationship: the abuser (China) desires the voluntary submissiveness of the abused (Japan), but insults and aggression only achieve a forced deference, which causes the abuser's frustration and violence to spiral out of control. See Denzin, "Phenomenology of Domestic Family Violence." Cited in Clark, "Emotions and Micropolitics in Everyday Life," p. 318.

39. Kobayashi, *Senso ron (On the War)*, pp. 151–71.

40. Kristof, "Burying the Past."

41. Japan's State Secretary for Foreign Affairs, Machimura Nobutaka, at the University of California, Berkeley, 25 January 1999.

42. Hein, "Doing the Really Hard Math."

43. "China Acknowledges U.S. Payment."

44. The following section draws from Gries, "Tears of Rage."

45. *Xu Xinghu Zhu Ying lieshi yongyuan huozai women de xinzhong! (Martyrs Xu Xinghu and Zhu Ying Will Live Forever in Our Hearts)*, letter 4.5. Subsequent references to the Web site in this chapter will be abbreviated as *Martyrs*.

46. Over five months later, on 17 October 1999, London's *Observer* did sug-

gest that NATO deliberately bombed the embassy after discovering that it was relaying Serbian military radio signals. See Sweeney and Holsoe, "NATO Bombed Chinese Deliberately." My thanks to Yu Bin for this reference. According to Fairness and Accuracy in Reporting (FAIR), the U.S. media reacted to the *Observer* story with a "deafening silence." The FAIR report was viewable at http://www.fair.org/activism/embassy.bombing.html, but is no longer up.

47. "China's True Colors."

48. Thomas Pettigrew originally dubbed this finding the "ultimate attribution error." Miles Hewstone has more recently and modestly labeled it the "intergroup attribution bias." See Pettigrew, "The Ultimate Attribution Error," and Hewstone "The 'Ultimate Attribution Error'?"

49. Li Zhaoxing, interview by Jim Lehrer.

50. *Martyrs,* letter 3.44.

51. *Martyrs,* letter 4.10.

52. *Martyrs,* letters 7.15 and 5.4.

53. See, for example, Crocker and Luhtanen, "Collective Self-Esteem and In-group Bias."

54. Shaver et al., "Emotion Knowledge," p. 1078.

55. *Martyrs,* letter 9.2.

56. *Martyrs,* letter 3.16.

57. *Martyrs,* letter 10.2.

58. *Martyrs,* letter 3.27.

59. *Martyrs,* letter 1.21. An October 2000 trip to the Fujian United Web site, http://www.fzfed.com.cn/fzfed/index.html, however, revealed both that they remained a " Microsoft-certified" solution provider, and that they still sold IBM computers.

60. *Martyrs,* letter 3.33.

61. *Martyrs,* letter 10.6.

62. Zhang Zhaozhong, *Xia yige mubiao shi shei (Who Is the Next Target?),* pp. 60 and 62.

63. *Martyrs,* letter 4.25.

64. *Martyrs,* letters 3.20 and 2.43.

65. *Martyrs,* letter 9.6.

66. *Martyrs,* letter 8.10.

67. *Martyrs,* letter 7.11.

68. *Martyrs,* letter 9.9.

69. See http://www.gmw.com.cn/2_zhuanti/jinian/jnzj/xzw/48.html. Accessed 25 March 2003.

70. *Martyrs,* letter 7.13.

71. For example, *Martyrs,* letters 2.28, 7.2, and 10.3.

72. *Martyrs,* letter 1.50.

73. *Martyrs,* letter 8.6.

74. *Martyrs,* letter 4.27. In the original Chinese, "but *[danshi]*" strongly emphasizes what follows it: not "peace" but the menacing "we do not fear war."

75. See, for example, *Martyrs,* letters 3.7, 5.4, 8.2, and 8.9. The Korean War was

also invoked during the 1996 Taiwan Strait crisis, when Chinese also needed confidence for a possible encounter with the U.S. military.

76. The full text of the letter is available online at http://www.cnn.com/2001/world/asiapcf/east/04/11/prueher.letter.text. Accessed 2 June 2003. The following section is based in part on Gries and Peng Kaiping, "Culture Clash?"

77. Huntington, *Clash of Civilizations*.

78. Hoagland, "Regarding China."

79. Butterfield, "China's Demand for Apology."

80. Kynge, "China Calls for Apology."

81. Suarez, "Spy Plane Standoff."

82. For a fine overview of the growing field of cross-cultural psychology, see Nisbett, *Geography of Thought*.

83. See Peng Kaiping, Ames, and Knowles, "Culture and Human Inference." Note that the very terms "East" and "West" *(Dong/Xi)* are mutually exclusive categories only in the Western mode of reasoning. "Easterners" would be more likely to see the distinction between East and West as relative—not absolute. Cross-cultural psychologists do not use these terms to reify them as exclusive categories; instead, their experimental work quantifies differences *of degree*. I use probabilistic phases like "more likely" and "tend to" to emphasize that these differences are not absolute.

84. "Commentary on Collision between U.S. Spy Plane and Chinese Military Jet." Cited in Mulvenon, "Civil-Military Relations and the EP-3 Crisis," p. 5.

85. Referring to the Akira Kurosawa movie in which a single event is told very differently by three different participants, James Mulvenon has called the different Chinese and American views of the incident a "Rashomon-like disconnect." See Mulvenon, "Civil-Military Relations and the EP-3 Crisis," p. 2.

86. Kagan and Kristol, "A National Humiliation."

87. Yan Xuetong, "Experts on Jet Collision Incident."

88. "Apology to China," The Nelson Report. I thank Rick Baum and Chinapol for this reference.

89. Cited by Lu Suping, "Nationalistic Feelings and Sports," pp. 518–519.

90. Lu Suping, "Nationalistic Feelings and Sports," pp. 518–519.

91. Lu Suping, "Nationalistic Feelings and Sports," pp. 521–52.

92. Yang, *A Chinese Village*, p. 167. Cited in Earley, *Face, Harmony, and Social Structure*, p. 43.

93. Zhai Xuewei, "'Mianzi' mianmianguan [The Faces of 'Face']," pp. 8–9. Cheng Boqing also defines *face* as "social capital," likely drawing from the work of Western sociologist James Coleman. See Coleman, *Foundations of Social Theory*, pp. 300–321.

94. Cited in Chang Hui-Ching and Holt, "A Chinese Perspective on Face," p. 122.

95. This helps explain why Chinese leaders so often appear so stiff and nervous in international settings.

96. Qian Ning, *Liuxue Meiguo (Studying in the USA)*, p. 244. For an English language review, see Gries, Review of *Zhongguo keyi shuobu*.

97. I agree with Russell Hardin that Mancur Olson's "collective action problem" can be overcome—the individual *can* benefit from group membership—and I apply Hardin's logic to the national group. Maintaining "national face" can be in the interest of the individual because his or her social credit *in international contexts* depends upon it. See Hardin, *One For All;* and Olson, *The Logic Of Collective Action.*

98. Lu Suping, "Nationalistic Feelings and Sports," p. 522. American press coverage of the Costas incident, in contrast, tended to criticize NBC for caving in to Chinese pressure.

99. Hu Guangyuan, "Yongbao Xianggang [Embrace Hong Kong]," p. 1.

100. CCTV dispatched fifty reporters to thirteen different countries to report on the handover celebrations of overseas Chinese and "foreign friends." See "Tongbu baodao huigui qingdian huodong [Celebrations around the World Will Be Broadcast Simultaneously]," p. 1.

101. See Friedman, "Comment on 'Nationalistic Feelings and Sports'"; Thomas Pixley, "Chinese Nationalists Rush the Net."

7. Popular Nationalism and the Fate of the Nation

1. *Xu Xinghu Zhu Ying lieshi yongyuan huozai women de xinzhong! (Martyrs Xu Xinghu and Zhu Ying Will Live Forever in Our Hearts!),* letter 3.32. Subsequent references to the Web site in this chapter will be abbreviated as *Martyrs.*

2. Dikötter, *Discourse of Race in Modern China,* p. 94.

3. Cohen, *History in Three Keys,* pp. 227–45.

4. It is Zheng Yongnian of the National University of Singapore, however, who has advanced the "state nationalism" view most recently. In *Discovering Chinese Nationalism in China,* Zheng maintains that the emergence of nationalism in China today is best understood as a statist response to the decentralization of state power that occurred under Deng's reforms. He thus downplays the role of the popular nationalists I highlight in this book.

5. Gellner, *Nations and Nationalism.*

6. To parallel Gellner's *Nations and Nationalism,* Fitzgerald might have entitled his lucid essay "States and Nationalism," rather than the forlorn "The Nationless State."

7. Fitzgerald, "Nationless State," pp. 57 and 58.

8. Gries, "Student Activists and the Politics of Persuasion."

9. Townsend, "Chinese Nationalism."

10. To be sure, Enlightenment intellectuals like Voltaire admired China—but to the same ends of criticizing European absolutisms and extolling the new Liberalism.

11. Elizabeth Perry has argued that a new "state-society" paradigm focusing on the nonstate has propelled scholarship out of the grasp of the "totalitarian" view. While writings informed by this new approach have advanced scholarship, assumptions from the totalitarian paradigm persist. State-society writings con-

tinue to take the form of "strong state, weak society" arguments. For example, Western scholars examining Chinese workers, peasants, and intellectuals have emphasized the dependency of these social groups on the state. On workers, see, for example, Andrew Walder's 1986 *Communist Neo-Traditionalism: Work and Authority in Chinese Industry.* (Brantly Womack is right that Walder's top-down approach to patron-client relations would be better labeled "neo-totalitarianism.") On peasants, Jean Oi takes a similar top-down approach to patron-client relations in the countryside. On intellectuals, Timothy Cheek and Carol Hamrin's 1986 conceptualization of "establishment intellectuals" also highlights the dependency of intellectuals on their political patrons. See Cheek and Hamrin, "Collaboration and Conflict in the Search for a New Order"; Oi, *State and Peasant in Contemporary China;* Perry, "Trends in the Study of Chinese Politics"; Walder, *Communist Neo-Traditionalism;* and Womack and Walder, "An Exchange of Views."

12. Madsen, *China and the American Dream.*

13. There are, of course, numerous exceptions. Susanne Rudolf and Vivienne Shue made important early critiques of the "state over society" view of Asian politics. In her 1987 Association of Asian Studies "Presidential Address," Rudolf criticized the Oriental despotism view for assuming too much state control over Asian societies. In *The Reach of the State,* Shue presented an early critique of the application of the totalitarian paradigm to China: "the new party/state *did not, could not,* and *plainly often did not wish to,* control everything." (Original emphasis.) See Rudolf, "Presidential Address," p. 737; and Shue, *The Reach of the State,* p. 104. My thanks to Kevin O'Brien for reminding me to mention these important exceptions to the rule.

14. Durkheim, *Suicide.*

15. See, for example, Hayes, *Nationalism: A Religion;* Kohn, *The Idea of Nationalism.*

16. The arguments of political scientist Benedict Anderson and historian Eric Hobsbawn fit together like hand in glove. But there is a clear division of labor. In his *Imagined Communities,* Anderson freezes time to highlight the construction of national *spaces* through print capitalism; in *The Invention of Tradition,* in contrast, Hobsbawm and Ranger highlight the construction of national *histories.*

17. Postcolonial historians would likely object most strongly to the latter half of my generalization that constructivist approaches to nationalism have been top-down. "Subaltern studies" approaches to nationalism, they might argue, have shifted attention from the colonizers to the colonized as the subjects of third world history. Such accounts, I contend, have nonetheless remained largely elitist: Indian intellectuals, for example, producing alternatives to the British vision of "India." See Chatterjee, *The Nation and Its Fragments;* and Kaviraj, "The Imaginary Institution of India." G. C. Spivak's lament that "the subaltern cannot speak" is reflective of a general postmodern emphasis on the elite production and mass consumption of discourse. See Spivak, "Can the Subaltern Speak?"

18. As Xu Ben has recently noted, "Nationalism in China is . . . a junction and node of contradiction, interaction, and integration between state and society." Xu Ben, "Chinese Populist Nationalism," p. 125.

19. Bendix, *Nation-Building and Citizenship;* Weber, *Theory of Social and Economic Organization.*

20. Wu Fang and Ray Zhang, "Dissident Called the Chinese Premier 'Incompetent.'"

21. "China Gets Wired as Cultural Blitz Planned." This project also suggests that the Internet in China is not the realm of a David civil society set against a Goliath state. The Internet is instead another site for nationalist politics, with actors both for and against the state vying for authority.

22. See, for example, Briscoe, "China Trying to Improve Image."

23. I will use the Chinese "Diaoyu," not to take China's side in the controversy, but because I approach the issue from a Chinese perspective.

24. Cited by Downs and Saunders, "Legitimacy and the Limits of Nationalism," pp. 134 and 135.

25. Song Qiang et al., *Zhongguo keyi shuobu (China Can Still Say No),* pp. 101, 88, and 89.

26. Zi Shui and Xiao Shi, *Jingti Riben diguo zhuyi! (Be Vigilant against Japanese Militarism!),* pp. 279–80, 278.

27. Hou Sijie, "Zai BaoDiao yundongzhong chengzhang [Growing Up in the Protect Diaoyu Movement]," pp. 9–12.

28. "Defend Diaoyutai," http://www.yitch.com/Baodiao/index2.html. Accessed 19 January 1999.

29. Sasaki, "Chinese Policy toward Hong Kong and Taiwan," p. 27.

30. Barmé and Ye, "Great Firewall of China," p. 176.

31. Liu Jiangyong, "Lun Diaoyudao de zhuquan guishu wenti [On the Sovereignty of the Diaoyu Islands]," *Riben xuekan (Japanese Studies),* p. 27.

32. See, for example, the section entitled "Japanese Shouldn't Do Stupid Things" in Zi Shui and Xiao Shi, *Jingti Riben diguo zhuyi! (Be Vigilant against Japanese Militarism!),* pp. 278–79.

33. Lilley, "The 'Fu Manchu' Problem."

34. "Beijing About-Turn."

35. Contrary to Chen Xiaomei's findings in her analysis of Occidentalism in 1980s China, pitting "official" against "anti-official" nationalisms during the "say no" sensation of the mid-1990s would obscure a basic similarity in the substance of Party and popular nationalism. In accordance with Chen's findings, however, both elite and popular Chinese actors sought to utilize images of America for distinct purposes. See Chen Xiaomei, *Occidentalism.*

36. Wang Lixiong, "Zhongguo yi shiqu 'zhuyi' lizu de jichu [China Has Already Lost the Foundation for Establishing a 'Doctrine']."

37. Chen Xiyan, "Guanfang meiti yu shangye chaozuo de huwei liyong [The Mutual Exploitation of the Official Media and Commercial Stir-Fried Works]," pp. 271–72.

38. Xiao Pang, ed., *Zhongguo ruhe miandui Xifang (How China Faces the West).*

39. "Weishenme bukeyi shuobu [Why Can't We Say No?]."

40. Chen Xiyan, "Guanfang meiti yu shangye chaozuo de huwei liyong [The Mutual Exploitation of the Official Media and Commercial Stir-Fried Works]," p. 268.

41. Liang Minwei, *"Zhongguo keyi shuobu* chuban qianhou [The Story of the Publication of *China Can Say No*]." Reprinted in Jia Qingguo, *Zhongguo bu jin-jin shubu (China Should Not Just Say No)*, pp. 251–253.

42. Song Qiang et al., *Disidairen de jingshen (Spirit of the Fourth Generation)*, pp. 88 and 86.

43. Song Qiang et al., *Zhongguo haishi neng sobu (China Can Still Say No)*, p. 92.

44. Xu Ben is certainly right that "While [popular nationalists] direct their attack explicitly against foreigners, the present government is held implicitly to account for yielding too readily to foreign political and commercial demands and for surrendering China's national dignity in the process." Xu Ben, "Chinese Populist Nationalism," p. 133.

45. I borrow "naysayers" from Xu Ben. See Xu Ben, "Chinese Populist Nationalism, p. 132.

46. Cheng Yue-ching, "Chinese Authorities Criticize Book."

47. For a concurring interpretation of the official nature of *China Should Not Play "Mr. No,"* see Fewsmith, "Historical Echoes and Chinese Politics," p. 21.

48. Shen Jiru, *Zhongguo budang "bu xiansheng" (China Should Not Play "Mr. No")*, pp. 56, 2–3, 57, 22.

49. Kynge, "Calculating Beijing Seeks to Harness Popular Outrage." Note that Kynge's article on the spy plane collision two years later, discussed in chapter 6, also emphasized the Beijing elites' calculated response to that crisis.

50. *Martyrs,* letter 6.10.

51. *Martyrs,* letter 4.10.

52. He Yu, "Zhonguo daxuesheng zhi Zhu Zongli de yifeng gongkaixin [An Open Letter from a Chinese University Student to Premier Zhu]."

53. Specifically, letters originated from twenty of China's twenty-three provinces (only Gansu, Qinghai, and Taiwan—the "twenty-third province"—are absent), three of China's five autonomous regions (three each from Inner Mongolia, Xinjiang, and Guangxi, but none from Tibet or Ningxia), and all three of China's municipalities: Beijing (the number one source with over forty letters), Shanghai (an unimpressive six), and Tianjin (four). These counts can only be estimates, however, as a few writers did not reveal their identities and either snail mailed or faxed their letters, or used service providers like "hotmail" whose users' geographical locations cannot be traced. More typically, however, it was possible to trace unidentified letters through e-mail addresses. An otherwise anonymous e-mail from hwwxmc@public2.zz.ha.cn, for instance, argues that "We must strive to make China a world superpower soon!" Pointing my browser to http://www.zz.ha.cn/ in June 1999, I discovered that the writer is from Zhengzhou City, Henan Province. See *Martyrs,* letter 4.8.

54. *Martyrs,* letters 2.8, 1.9, 2.8, 1.9, 1.47, 3.32, 4.16, 2.31, 1.43, 1.13, 2.4, 6.2, 1.6, 1.38, 5.8.

55. *Martyrs,* letters 2.29 and 2.20.

56. See http://web1.peopledaily.com.cn/item/kangyi/tpxw/051102.html. Accessed 25 March 2003.

57. "Workers Turning Anger into Motivation."

58. "Students Turn Indignation into Motivation."
59. Gries, "Tears of Rage."
60. Jin Hui, *Tongwen cangzang (Wailing at the Heavens)*, pp. iv and 465.
61. See the MFA's Chinese-language Web page at http://www.fmprc.gov
.cn/chn/. The pop-up on the index page leads to http://bbs.fmprc.gov.cn/index.jsp.
The English-language site is at http://www.fmprc.gov.cn/eng/. All three were accessed on 25 March 2003.
62. Keefe, "Anatomy of the EP-3 Incident," p. 10.

8. Chinese Nationalism and U.S.-China Relations in the Twenty-First Century

1. Ross, "Engagement in U.S. China Policy," p. 183.
2. See Gill and O'Hanlon, "China's Hollow Military"; O'Hanlon, "Why China Cannot Conquer Taiwan"; and Segal, "Does China Matter?"
3. Christensen, "Posing Problems without Catching Up." For an extended critique, see Gries, "Power and Resolve in U.S. China Policy."
4. Schweller, "Managing the Rise of Great Powers," pp. 25, 26.
5. Wang Hainan, "The Current Situation and Future Prospect of Sino-U.S. Relations," p. 24. Cited in Rosalie Chen, "China Perceives America," p. 296.
6. With the dominance of first behaviorism and then rational choice theory, emotions were largely excluded from twentieth-century social science. International relations theory was no exception. There are signs, however, of a revival in emotions research. For instance, Neta Crawford has recently argued that "the perceptions of others and the attribution of their motives will depend on actors' preexisting emotions." See Crawford, "Passion of World Politics," p. 119.
7. Kagan and Kristol, "A National Humiliation."
8. Qin Yaqing, "Response to Yong Deng," pp. 157 and 158.
9. Paul Kennedy, *Rise and Fall of the Great Powers.*
10. Huntington, *Clash of Civilizations.* See also Mercer, "Anarchy and Identity."
11. For example, studies of racism in the United States and Europe have found evidence of a "symbolic" or "aversive" racism that involves pro-white, rather than anti-black, attitudes and behaviors. Kinder and Sears, "Prejudice and Politics"; Murrell et al., "Aversive Racism and Resistance to Affirmative Action."
12. Brewer, "Ingroup Identification and Intergroup Conflict," p. 35.
13. Said, *Orientalism*, p. 45.
14. Sax, "Hall of Mirrors," p. 294.
15. Kelman, "Interdependence of Israeli and Palestinian National Identities," pp. 588 and 591.
16. Xi Yongjun and Ma Zaizhun, *Chaoyue Meiguo (Surpassing the USA)*, pp. 3–4.
17. Xi Yongjun and Ma Zaizhun, *Chaoyue Meiguo (Surpassing the USA)*, pp. 148–189, 229.
18. Wang Yuesheng, "Shehui qingxu [Social Sentiment]," p. 131.
19. Wang Ning, "Orientalism vs. Occidentalism?," p. 64.

20. Deng Yong, "Hegemon on the Offensive," p. 352. See also Deng Yong, "Chinese Perceptions of U.S. Power and Strategy."

21. "American Empire Steps Up Fourth Expansion," *People's Daily,* 11 March 2003.

22. Guangming Daily, *Xu Xinghu Zhu Ying lieshi yongyuan huozai women de xinzhong! (Martyrs Xu Xinghu and Zhu Ying Will Live Forever in Our Hearts!),* letter 10.5. Subsequent references to the Web site in this chapter will be abbreviated as *Martyrs.*

23. *Martyrs,* letter 10.7.

24. Madsen, *China and the American Dream.*

25. For a biting critique of the Western media's attempts to "discipline" China, see Chow, "King Kong in Hong Kong."

26. Waldron, "China and America Were Lucky."

27. Dower, *War Without Mercy.*

28. Li Xiguang and Liu Kang, *Yaomohua Zhongguo de beiho (Plot to Demonize China),* p. 83.

29. See Gries, "Tears of Rage."

30. See Kahneman and Tversky, "Prospect Theory"; and Levy, "Prospect Theory."

31. Kagan and Kristol, "A National Humiliation," p. 14.

32. Hopf, *Peripheral Visions.*

33. Mercer, *Reputation and International Politics,* p. 227.

34. Zhang Yimou, dir., *Qiu Ju da guanzi [The Story of Qiu Ju],* 1992.

35. Allport, *Nature of Prejudice.*

36. Prentice and Miller, "Psychology of Cultural Contact," p. 2.

37. Li Xiguang and Liu Kang, *Yaomohua Zhongguo de beiho (Plot to Demonize China),* p. 5.

38. Bernstein and Munro, "Coming Conflict with China."

39. Hewstone and Brown, "Contact Is Not Enough."

40. Gaertner et al., "Across Cultural Divides."

41. *Martyrs,* letter 9.5.

Bibliography

"Aiguozhuyi he geming yingxiongzhuyi de buxiu fengpai—jinian Zhongguo
   renmin zhiyuanjun KangMei YuanChao chuguo zuozhan 50 zhounian [The
   Eternal Banner of Patriotism and Revolutionary Heroism: Commemorating
   the Fiftieth Anniversary of the Chinese People's Volunteers' Setting Off to do
   Battle in the War to Resist America and Aid Korea]." Editorial, *Renmin ribao*
   (People's Daily), 25 October 2000, 1.
Allport, Gordon W. *The Nature of Prejudice*. Cambridge, Mass.: Addison-Wesley
   Publishing Company, 1954.
Anderson, Benedict. *Imagined Communities: Reflections on the Origins and Spread
   of Nationalism*. New York: Verso, 1993. Originally published in 1983.
"Apology to China." The Nelson Report. 2001.
"'Apology' Without Sincerity Cannot Be Accepted." Editorial, *Ta Kung Pao*, 12
   May 1999, A2.
Barbalet, J. M. *Emotion, Social Theory, and Social Structure: A Macrosociological Ap-
   proach*. Cambridge: Cambridge University Press, 1998.
Barmé, Geremie. "History for the Masses." In *Using the Past to Serve the Present:
   Historiography and Politics in Contemporary China*, edited by Jonathan Unger.
   Armonk, N.Y.: M. E. Sharpe, 1993.
———. *In the Red: On Contemporary Chinese Culture*. New York: Columbia Uni-
   versity Press, 1999.
———. "To Screw Foreigners Is Patriotic: China's Avant-Garde Nationalists." *The
   China Journal* 34 (July 1995):209–234.
Barmé, Geremie, and Sang Ye. "The Great Firewall of China." *Wired* (June 1997).
Barshay, Andrew. "To the Editor." *New York Times*, 4 January 1998.
Beck, Simon. "No Protester Died in Tiananmen, Says Chi." *South China Morn-
   ing Post*, 12 December 1996, p. 8.
"Beijing About-Turn, Says 'No' to US-Bashing Bestseller." *Straits Times*, 12 De-
   cember 1996, 24.

"BeiYue zha shiguan; Zhongguo aoqi fan Meichao [NATO Bombs Their Embassy and China Experiences a Wave of Anti-Americanism]." *Pingguo ribao (Apple Daily)*, 9 May 1999. Reprinted in Huaxia Wenzhai Supplement #178–1 (11 May 1999). Viewable at http://www.cnd.org/HXWZ/ZK99/zk178–1.hz8 .html. Accessed 26 March 2003.

"A Belgrade Bombing Explodes in Beijing." Editorial, *San Francisco Chronicle*, 11 May 1999, A 20.

Bendix, Reinhard. *Nation-Building and Citizenship: Studies of our Changing Social Order.* New enlarged edition. Berkeley: University of California Press, 1977.

Berkow, Ira. "A Mask for Bad Behavior." *New York Times,* 9 December 1997.

Berlin, Isaiah. *Four Essays on Liberty.* London: Oxford University Press, 1969.

Bernstein, Richard, and Ross Munro. "The Coming Conflict with China." *Foreign Affairs* 76, no. 2 (1997):18–32.

Bertram, James. *Buke zhengfu de renmen: Yige waiguoren yanzhong de Zhongguo kangzhan (Unconquered: China's War of Resistance in the Eyes of a Foreigner).* Beijing: Qiushi chubanshe, 1988. Originally published in 1939 in English.

"Beyond Apologies." Editorial, *South China Morning Post,* 11 October 1998.

Branscombe, Nyla R., and Daniel L. Wann. "Collective Self-Esteem Consequences of Outgroup Derogation When a Valued Social Identity Is on Trial." *European Journal of Social Psychology* 24, no. 6 (1994):641–657.

Brewer, Marilynn B. "Ingroup Identification and Intergroup Conflict: When Does Ingroup Love Become Outgroup Hate?" In *Social Identity, Intergroup Conflict, and Conflict Resolution,* edited by R. Ashmore, L. Jussim, and D. Wilder. Oxford: Oxford University Press, 2001.

Briscoe, David. "China Trying to Improve Image with Ordinary Americans, Still Wary of Government." *Associated Press,* 30 August 2000.

Buruma, Ian. *Bad Elements: Chinese Rebels from Los Angeles to Beijing.* New York: Random House, 2001.

Butterfield, Fox. "China's Demand for Apology Is Rooted in Tradition." *New York Times,* 7 April 2001.

Cai Rong. "Problematizing the Foreign Other: Mother, Father, and the Bastard in Mo Yan's *Large Breasts and Full Hips.*" *Modern China* 29, no. 1 (2003).

Chai Zemin. "Daixu [Preface]." In *ZhongMei jiaoliang daxiexhen (The True Story of the Sino-American Contest),* edited by Chen Feng and Huang Zhaoyu. Beijing: Zhongguo renshi chubanshe, 1996.

Chan, Sau. "Nanking Chronicles the 'Forgotten Holocaust.'" *Associated Press,* 10 April 1998.

Chang, Iris. *The Rape of Nanking: The Forgotten Holocaust of World War II.* New York: BasicBooks, 1997.

Chang Hui-Ching and G. Richard Holt, "A Chinese Perspective on Face as Inter-Relational Concern." In *The Challenge of Facework: Cross-Cultural and Interpersonal Issues,* edited by Stella Ting-Toomey. Albany: State University of New York Press, 1994.

Chartier, Roger. "Texts, Printing, Readings." In *The New Cultural History,* edited by Lynn Hunt. Berkeley: University of California Press, 1989.

Chatterjee, Partha. *The Nation and Its Fragments: Colonial and Postcolonial Histories*. Princeton, N.J.: Princeton University Press, 1993.

Cheek, Timothy, and Carol Hamrin. "Introduction: Collaboration and Conflict in the Search for a New Order." In *China's Establishment Intellectuals*, edited by Timothy Cheek and Carol Hamrin. Armonk, N.Y.: M. E. Sharpe, 1986.

Chen, Rosalie. "China Perceives America: Perspectives of International Relations Experts." *Journal of Contemporary China* 12, no. 35 (2003).

Chen, Xiaomei. *Occidentalism: A Theory of Counter-Discourse in Post-Mao China*. New York: Oxford University Press, 1995.

Chen Feng, Huang Zhaoyu, and Chai Zemin (consultant). *ZhongMei jiaoliang daxiexhen (The True Story of the Sino-American Contest)*. 2 vols. Beijing: Zhongguo renshi chubanshe, 1996.

Chen Jian'an, Xu Jingbo, and Hu Lingyun. "Xiandai Zhongguoren de Ribenguan [The Contemporary Chinese View of Japan]." *Riben yanjiu jikan (Japan Research Quarterly)* 1 (1996):1–4.

Chen Xiyan. "Guanfang meiti yu shangye chaozuo de huwei liyong [The Mutual Exploitation of the Official Media and Commercial Stir-Fried Works]." In *Zhonguo ruhe miandui Xifang (How China Faces the West)*, edited by Xiao Pang. Hong Kong: Mirror Books, 1997.

Cheng Yue-ching. "Chinese Authorities Criticize Book *China Can Say No*." *Mingbao*, 10 December 1996, 12. Translated in BBC, 13 December 1996.

"China Acknowledges U.S. Payment for Belgrade Embassy Bombing." *Kyodo*, 20 January 2001.

"China Gets Wired as Cultural Blitz Planned." *China News Digest*, 1998.

"China Massacre Brought into Focus." *China Daily*, 12 October 1998.

"China's True Colors." Editorial, *Washington Post*, 11 May 1999, A20.

Chow, Rey. "King Kong in Hong Kong: Watching the 'Handover' from the USA." *Social Text* 16, no. 2 (1998):93–108.

Christensen, Thomas. "Chinese Realpolitik." *Foreign Affairs* 75, no. 5 (1996):37–52.

———. "Posing Problems without Catching Up: China's Rise and Challenges for U.S. Security Policy." *International Security* 25, no. 4 (2001):5–40.

"Chuban congshu zongzhi [Series Preface]." In *Wuwang guochi lishi congshu (Do Not Forget the National Humiliation Historical Series)*. Beijing: Zhongguo huaqiao chubanshe, 1991.

Church, George J. "Deng Xiaoping Leads a Far-Reaching, Audacious but Risky Second Revolution." *Time*, 6 January 1986.

Cialdini, Robert B. "Basking in Reflected Glory: Three (Football) Field Studies." *Journal of Personality and Social Psychology* 34, no. 3 (1976):366–375.

Clark, Candace. "Emotions and Micropolitics in Everyday Life." In *Research Agendas in the Sociology of Emotions*, ed. Theodore D. Kemper. Albany: State University of New York Press, 1990.

Cohen, Paul A. *History in Three Keys: The Boxers as Event, Experience, and Myth*. New York: Columbia University Press, 1997.

———. "Remembering and Forgetting: National Humiliation in Twentieth-Century China." *Twentieth-Century China* 27, no. 2 (2002):1–39.

Coleman, James S. *Foundations of Social Theory*. Cambridge, Mass.: Harvard University Press, 1990.

Collier, David, and James Mahoney. "Insights and Pitfalls: Selection Bias in Qualitative Research." *World Politics* 49 (1996):56–91.

"Commentary on Collision between U.S. Spy Plane and Chinese Military Jet." Editorial, *Renmin ribao (People's Daily)*, 3 April 2001.

Cooley, Charles Horton. *Human Nature and the Social Order*. New York: Scribner, 1922. Originally published in 1902.

Crawford, Neta C. "The Passion of World Politics: Propositions on Emotion and Emotional Relationships." *International Security* 24, no. 4 (2000):116–156.

Crocker, Jennifer, and Riia Luhtanen. "Collective Self-Esteem and Ingroup Bias." *Journal of Personality and Social Psychology* 58, no. 1 (1990):60–67.

Dai Xiaohua. "Interview with 'Senior Diplomat' Ji Chaozhu: Witnessing the Establishment of Sino–U.S. Relations." *Beijing Review* 3 (1999):8–11.

Damasio, Antonio R. *Descartes' Error: Emotion, Reason, and the Human Brain*. New York: G. P. Putnam, 1994.

"Defusing the Crisis with China." Editorial, *Boston Globe*, 11 May 1999, A18.

Deng Yong. "Chinese Perceptions of U.S. Power and Strategy." *Asian Affairs, An American Review* 28, no. 3 (2001):150–4.

———. "Chinese Relations with Japan: Implications for Asia-Pacific Regionalism." *Pacific Affairs* 70, no. 3 (1997):373–91.

———. "Hegemon on the Offensive: China Perspectives on U.S. Global Strategy." *Political Science Quarterly* 116, no. 3 (2001):343–65.

Denzin, Norman K. "Toward a Phenomenology of Domestic Family Violence." *American Journal of Sociology* 90, no. 3 (1984):483–513.

Department of Defense. *Annual Report on the Military Power of the People's Republic of China*. Washington, D.C., 2002.

Derbyshire, John. "Communist, Nationalist, and Dangerous." *National Review*, 30 April 2001, 31–33.

Diamant, Neil Jeffrey. *Revolutionizing the Family: Politics, Love, and Divorce in Urban and Rural China, 1949–1968*. Berkeley: University of California Press, 2000.

Dikötter, Frank. *The Discourse of Race in Modern China*. Stanford, Calif.: Stanford University Press, 1992.

Dirlik, Arif. "'Past Experience, If Not Forgotten, Is a Guide to the Future'; or, What Is in a Text? The Politics of History in Chinese-Japanese Relations." In *Japan in the World*, ed. Miyoshi Masao and H. D. Harootunian. Durham, N.C.: Duke University Press, 1993.

Dower, John. *War Without Mercy*. New York: Pantheon Books, 1986.

Downs, Erica Strecker, and Phillip C. Saunders. "Legitimacy and the Limits of Nationalism: China and the Diaoyu Islands." *International Security* 23, no. 3 (1998/1999):114–146.

Duara, Prasenjit. "Deconstructing the Chinese Nation." Manuscript chapter for *Rescuing History from the Nation: Questioning Narratives of Modern China*. Chicago: University of Chicago Press, 1995.

———. "Nationalists among Transnationals: Overseas Chinese and the Idea of

China." In *Ungrounded Empires: The Cultural Politics of Modern Chinese Transnationalism,* edited by Aihwa Ong and Donald Nonini. New York and London: Routledge, 1997.

———. "Superscribing Symbols: The Myth of Guandi." *Journal of Asian Studies* 41, no. 4 (1988):778–95.

Durkheim, Emile. *Suicide: A Study in Sociology.* Translated by John A. Spaulding and George Simpson, edited by George Simpson. New York: Free Press, 1966.

Earley, P. Christopher. *Face, Harmony, and Social Structure: An Analysis of Organizational Behavior Across Cultures.* New York and Oxford: Oxford University Press, 1997.

Eckholm, Erik. "China Faults the U.S. and Calls for an Apology." *New York Times,* 4 April 2001.

Eichler, Margrit. *The Double Standard: A Feminist Critique of Feminist Social Science.* New York: St. Martin's Press, 1979.

Fanon, Frantz. *The Wretched of the Earth.* New York: Grove Press, 1968.

Farnsworth, Elizabeth. "I'm Sorry?" *The NewsHour with Jim Lehrer,* Public Broadcasting Service, 1 December 1998.

Feng Ping. "'Xiezui waijiao' yu 'shiyan waijiao' ['Apology diplomacy' and 'Misstatement diplomacy']." *Riben Xuekan (Japanese Studies)* 1 (1995):16.

Feng Zhaokui. "Xulun [Introduction]." In *Riben de jingyan yu Zhongguo de gaige (Japan's Experience and China's Reforms),* ed. The CASS Institute for Japanese Studies "Lessons from Japan's Economic Development Experience" Study Group. Beijing: Jingji kexue chubanshe, 1993.

Ferguson, Paul. "Barbarism under Fire: A Flawed Account of a Shameful Episode." *Asiaweek,* 12 June 1998, 32.

Festinger, Leon. "A Theory of Social Comparison Processes." *Human Relations* 7 (1954):117–140.

Fewsmith, Joseph. "Historical Echoes and Chinese Politics: Can China Leave the Twentieth Century Behind?" In *China Briefing 2000: The Continuing Transformation,* edited by Tyrene White. Armonk, N.Y.: M. E. Sharpe, 2000.

Film Censorship Committee of the Bureau of Film and Television Broadcasting. "Pianzi *Guizi laile* yu pijun lixiang juben zhuyao butong zhichu [Places Where the Film *Devils on the Doorstep* Deviates from the Approved Script]." 2000.

Fitzgerald, John. "China and the Quest for Dignity." *National Interest* 55 (1999): 47–59.

———. "The Nationless State: the Search for a Nation in Modern Chinese Nationalism." In *Chinese Nationalism,* ed. Jonathan Unger. Armonk, N.Y.: M. E. Sharpe, 1996.

Fogel, Joshua A. *The Cultural Dimension of Sino-Japanese Relations: Essays on the Nineteenth and Twentieth Centuries.* Armonk, N.Y.: M. E. Sharpe, 1995.

———. Review of Iris Chang's *The Rape of Nanking: The Forgotten Holocaust of World War II* and *Japan's War Memories: Amnesia or Concealment? Journal of Asian Studies* 57, no. 3 (1998):818–20.

———. Review of *Japan's Orient. Monumenta Nipponica* 49, no. 1 (1993):112.

Foot, Rosemary. *The Practice of Power: US Relations with China since 1949*. Oxford: Oxford University and Clarendon Presses, 1995.

Friedman, Edward. "Comment on 'Nationalistic Feelings and Sports,'" *Journal of Contemporary China* 8, no. 22 (November 1999):535–538.

———. *National Identity and Democratic Prospects in Socialist China*. Armonk, N.Y.: M. E. Sharpe, 1995.

Fu Hao. "A Ruling Given by History—Marking the 25th Anniversary of China's Restoration of its Legitimate Seat in United Nations." *Renmin Ribao (People's Daily)*, 23 October 1996, 6. Translated by the Foreign Broadcast Information Service under FBIS-CHI-96-212.

Gaertner, Samuel L., John F. Dovidio, Jason A. Nier, Christine M. Ward, and Brenda S. Banker. "Across Cultural Divides: The Value of a Superordinate Identity." In *Cultural Divides: Understanding and Overcoming Group Conflict*, edited by Deborah A. Prentice and Dale T. Miller. New York: Russell Sage Foundation, 1999.

Gao Ping, Tang Yun, and Yang Yu. *Xuezhai: Dui Riben suopei jishi (Blood Debt: Chinese Claims for Reparations)*. Beijing: Guoji wenhua chuban gongsi, 1997.

Gao Zengjie. "ZhongRi guanxizhong wenhua yinsu de yiyi [The Significance of Cultural Factors in Sino-Japanese Relations]." *Riben xuekan (Japanese Studies)* 1 (1996):97–109.

Garver, John W. *Face Off: China, the United States, and Taiwan's Democratization*. Seattle: University of Washington Press, 1997.

Ge Xin. *ZhongRi youhao shilue (A Brief History of Sino-Japanese Friendship)*. Shanghai: Xuelin chubanshe, 1992.

Gellner, Ernest. *Nations and Nationalism*. Ithaca, N.Y.: Cornell University Press, 1983.

Gergen, David. "The Forgotten Holocaust." *The NewsHour with Jim Lehrer*, Public Broadcasting Service, 20 February 1998.

Gertz, Bill. *The China Threat: How the People's Republic Targets America*. Washington, D.C.: Regnery Publishers, 2000.

———. "China Whistleblower Says FBI Harassment Was Payback." *Washington Times*, 14 November 2000.

Giddens, Anthony. *Modernity and Self-Identity: Self and Society in the Late Modern Age*. Stanford, Calif.: Stanford University Press, 1991.

Gill, Bates, and Michael O'Hanlon. "China's Hollow Military." *The National Interest* 56 (1999):55–62.

Goffman, Erving. *Interaction Ritual: Essays on Face-to-Face Behavior*. New York: Pantheon Books, 1982. Originally published in 1967.

Golden Disc Ltd. *Yapian Zhanzheng (The Opium War)*. Computer game, 1997.

Greenfeld, Liah. *Nationalism: Five Roads to Modernity*. Cambridge, Mass.: Harvard University Press, 1992.

Gries, Peter Hays. "A 'China Threat'? Power and Passion in Chinese 'Face Nationalism.'" *World Affairs* 162, no. 2 (1999):63–75.

———. "Correspondence: Power and Resolve in U.S. China Policy." *International Security* 26, no. 2 (2001):155–160.

———. Review of *Zhongguo keyi shuobu (China Can Say No)*, *Zhongguo haishineng shuobu (China Can Still Say No)*, and *Liuxue Meiguo (Studying in the USA)*. *China Journal* 37 (1997):180–185.

———. "Student Activists and the Politics of Persuasion: Chinese Nationalistic Mobilization during the December Ninth Movement of 1935." Masters essay, Department of Political Science, University of California, Berkeley, 1994.

———. "Tears of Rage: Chinese Nationalism and the Belgrade Embassy Bombing." *The China Journal* 46 (2001):25–43.

Gries, Peter Hays, and Peng Kaiping. "Culture Clash? Apologies East and West." *The Journal of Contemporary China* 11, no. 30 (2002):173–178.

Guan Shijie. "Cultural Collisions Foster Understanding." *China Daily*, 2 September 1996, 4.

Guangming Daily. "Xu Xinghu Zhu Ying lieshi yongyuan huozai women de xinzhong! (Martyrs Xu Xinghu and Zhu Ying Will Live Forever in Our Hearts!)," 1999. Viewable at http://www.gmdaily.com.cn/2_zhuanti/jinian/jnzj/jnzj.html. Accessed 1 August 2002.

Halbwachs, Maurice. *The Collective Memory.* New York: Harper & Row, 1980.

Han Zhongkun. "Zhongguo, bushi yibajiujiu [This Is Not 1899 China]." *Renmin Ribao [People's Daily]*, 12 May 1999.

Hardin, Russell. *One For All: The Logic of Group Conflict.* Princeton, N.J.: Princeton University Press, 1995.

Harding, Harry. *A Fragile Relationship: The United States and China since 1972.* Washington, D.C.: Brookings Institution, 1992.

Harmsen, Peter. "EU's Patten No Longer 'a Thousand-Year Sinner' in Chinese Eyes." *Agence France Presse*, 2 April 2002.

Harootunian, Harry. "The Functions of China in Tokugawa Thought." In *The Chinese and the Japanese: Essays in Political and Cultural Interactions*, edited by Akira Iriye. Princeton, N.J.: Princeton University Press, 1980.

Hayes, Carlton. *Nationalism: A Religion.* New York: Macmillan, 1960.

He Yu. "Zhonguo daxuesheng zhi Zhu Zongli de yifeng gongkaixin [An Open Letter from a Chinese University Student to Premier Zhu]." Accessed at www.chinabulletin.com/luntan/58/heyu.gb in November 1999.

Hein, Laura. "Doing the Really Hard Math." *Association of Asian Studies Newsletter*, 13 March 1998.

Hevia, James Louis. *Cherishing Men from Afar: Qing Guest Ritual and the Macartney Embassy of 1793.* Durham, N.C.: Duke University Press, 1995.

Hewstone, Miles. "The 'Ultimate Attribution Error'? A Review of the Literature on Intergroup Causal Attribution." *European Journal of Social Psychology* 20, no. 4 (1990):311–35.

Hewstone, Miles, and Rupert Brown. "Contact Is Not Enough: An Intergroup Perspective on the 'Contact Hypothesis.'" In *Contact and Conflict in Intergroup Encounters*, edited by Miles Hewstone and Rupert Brown. Oxford, England: Basil Blackwell, 1986.

Hirt, Edward R., Dolf Zillmann, Grant A. Erickson, and Chris Kennedy. "Costs and Benefits of Allegiance: Changes in Fans' Self-Ascribed Competencies After Team Victory Versus Defeat." *Journal of Personality and Social Psychology* 63, no. 5 (1992):724–738.

Ho, David Y. F. "On the Concept of Face." *American Journal of Sociology* 81 (1976):867–884.

Hoagland, Jim. "Regarding China, Is It Getting Personal?" *Washington Post*, 4 April 2001, A23.

Hobsbawm, E. J., and T. O. Ranger, eds. *The Invention of Tradition*. Cambridge: Cambridge University Press, 1983.

Holdridge, John H. *Crossing the Divide: An Insider's Account of Normalization of U.S.–China Relations*. Lanham, M.D.: Rowman & Littlefield Publishers, 1997.

Hopf, Ted. *Peripheral Visions: Deterrence Theory and American Foreign Policy in the Third World, 1965–1990*. Ann Arbor: University of Michigan Press, 1994.

Horkheimer, Max, and Theodor W. Adorno. *Dialectic of Enlightenment: Philosophical Fragments, Cultural Memory in the Present*. Stanford, Calif.: Stanford University Press, 2002. Originally published in English in 1972.

Hou Sijie. "Zai BaoDiao yundongzhong chengzhang [Growing Up in the Protect Diaoyu Movement]." *Mingbao yuekan* 10 (1996):9–12.

Howard, Michael Eliot. *The Causes of Wars and Other Essays*. Cambridge, Mass.: Harvard University Press, 1983.

Howland, Douglas. *Borders of Chinese Civilization: Geography and History at Empire's End*. Durham, N.C.: Duke University Press, 1996.

Hu Guangyuan. "Yongbao Xianggang [Embrace Hong Kong]." "Hong Kong's Return," special issue of *Huangjin shidai (Golden Age)*. Canton, June 1997.

Hu Hsien-chin. "The Chinese Concepts of 'Face.'" *American Anthropologist* 46 (1944):45–64.

Hu Sheng. "Zhonghua minzu de ningjuli [The Chinese Race's Power to Coalesce]." *KangRi zhanzheng yanjiu (The Journal of Studies of China's Resistance War Against Japan)* 2 (1991):4–7.

Huntington, Samuel P. *The Clash of Civilizations and the Remaking of World Order*. New York: Simon & Schuster, 1996.

Iritani, Evelyn. "News Corp Heir Woos China with Show of Support." *Los Angeles Times*, 23 March 2001, C1.

Iritani, Toshio. *Group Psychology of the Japanese in Wartime*. London: Kegan Paul International, 1991.

"It's Not Over." *New Republic* 225, no. 17 (23 April 2001):9.

Jenner, W. J. F. *The Tyranny of History: The Roots of China's Crisis*. London: Allen Lane, 1992.

Jervis, Robert. *The Logic of Images in International Relations*. Princeton, N.J.: Princeton University Press, 1970.

———. *Perception and Misperception in International Politics*. Princeton, N.J.: Princeton University Press, 1976.

Jia Qingguo. *Zhongguo bu jinjin shubu (China Should Not Just Say No)*. Beijing: Zhonghua gongshang lianhe chubanshe, 1996.

Jiang Lifeng, Ji Zhaocui, Liu Shilong, and Jin Zhaode. *ZhongRi guanxi sanlun*

(Three Essays on Sino-Japanese Relations). Harbin: Heilongjiang jiaoyu chubanshe, 1996.

Jiang Wen, dir. *Devils on the Doorstep*. 35mm, 166 min. China, 2000.

Jin Hui. *Tongwen cangzang: Rijun qinHua baoxing beiwanglu (Wailing at the Heavens: The Violence of the Japanese Invasion of China)*. Beijing: Jiefangjun wenyi chubanshe, 1995.

Jin Junhui. "Clash of Civilizations Theory No Accident." *Shijie Zhishi (World Affairs)* 9 (1995):4–12.

Jin Niu. "Zhongguo ruhe shuobu? [How Should China Say No?]." In *Zhongguo ruhe shuobu? (How Should China Say No?)*, ed. Meiguo daguan (America the Beautiful). Beijing: CASS Institute of American Studies, 1996.

Jing Zhong. "KangRi zhanzhengshi yanjiu shulue [Research on the History of the War of Resistance against Japan]." In *KangRi zhanzheng shengli wushi zhounian jinianji (A Collection Commemorating the Fiftieth Anniversary of Victory in the War of Resistance Against Japan)*, edited by the Research on the War of Resistance against Japan Editorial Board. Beijing: Jindaishi yanjiu zazhishe, 1995.

Johnson, Chalmers A. *Peasant Nationalism and Communist Power: The Emergence of Revolutionary China*. Stanford, Calif.: Stanford University Press, 1962.

Johnston, Alastair I. *Cultural Realism: Strategic Culture and Grand Strategy in Chinese History*. Princeton, N.J.: Princeton University Press, 1995.

Kagan, Robert, and William Kristol. "A National Humiliation." *Weekly Standard*, 16–23 April 2001, 11–16.

Kahneman, D., and A. Tversky. "Prospect Theory: An Analysis of Decision under Risk." *Econometrica* 47 (1979):263–291.

Kaiser, Robert G., and Steven Mufson. "'Blue Team' Draws a Hard Line on Beijing; Action on Hill Reflects Informal Group's Clout." *Washington Post*, 22 February 2000, A1.

Kant, Immanuel. *Critique of Pure Reason*. Cambridge: Cambridge University Press, 1998.

Karl, Rebecca E. "The Burdens of History: *Lin Zexu* (1959) and the *Opium War* (1997)." In *Whither China? Intellectual Politics in Contemporary China*, edited by Zhang Xudong. Durham, N.C.: Duke University Press, 2001.

Kaviraj, Sudipta. "The Imaginary Institution of India." In *Subaltern Studies VII: Writings on South Asian History and Society*, edited by Partha Chatterjee and Gyanendra Pandley. New York: Oxford University Press, 1992.

Kedourie, Elie. *Nationalism*. Oxford, England, and Cambridge, Mass.: Blackwell, 1993. Originally published in 1960.

Keefe, John. "Anatomy of the EP-3 Incident, April 2001." Alexandria, Va.: Center for Naval Analysis, 2001.

Keene, Donald. "The Sino-Japanese War of 1894–95 and Its Cultural Effects in Japan." In *Tradition and Modernization in Japanese Culture*, edited by Donald Howard Shively. Princeton, N.J.: Princeton University Press, 1971.

Kelman, Herbert C. "The Interdependence of Israeli and Palestinian National Identities: The Role of the Other in Existential Conflicts." *Journal of Social Issues* 55, no. 3 (1999):581–98.

Kennedy, David M. Review of Iris Chang's *The Rape of Nanking*. *Atlantic Monthly* 281, no. 4 (1998).

Kennedy, Paul M. *The Rise and Fall of the Great Powers: Economic Change and Military Conflict from 1500 to 2000*. New York: Random House, 1987.

Kinder, Donald R., and David O. Sears. "Prejudice and Politics: Symbolic Racism Versus Racial Threats to the Good Life." *Journal of Personality and Social Psychology* 40, no. 3 (1981):414–431.

Kipnis, Andrew B. "'Face': An Adaptable Discourse of Social Surfaces." *Positions* 3, no. 3 (1995):119–148.

———. *Producing Guanxi: Sentiment, Self, and Subculture in a North China Village*. Durham, N.C.: Duke University Press, 1997.

Kissinger, Henry. "The Drama in Beijing." *Washington Post*, 11 June 1989.

———. "The Folly of Bullying Beijing." *Los Angeles Times*, 6 July 1997.

———. "No Place for Nostalgia in Our China Dealings." *Houston Chronicle*, 28 June 1998.

———. "Storm Clouds Gathering: The Unnecessary Rush toward Confrontation Must be Reversed by Both China and the United States." *Washington Post*, 7 September 1999.

———. *The White House Years*. Boston: Little, Brown, 1979.

Kobayashi Yoshinori. *Senso ron (On the War)*. Tokyo: Gentosha, 1998.

Kohn, Hans. *The Idea of Nationalism: A Study in Its Origins and Background*. New York: Macmillan Co., 1944.

Kristof, Nicholas D. "Burying the Past: War Guilt Haunts Japan." *New York Times*, 30 November 1998, 1.

———. "The Problem of Memory." *Foreign Affairs* 77, no. 6 (1998).

Kokubun Ryosei. "Beyond Normalization: Thirty Years of Sino-Japanese Diplomacy." *Gaiko Forum* 2, no. 4 (2003):31–39.

Kynge, James. "Calculating Beijing Seeks to Harness Popular Outrage." *Financial Times*, 17 May 1999.

———. "China Calls for Apology Over Collision." *Financial Times*, 4 April 2001, 12.

LaCapra, Dominick. *History and Memory after Auschwitz*. Ithaca, N.Y.: Cornell University Press, 1998.

Lam, Willy Wo-Lap. "Behind the Scenes in Beijing's Corridors of Power." *CNN*, 11 April 2001. Viewable at http://www.cnn.com/2001/WORLD/asiapcf/east/04/11/china.plane.wlam/index.html. Accessed 2 April 2003.

Lampton, David. "A Growing China in a Shrinking World: Beijing and the Global Order." In *Living with China: U.S./China Relations in the Twenty-First Century*, edited by Ezra F. Vogel. New York: W. W. Norton, 1997.

———. *Same Bed, Different Dreams: Managing U.S.–China Relations, 1989–2000*. Berkeley: University of California Press, 2001.

Lee, Chae-Jin. *China and Japan: New Economic Diplomacy*. Stanford, Calif.: Hoover Institute Press, 1984.

———. *Japan Faces China: Political and Economic Relations in the Postwar Era*. Baltimore, M.D.: Johns Hopkins University Press, 1976.

Lei Yi. "Xiandai de 'Huaxia zhongxinguan' yu 'minzu zhuyi' [Modern 'Sinocentrism' and 'Nationalism']." In *Zhonguo ruhe miandui Xifang (How China Faces the West)*, edited by Xiao Pang. Hong Kong: Mirror Books, 1997.

"A Lesson in Diplomacy." Editorial, *Washington Post*, 16 April 2000, B2.

Levine, Steven. "Sino-American Relations: Testing the Limits." In *China and the World: Chinese Foreign Relations in the Post–Cold War era*, edited by Samuel S. Kim. Boulder, Colo.: Westview Press, 1994.

Levy, Jack S. "Prospect Theory, Rational Choice, and International Relations." *International Studies Quarterly* 41, no. 1 (1997):87–112.

Li Cheng. *China's Leaders: The New Generation*. Lanham, M.D.: Rowman & Littlefield Publishers, 2001.

Li Fang. "Chongnianshi de Meiguo xingxiang [Childhood Images of America]." *Zhongguo ruhe shuobu (How China Should Say No)*. Special issue of *Zuojia tiandi (Writer's World)*, 1996.

———. "Chongjian Zhongguo youxi guize [Rewriting China's Rules of the Game]." *Zhongguo ruhe shuobu (How China Should Say No)*. Special issue of *Zuojia tiandi (Writer's World)*, 1996.

———. "Women zhe yidairen de Meiguo qingjie [Our Generation's America Complex]." *Zhongguo ruhe shuobu (How China Should Say No)*. Special issue of *Zuojia tiandi (Writer's World)*, 1996.

Li Haibo. "China and Its Century." *Beijing Review*, 18 October 1999.

Li Shenzhi. "Fear Under Numerical Superiority." *Dushu (Reading)* (Beijing) 6 (1997): 31–38.

Li Xiaofei and Shao Longyu. *Zhonghun: Jiawu zhanzheng de gushi (Loyal Souls: The Story of the Jiawu War)*. The Jiawu National Shame Series, vol. III. Beijing: Zhongyang minzu daxue chubanshe, 1997.

Li Xiguang and Liu Kang. *Yaomohua Zhongguo de beiho (The Plot to Demonize China)*. Beijing: Zhongguo shehui kexue chubanshe, 1996.

Li Yunfei. "Zhou Enlai Was the Most Outstanding Politician — Interviewing Former U.S. Secretary of State Dr. Kissinger." *Renmin Ribao (People's Daily)*, 3 March 1998, p 6. Translated in FBIS-CHI-98–089, 30 March 1998.

Li Zhaoxing, interview by Jim Lehrer, *The NewsHour with Jim Lehrer*, Public Broadcasting Service, 10 May 1999.

Li Zhengtang. *Weishenme Riben bu renzhang: Ribenguo zhanzheng peishang wanglu (Why Japan Won't Settle Accounts: A Record of Japanese War Reparations)*. Beijing: Shishi chubanshe, 1997.

Liang Minwei. "*Zhongguo keyi shuobu* chuban qianhou [The Story of the Publication of *China Can Say No*]." *Lianhe zaobao*, 20 August 1996.

Liang Qianxiang. *KangMei YuanChao zhanzheng huajuan (A Pictorial History of the War of Resistance Against America in Aid of Korea)*. Beijing: KangMei Yuan-Chao jinianguan and Zhongguo wenlian chuban gongsi, 1990.

"Lieberman: China Played 'Aggressive Game of Aerial Chicken,'" CNN, 4 April 2001.

Lilley, James R. "The 'Fu Manchu' Problem." *Newsweek*, 24 February 1997.

Lin Qiang. "Zhonghua minzu zouxiang shijie de lishi zhuanzhe [The Historical Turn of the Chinese Nation towards the World]." *Zhonggong dangshi yanjiu (Research on the History of the Chinese Communist Party)* 4 (1995):21–26.

Ling Qing. "Wo xiang Lianheguo dijiao 'ZhongYing lianhe shengming' [I Submitted the 'Sino-British Joint Declaration' to the United Nations]." *Zongheng* 5 (1997):18–19.

Lipsyte, Robert. "Backtalk, Ball of Confusion: That's What the Sports World Is Today." *New York Times*, 14 December 1997.

Liu, Lydia. "The Female Body and Nationalist Discourse: Manchuria in Xiao Hong's *Field of Life and Death*." In *Body, Subject & Power in China*, edited by Angela Zito and Tani E. Barlow. Chicago: University of Chicago Press, 1994.

Liu Jiangyong. "Lun Diaoyudao de zhuquan guishu wenti [On the Sovereignty of the Diaoyu Islands]." *Riben xuekan (Japanese Studies)* 6 (1996): 13–28.

Lu Junhua. *Lun Ah Q jingshen shenglifa de zheli he xinli neihan (On the Philosophical and Psychological Meaning of Ah Q's Psychological Victory Technique)*. Xian: Jiangxi renmin chubanshe, 1982.

Lu Suping. "Nationalistic Feelings and Sports: The Incident of Overseas Chinese Protest against NBC's Coverage of the Centennial Olympic Games." *Journal of Contemporary China* 8, no. 22 (November 1999).

Lu Xun. "The True Story of Ah Q." In *A Call to Arms*. Beijing: Foreign Languages Press, 1981.

Lu Zhong, ed. "Baguo lianjun yexing milu [The Secret Records of the Eight Nation Force's Bestiality]." *Rainbow Magazine* 8 (1994 special issue).

Luhtanen, Riia, and Jennifer Crocker. "Self-Esteem and Intergroup Comparison: Towards a Theory of Collective Self-Esteem." In *Social Comparison: Contemporary Theory and Research*, edited by Jerry Suls and Thomas Wills. Hillsdale, N.J.: Lawrence Erlbaum, 1991.

Luo Huanzhang. "Zhonguo gongchangdang dui cujin shijie fan faxisi tongyi zhanxian de gongxian [The Contribution the Chinese Communist Party Made to the World Anti-Fascist United Front]." In *Zhongguo renmin KangRi zhanzheng jinianguan wencong (Chinese People's War of Resistance against Japan Museum Compilation)*. Beijing: Beijing chubanshe, 1995.

———. "Zhongguo KangRi zhanzheng dui dabai Riben diguo zhuyi de weida gongxian [The Great Contribution the War of Resistance against Japan Made to the Defeat of Japanese Imperialism]." *KangRi zhanzheng yanjiu (Journal of Studies of China's Resistance War against Japan)* 2 (1991):26–47.

McAdams, Dan P. *The Stories We Live By: Personal Myths and the Making of the Self.* New York: Guilford Press, 1996.

Madsen, Richard. *China and the American Dream: A Moral Inquiry.* Berkeley: University of California Press, 1995.

Mann, Jim. *About Face: A History of America's Curious Relationship with China from Nixon to Clinton.* New York: Alfred Knopf, 1999.

Mannheim, Karl. *Essays on the Sociology of Knowledge.* London: Routledge & Kegan Paul, 1952.

Mao Haijian. *Tianchao de bengkui: Yapian zhanzheng zai yanjiu (The Collapse of the Heavenly Kingdom: Rethinking the Opium War)*. Beijing: Sanlian chubanshe, 1995.

Marrus, Michael Robert. *The Holocaust in History.* Hanover, N.H.: Published for Brandeis University Press by University Press of New England, 1987.

Matsumoto, David. *Unmasking Japan: Myths and Realities about the Emotions of the Japanese.* Stanford, Calif.: Stanford University Press, 1996.

Mead, George Herbert. *Mind, Self & Society From the Standpoint of a Social Behaviorist.* Chicago: University of Chicago Press, 1934.

Meng Guoxiang and Yu Dewen. *Zhongguo kangzhan sunshi yu zhanhou suopei shimo (Losses in China's War of Resistance and the Full Story of Postwar Reparations Efforts).* Hefei: Anhui renmin chubanshe, 1995.

Mercer, Jonathan. "Anarchy and Identity." *International Organization* 49, no. 2 (1995):229–252.

———. *Reputation and International Politics.* Cornell Studies in Security Affairs. Ithaca, N.Y.: Cornell University Press, 1996.

Metzger, Thomas A., and Ramon H. Myers. "Chinese Nationalism and American Policy." *Orbis* 42, no. 1 (1998):21–37.

Miike, Takashi, dir. *Bird People of China.* Color, 118 min. 1997.

Milner, Murray. *Status and Sacredness: A General Theory of Status Relations and an Analysis of Indian Culture.* New York: Oxford University Press, 1994.

Moore, Barrington. *Injustice: The Social Bases of Obedience and Revolt.* White Plains, N.Y.: M. E. Sharpe, 1978.

Mulvenon, James. "Civil-Military Relations and the EP-3 Crisis: A Content Analysis." *China Leadership Monitor* 1 (2002).

Murrell, Audrey J., Beth L. Dietz-Uhler, John F. Dovidio, and Samuel L. Gaertner. "Aversive Racism and Resistance to Affirmative Action: Perceptions of Justice Are Not Necessarily Color Blind." *Basic and Applied Social Psychology* 15, nos. 1–2 (1994):71–86.

Nanjing Massacre Historical Materials Editorial Committee. *QinHua Rijun Nanjing datusha shigao (Draft Manuscript of the History Relating to the Horrible Massacre Committed by the Japanese Troops in Nanjing in December 1937).* Nanjing: Jiangsu wenyi chubanshe, 1987.

Nisbett, Richard E. *The Geography of Thought: Why We Think the Way We Do.* New York: Free Press, 2003.

Nisbett, Richard E., and Dov Cohen. *Culture of Honor: The Psychology of Violence in the South.* Boulder, Colo.: Westview Press, 1996.

Novick, Peter. *The Holocaust in American Life.* Boston: Houghton Mifflin, 1999.

O'Hanlon, Michael. "Why China Cannot Conquer Taiwan." *International Security* 25, no. 2 (2000):51–86.

Oi, Jean Chun. *State and Peasant in Contemporary China: The Political Economy of Village Government.* Berkeley: University of California Press, 1989.

Olick, Jeffrey, and Joyce Robbins. "Social Memory Studies: From 'Collective Memory' to the Historical Sociology of Mnemonic Practices." *Annual Review of Sociology* 24 (1998):105–140.

Olson, Mancur. *The Logic of Collective Action: Public Goods and the Theory of Groups.* Cambridge, Mass.: Harvard University Press, 1965.

Peng Kaiping, Daniel Ames, and Eric Knowles. "Culture and Human Inference: Perspectives from Three Traditions." In *Handbook of Cross-Cultural Psychology.* Oxford: Oxford University Press, 2001.

Peng Qian, Yang Mingjie, and Xu Deren. *Zhongguo weishenme shuo bu? Leng-*

zhanhou Meiguo duiHua zhengce de cuowu (Why Does China Say No? Mistakes in Post–Cold War American Foreign Policy). Beijing: Xinshijie chubanshe, 1996.

Perry, Elizabeth. "Trends in the Study of Chinese Politics: State-Society Relations." *China Quarterly* 139 (1994):704–14.

Pettigrew, Thomas F. "The Ultimate Attribution Error: Extending Allport's Cognitive Analysis of Prejudice." *Personality and Social Psychology Bulletin* 5, no. 4 (1979):461–76.

Pixley, Thomas. "Chinese Nationalists Rush the Net." *Asian Wall Street Journal*, 26 August 1996.

Pollack, David. *The Fracture of Meaning: Japan's Synthesis of China from the Eighth through the Eighteenth Centuries*. Princeton, N.J.: Princeton University Press, 1986.

Prentice, Deborah A., and Dale T. Miller. "The Psychology of Cultural Contact." In *Cultural Divides: Understanding and Overcoming Group Conflict*, edited by Deborah A. Prentice and Dale T. Miller. New York: Russell Sage Foundation, 1999.

Qiao Haitian and Ma Zongping. *Maguan qichi (The Extraordinary Humiliation at Shimonoseki)*. Beijing: Zhongguo huaqiao chubanshe, 1991.

Qian Ning. *Liuxue Meiguo (Studying in the USA)*. Nanjing: Jiangsu wenyi chubanshe, 1996.

Qin Yaqing. "A Response to Yong Deng: Power, Perception, and the Cultural Lens." *Asian Affairs, An American Review* 28, no. 3 (2001):155–9.

Rennie, David, and Juliet Hindell. "Jiang Attacked over War Apology Failure." *The Daily Telegraph*, 27 November 1998, 16.

Ringle, Ken. "You Think You Know What Evil Is, says Iris Chang. But Nothing Prepared Me for What I Found." *Newsday*, 8 January 1998.

Ross, Robert. "Engagement in U.S. China Policy." In *Engaging China: The Management of an Emerging Power*, edited by Alastair I. Johnston and Robert S. Ross. London and New York: Routledge, 1999.

Rudolf, Susanne. "Presidential Address." *Journal of Asian Studies* 46, no. 4 (1987).

Said, Edward W. *Orientalism*. New York: Pantheon Books, 1978.

Sandelands, Lloyd. *Feeling and Form in Social Life*. New York: Rowman and Littlefield, 1998.

Sanger, David E. "Powell Sees No Need for Apology." *New York Times*, 4 April 2001.

Sasaki, Norihiro. "Chinese Policy toward Hong Kong and Taiwan: Present and Future." In *One Country, Two Systems: China's Dilemma*, edited by Yasuo Onishi. Tokyo: Institute of Developing Economies, 1997.

Sautman, Barry. "Racial Nationalism and China's External Behavior." *World Affairs* 160, no. 2 (Fall 1997).

Sax, William S. "The Hall of Mirrors: Orientalism, Anthropology, and the Other." *American Anthropologist* 100, no. 2 (1998):292–301.

Scheff, Thomas J. *Bloody Revenge: Emotions, Nationalism, and War*. Boulder, Colo.: Westview Press, 1994.

———. "Shame and Conformity: The Deference-Emotion System." *American Sociological Review* 53, no. 3 (1988):395–406.

Schell, Orville. "Bearing Witness: The Granddaughter of Survivors of the Japanese Massacre of Chinese in Nanjing Chronicles the Horrors." *New York Times,* 14 December 1997.

———. *Virtual Tibet: Searching for Shangri-la from the Himalayas to Hollywood.* New York: Metropolitan Books, 2000.

Schwarcz, Vera. *Bridge across Broken Time: Chinese and Jewish Cultural Memory.* New Haven, Conn.: Yale University Press, 1998.

Schwartz, Benjamin Isadore. *In Search of Wealth and Power: Yen Fu and the West.* Harvard East Asian Series 16. Cambridge, Mass.: Belknap Press of Harvard University Press, 1964.

Schweller, Randall. "Managing the Rise of Great Powers: History and Theory." In *Engaging China: The Management of an Emerging Power,* edited by Alastair I. Johnston and Robert S. Ross. London: Routledge, 1999.

Scott, James C. *Weapons of the Weak: Everyday Forms of Peasant Resistance.* New Haven, Conn.: Yale University Press, 1985.

Segal, Gerald. "Does China Matter?" *Foreign Affairs* 78, no. 5 (1999):24–37.

Segev, Tom. *The Seventh Million: The Israelis and the Holocaust.* New York: Hill and Wang, 1993.

Shambaugh, David L. *Beautiful Imperialist: China Perceives America, 1972–1990.* Princeton, N.J.: Princeton University Press, 1991.

Shaver, Phillip, Judith Schwartz, Donald Kirson, and Cary O'Connor. "Emotion Knowledge: Further Exploration of a Prototype Approach." *Journal of Personality and Social Psychology* 52, no. 6 (1987).

Shen Jiru. *Zhongguo budang "bu xiansheng"—Dangdai Zhongguo de guoji zhanlue wenti (China Should Not Play "Mr. No": The Problem of China's Contemporary International Strategy).* Beijing: Jinri Zhongguo chubanshe, 1998.

Shi Zhong (Wang Xiaodong). "Xifangren yanzhongde 'Zhongguo minzuzhuyi' ['Chinese Nationalism' in the Eyes of Westerners]." *Zhanlue yu guanli (Strategy and Management)* 1 (1996).

Shue, Vivienne. *The Reach of the State: Sketches of the Chinese Body Politic.* Stanford, Calif.: Stanford University Press, 1988.

Singer, Jefferson A., and Peter Salovey. *The Remembered Self: Emotion and Memory in Personality.* New York: Free Press, 1993.

Skinner, William. "Marketing and Social Structure in Rural China," parts 1–3, *Journal of Asian Studies* 24, no. 1 (November 1964):3–43; no. 2 (February 1965):195–228; no. 3 (May 1965):363–399.

Somers, Margaret R. "The Narrative Constitution of Identity: A Relational and Network Approach." *Theory and Society* 23 (1994):605–649.

Song Qiang, Qiao Bian, Caiwang Naoru, Xia Jilin, and Liu Hui. *Disidairen de jingshen: Xiandai Zhongguoren de jiushi qingjie (The Spirit of the Fourth Generation: The Savior Complex of Modern Chinese).* Lanzhou: Gansu wenhua chubanshe, 1997.

Song Qiang et al. *Zhongguo keyi shuobu (China Can Say No).* Beijing: Zhonghua gongshang lianhe chubanshe, 1996.

Song Qiang, Zhang Zangzang, Qiao Bian, Tang Zhengyu, and Gu Qingsheng. *Zhongguo haishi neng shuobu (China Can Still Say No)*. Beijing: Zhongguo wenlian chubanshe, 1996.

Speier, Hans. "Honor and Social Structure." *Social Research* 2 (1935). Rpt. in *The Truth in Hell and Other Essays on Politics and Culture, 1935–1987*. New York: Oxford University Press, 1989.

Spivak, G. C. "Can the Subaltern Speak?" In *Marxism and the Interpretation of Culture*, edited by Cary Nelson and Lawrence Grossberg. Urbana: University of Illinois Press, 1988.

"Students Turn Indignation into Motivation." *Xinhua*, 11 May 1999.

Suarez, Ray. "Spy Plane Standoff." *The NewsHour with Jim Lehrer*, Public Broadcasting Service, 3 April 2001.

Sullivan, Kevin. "In a First, Japan Leaders Apologize to Kim for Occupation of Korea." *International Herald Tribune*, 9 October 1998.

Sun Zhongyi. *Juexing: Riben zhanfan gaizao jishi (Awakening: A Record of Educating and Reforming of the Japanese War Criminals)*. Beijing and Hong Kong: Qunzhong chubanshe and Great Wall Publishing, 1991.

Sweeney, John, and Jens Holsoe. "Nato Bombed Chinese Deliberately." *Observer*, 17 October 1999.

Szonyi, Michael. "The Illusion of Standardizing the Gods: The Cult of the Five Emperors in Late Imperial China." *Journal of Asian Studies* 56, no. 1 (February 1997):113–35.

Tajfel, Henri. *Human Groups and Social Categories: Studies in Social Psychology*. Cambridge: Cambridge University Press, 1981.

Tanaka, Stefan. *Japan's Orient: Rendering Pasts into History*. Berkeley: University of California Press, 1993.

Taylor, Shelley E. "The Social Being in Social Psychology." In *The Handbook of Social Psychology*, 2 vols., 4th edition, ed. Daniel Gilbert, Susan Fiske, and Gardner Lindsey. Boston: McGraw-Hill, 1998.

Tell, David. "None Dare Call It Tyranny." *Weekly Standard*, 16–23 April 2001, 16–17.

Timperlake, Edward and William C. Triplett. *Year of the Rat: How Bill Clinton Compromised U.S. Security for Chinese Cash*. Washington, D.C.: Regenery Pub., 1998.

Ting-Toomey, Stella. *The Challenge of Facework: Cross-Cultural and Interpersonal Issues*. SUNY Series in Human Communication Processes. Albany: State University of New York Press, 1994.

de Tocqueville, Alexis. *Democracy in America*. Chicago: University of Chicago Press, 2000. Originally published in 1835.

"Tongbu baodao huigui qingdian huodong" [Celebrations around the World Will be Broadcast Simultaneously]." *Zhongguo dianshibao (China TV News)*, 2 June 1997.

Townsend, James. "Chinese Nationalism." In *Chinese Nationalism*, edited by Jonathan Unger. Armonk, N.Y.: M. E. Sharpe, 1996.

Tu Wei-ming. "Cultural China: The Periphery as the Center." *Daedalus* (Spring 1991), issue entitled *The Living Tree: The Changing Meaning of Being Chinese Today*.

Tyler, Patrick. 1999. *A Great Wall: Six Presidents and China, An Investigative History.* New York: PublicAffairs, 1999.

Unger, Jonathan, ed. *Using the Past to Serve the Present: Historiography and Politics in Contemporary China.* Armonk, N.Y.: M. E. Sharpe, 1993.

Unger, Roberto. *Knowledge and Politics.* New York and London: Macmillan, 1975.

U.S.–China Security Review Commission. *Report to Congress of the U.S.–China Security Review Commission: The National Security Implications of the Economic Relationship between the United States and China.* Washington, D.C., 2002.

van der Veer, Peter. "The Foreign Hand: Orientalist Discourse in Sociology and Communalism." In *Orientalism and the Postcolonial Predicament: Perspectives on South Asia,* ed. Carol A. Breckenridge and Peter van der Veer. Philadelphia: University of Pennsylvania Press, 1993.

"Viewing Nanking: Perspectives from Japan." Panel, "Nanking, 1937" Princeton conference, 22 November 1997.

Volkan, Vamik, and Norman Itzkowitz. *Turks and Greeks: Neighbors in Conflict.* Cambridgeshire, England: Ethoden, 1994.

Walder, Andrew G. *Communist Neo-Traditionalism: Work and Authority in Chinese Industry.* Berkeley: University of California Press, 1986.

Waldron, Arthur. "China and America Were Lucky." *The Daily Telegraph,* 12 April 2001, 30.

Wang Bin. *Jinshu, wenziyu (Censorship and Imprisonment for Political Expression).* Beijing: Zhongguo gongren chubanshe, 1992.

Wang Hailiang. "ZhongRi guanxi 150 nian zhi wojian: Yu Shantian Zhenxiong xiansheng shangquan [My View of 150 Years of Sino-Japanese Relations: A Discussion with Yamada Tatsuo]." *Yatai luntan (Asia-Pacific Forum)* 5 (1996): 19–23.

Wang Hainan. "The Current Situation and Future Prospect of Sino-U.S. Relations." *International Studies* 12–13 (1998).

Wang Jing. *High Culture Fever: Politics, Aesthetics, and Ideology in Deng's China.* Berkeley: University of California Press, 1996.

Wang Jisi. "Why Such Strong Reactions to Clash of Civilizations?" *Shijie Zhishi (World Affairs)* 9 (1995):4–12.

Wang Jisi, ed. *Wenming yu guoji zhengzhi: Zhongguo xuezhe ping Hundingdun de wenming chongtulun (Civilizations and International Politics: Chinese Scholars Critique Huntington's Clash of Civilizations Thesis).* Shanghai: Shanghai renmin chubanshe, 1995.

Wang Junyan. *Jingti Riben: Zuori de qinlue yu jinri de kuozhang (Be Vigilant against Japan: Yesterday's Aggression and Today's Expansion),* 2 vols. Tianjin: Neimengu renmin chubanshe, 1997.

Wang Lixiong. "Zhongguo yi shiqu 'zhuyi' lizu de jichu [China Has Already Lost the Foundation for Establishing a 'Doctrine']." In *Zhonguo ruhe miandui Xifang (How China Faces the West),* edited by Xiao Pang. Hong Kong: Mirror Books, 1997.

Wang Ning. "Orientalism vs. Occidentalism?" *New Literary History* 28, no. 1 (1997):57–68.

Wang Xiuhua. "Qingtu bujin de ganqing [An Emotion We Just Can't Get Out]." *Riben yanjiu (Japanese Studies)* 2 (1991):86–88.

Wang Yuesheng. "Shehui qingxu, wenming jiaowang yu gongtong jiazhi [Social Sentiment, the Exchange of Civilizations, and Common Values]." In *Zhongguo ruhe miandui Xifang (How China Faces the West),* edited by Xiao Pang. Hong Kong: Mirror Books, 1997.

"Washington Times Carries Article with Sinister Intention." *People's Daily online,* 26 December 2001.

Watson, James. "Standardizing the Gods: The Promotion of T'ien Hou [Empress of Heaven] along the South China Coast, 960–1960." In *Popular Culture in Late Imperial China,* David Johnson et al., eds. Berkeley: University of California Press, 1985.

Weber, Max. *The Theory of Social and Economic Organization.* New York: Free Press, 1964.

Weinstein, Eugene A., and Paul Deutschberger. "Some Dimensions of Altercasting." *Sociometry* 26, no. 4 (1963):454–466.

"Weishenme bukeyi shuobu [Why Can't We Say No?]." *Zhonghua dushubao (Reader's Daily),* 4 September 1996.

Wen Ming. "Misguidance in Vain." *Beijing Review* 40, nos. 7–8 (1997):7–8.

Whiting, Allen. *China Eyes Japan.* Berkeley: University of California Press, 1989.

Wixted, J. Timothy. "Reverse Orientalism." *Sino-Japanese Studies* 2, no. 1 (1989): 17–27.

Womack, Brantly, and Andrew Walder. "An Exchange of Views about Basic Chinese Social Organization." *China Quarterly* 126 (1991):313–30.

"Women you zui youxiu de rennao [We have the best brains]." *Beijing qingnian zhoukan (Beijing Youth Weekly)* 98, 20 May 1997.

"Workers Turning Anger into Motivation." *Xinhua,* 10 May 1999.

Wu Fang, and Ray Zhang. "Dissident Called the Chinese Premier 'Incompetent.'" *China News Digest,* 13 February 1998.

Wu Xinhua. "Kaipian [Introduction]" and "Jieshupian [Conclusion]." In *Zhongguo qizhi shuobu: ZhongMei jiaoliang (China Shouldn't Just Say No: The Sino-American Contest);* special issue of *Ai wo Zhonghua (Love Our China),* edited by Yu Shaohua, Feng Sanda and Chen Neimin. Hefei, 1996.

"Wuwang lishi, zhenxing Zhonghua [Do Not Forget History; Arouse China]." Editorial, *Jiefangjun bao (People's Liberation Army Daily),* 7 September 1987.

Xi Yongjun and Ma Zaizhun. *Chaoyue Meiguo: Meiguo shenhua de zhongjie (Surpassing the USA: The End of the American Myth).* Harbin: Neimenggu daxue chubanshe, 1996.

Xiao Gongqing. "Cong minzuzhuyi zhong jiequ guojia ningjuli de xinziyuan [Deriving from Nationalism a New Resource that Congeals the State]." *Zhanlue yu guanli (Strategy and Management)* 4 (1994). Cited in Chen Feng, "Order and Stability in Social Transition: Neoconservative Political Thought in Post-1989 China," *China Quarterly* 151 (September 1997):593–613.

Xiao Pang, ed. *Zhongguo ruhe miandui Xifang (How China Faces the West).* Hong Kong: Mirror Books, 1997.

Xiao Tong and Du Li. *Longli, 1978–1996: Zhuanxingqi Zhongguo baixing xinjilu (Dragon History: The True Feelings of the Chinese People during a Time of Transition, 1978–1996)*. Beijing: Gaige chubanshe, 1997.

Xing Xiangyang, ed. *Bainian enchou: Liange Dongya daguo xiandaihua bijiao de dingzi baogao (A Century of Hatred: A 1996 Report Comparing the Modernization of Two East Asian Powers)*. 2 vols., "National Affairs" Series. Beijing: Zhongguo shehui chubanshe, 1996.

Xu Ben. "Chinese Populist Nationalism: Its Intellectual Politics and Moral Dilemma." *Representations* 76, no. 1 (2001):120–140.

———. "Contesting Memory for Intellectual Self-Positioning: The 1990s' New Cultural Conservatism in China." *Modern Chinese Literature and Culture* 11, no. 1 (1999):157–92.

Xu Bin. *'97 Xianggang huigui fengyun (Hong Kong's Stormy '97 Return)*. Changchun: Jilin Sheying chubanshe, 1996.

Xue Yunfeng. Talk given at the Beijing Conference Commemorating the Sixtieth Anniversary of the Marco Polo Bridge Incident, 1997.

Yan Tao and Liu Ruting. "Zhongguo renmin shi buke zhansheng de! [The Chinese People Cannot be Defeated!]." *Xinhua*, 11 May 1999. Viewable at http://www.peopledaily.com.cn/item/kangyi/199905/12/051252.html. Accessed 25 March 2003.

Yan Xuetong. "Experts on Jet Collision Incident and Overall Situation in Sino–U.S. Relations." *Liaowang* 16 (2001):6–8. Cited in FBIS-CHI-2001-042616.

Yang, Martin Mao-chun. *A Chinese Village*. New York: Columbia University Press, 1945.

Yang Dezhi. "Qianyan [Preface]." In *KangMei YuanChao de kaige (A Paean to the War to Resist America and Aid Korea)*. Beijing: Zhongguo da baike chuanshu chubanshe, 1990.

Yeh, Michelle. "International Theory and the Transnational Critic: China in the Age of Multiculturalism." *Boundary 2* 25, no. 3 (1998):193–222.

Yu Shaohua, Feng Sanda, and Chen Neimin. *Zhongguo qizhi shuobu: ZhongMei jiaoliang (China Shouldn't Just Say No: The Sino-American Contest)*. Special issue of *Ai wo Zhonghua (Love Our China)* 3–4. Hefei, 1996.

Yuan Jiaxin. Talk given at the Beijing conference commemorating the sixtieth anniversary of the Marco Polo Bridge Incident, 4 July 1997.

Zeng Jingzhong. "1995 nian KangRi Zhanzhengshi yanjiu de jinzhan [1995 Developments in Research on the War of Resistance against Japan]." *KangRi Zhanzheng yanjiu (Studies on the War of Resistance against Japan)* 2 (1995):216–234.

Zerubavel, Yael. *Recovered Roots: Collective Memory and the Making of Israeli National Tradition*. Chicago: University of Chicago Press, 1995.

Zhai Xuewei. "'Mianzi' mianmianguan [The Faces of 'Face']." *Dongfang wenhua zhoukan (Oriental Culture Weekly)* 12 (1997):8–9.

Zhang Tianwei. "Jiyi jiushi yizhong xianshi [Memory Is a Type of Present Reality]." *Beijing Qingnianbao (Beijing Youth Daily)*, 29 June 2000, 34.

Zhang Yimou, dir. *Qiu Ju da guansi (The Story of Qiu Ju)*. Color, 100 min. 1992.

Zhang Zhaozhong. *Xia yige mubiao shi shei (Who Is the Next Target?)*. Beijing: Zhongguo qingnian chubanshe, 2000.

Zhang Zhuhong, ed. *Guoji youren yu KangRi zhanzheng (International Friends and the War of Resistance against Japan)*. Beijing: Yanshan chubanshe, 1997.

———. "Taierzhuang zhanshe de guoji yinxiang [The International Influence of the Battle of Taierzhuang]." In *Zhongguo renmin KangRi zhanzheng jinianguan wencong (Chinese People's War of Resistance against Japan Museum Compilation)*. Beijing: Beijing chubanshe, 1995.

Zhao Dingxin. "An Angle on Nationalism in China Today: Attitudes among Beijing Students after Belgrade 1999." *China Quarterly* 172 (December 2002): 885–905.

Zhao Suisheng. "Chinese Intellectuals' Quest for National Greatness and Nationalistic Writing in the 1990s." *China Quarterly* 152 (1997):725–745.

———. "Chinese Nationalism and Its International Orientations." *Political Science Quarterly* 115, no. 1 (2000):1–33.

Zhao Wenli. "Aidejia Sinuo yu Zhongguo Kangzhan [Edgar Snow and the Chinese War of Resistance]." In *Zhongguo renmin KangRi zhanzheng jinianguan wencong (Chinese People's War of Resistance against Japan Museum Compilation)*. Beijing: Beijing chubanshe, 1995.

Zheng Xinshui. "Lu Xun lun mianzi wenhua [Lu Xun on *mianzi* Culture]." *Lu Xun yanjiu yuekan* 4 (1996):19–26.

Zheng Yongnian. *Discovering Chinese Nationalism in China: Modernization, Identity, and International Relations*. Cambridge Asia-Pacific Studies. Cambridge: Cambridge University Press, 1999.

"Zhonghua minzu shi yinggutou—Fang Yuan Shengping Jiangjun [The Chinese race is dauntless: An interview with general Yuan Shengping]," *Xinhua (New China News Agency)*, 6 October 2000.

Zhu Jiamu, and An Jianshe, eds. *Zhenhan shijie de 20 tian: Waiguo jizhe bixia de Zhou Enlai shishi (20 Days that Shook the World: Zhou Enlai's Passing in the Writings of Foreign Reporters)*. Beijing: Zhongyang wenxian chubanshe, 1999.

Zi Shui and Xiao Shi. *Jingti Riben diguo zhuyi! (Be Vigilant against Japanese Militarism!)*. Beijing: Jincheng chubanshe, 1997.

Zi Zhongyun. "The Impact and Clash of Ideologies: Sino-US Relations from a Historical Perspective." *Journal of Contemporary China* 16 (November 1997): 531–550.

Acknowledgments

My interest in China began when I was a ten- and eleven-year-old in Beijing. After placing fifth in the city in hand grenade throwing, I was hooked! I thank Shi Laoshi, my teacher at Chinese public elementary school, who first taught me how to memorize and recite Chinese stories—and how to get along with my North Korean classmates. My interest in Chinese history arose through trading stamps with the Chinese collectors who gathered outside the now-long-gone stamp store in Wangfujing in downtown Beijing. Why was the man sitting next to Mao in so many stamps always defaced? Perhaps it was the tragic fate of Lin Biao, Mao's Cultural Revolution successor turned "traitor," that first aroused my interest in *face*!

In high school in Washington, D.C., Morris Abrams taught me far more than geometry, and Sue Ikenbery taught me that there was the American past, and then there were conflicting histories about that past. Given my interest in biology and experience living in China, my high school yearbook predicted that in the future I would "teach dolphins to speak Chinese." They got the teaching part right.

At Middlebury College, I thank Nicholas Clifford and Hiroshi Miyagi for passing on their passion for Asian history and philosophy, and especially Clara Yu, whose intellectual and personal support have been invaluable over many years. During my junior year abroad at Beijing University, Coach Yuan and my men's volleyball teammates taught me much more than how to spike. At Michigan, the late Michael Oksenberg inspired an excitement about studying China; Donald Munro provided a model for more than just an academic career; and Qian Ning's generosity and humor in guiding me through the maze of twentieth-century intellectual history motivated me to further scholarship.

The origins of this particular book, however, are to be found in the political science and Chinese studies communities at Berkeley. First and foremost, Kevin O'Brien has been a good friend and mentor ever since I returned from fieldwork in China in 1997. His support was invaluable in bringing this book to its fruition. Annie Zhang and the Center for Chinese Studies Library staff at Berkeley not only aided in my research, but created a home away from home for an overworked Ph.D. student. Thanks also to Professor Ken Jowitt, whose fire for teaching has inspired my own lectures here in Colorado.

I began researching this book in 1996–1997 as a visiting fellow at the Center for Japanese Studies of the Chinese Academy of Social Sciences in Beijing. I thank Director Zhang Yunling and the entire center staff for their hospitality. I greatly enjoyed our "badminton diplomacy"! The Chinese and Western friends who helped me with my research over many beers in Beijing should be the coauthors of this volume. To the University of California Office of the President thanks is due for the Pacific Rim Research Fellowship that supported my research abroad. For intellectual and emotional support during the writing phase in Berkeley, thanks to Wang Boqing, Daphne Anshel, John Emerson, Elizabeth Rudd, and Gretchen Jones, my "dissertation partner." Mônica, a wedding in Brazil, and a honeymoon in Europe more than inspired the final push to finish.

I conducted the bulk of the research and writing of this book as a postdoctoral fellow at the Mershon Center for International Security Studies at Ohio State University. Director Ned Lebow and colleagues there, including Rick Herrman, Marilyn Brewer, Emannuelle Castano, Peter Furia, Maria Fanis, and Ted Hopf, provided intellectual stimulation, support, and camaraderie. Paul Cohen, Josh Fogel, Ed Friedman, and David Shambaugh commented on portions of earlier versions of the manuscript, and provided much-needed encouragement and support.

Colleagues at the University of Colorado have provided a supportive and stimulating atmosphere in which to complete the book. In particular, I would like to thank Sven Steinmo, David Maple, Steve Chan, Colin Dueck, Roland Paris, and Tim Weston. Stan Rosen, with whom I coedited *State and Society in 21st Century China: Crisis, Contention, and Legitimation,* also provided advice and good cheer as I completed this book.

I thank four anonymous reviewers for their constructive criticism and generous encouragement. At the University of California Press, many thanks are also owed to acquisitions editor Reed Malcolm (who deserves combat pay), development editor Doug Abrams, production editor

Suzanne Knott, copyeditor Laura Schattschneider, and publicist Alex Dahne. All contributed to improving the book immensely.

For permission to reproduce their photographs, I thank Richard Smith, Scott Kennedy, Hein Thorsten, and Du Jiang of the *People's Daily Online*, AP/Wide World Photos, and AFP. Portions of chapters 6 and 8 are based on work that has been previously published in *The China Journal, The Journal of Contemporary China,* and *International Security.* I thank all three journals for permissions to reproduce them here.

Without support from my family, I doubt I could have completed this journey. Thanks to Mônica, Mom, Dad, Puckie, Caroline, Susannah, and our collie Zeus.

Index

Text:	10/13 Galliard
Display:	Galliard
Indexer:	Jean Mann
Compositor:	Integrated Composition Systems
Printer:	Maple-Vail Manufacturing Group